# COVER ME

# COVER ME

## THE STORIES BEHIND THE GREATEST COVER SONGS OF ALL TIME

**RAY PADGETT**

**FOUNDER AND EDITOR OF THE BLOG *COVER ME***

STERLING
New York

STERLING
New York

An Imprint of Sterling Publishing Co., Inc.
1166 Avenue of the Americas
New York, NY 10036

ISBN 978-1-4549-2250-6

Distributed in Canada by Sterling Publishing Co., Inc.
c/o Canadian Manda Group, 664 Annette Street
Toronto, Ontario, Canada M6S 2C8
Distributed in the United Kingdom by GMC Distribution Services
Castle Place, 166 High Street, Lewes, East Sussex, England BN7 1XU
Distributed in Australia by NewSouth Books
45 Beach Street, Coogee, NSW 2034, Australia

For information about custom editions, special sales, and premium and corporate purchases, please contact Sterling Special Sales at 800-805-5489 or specialsales@sterlingpublishing.com.

Manufactured in China

2  4  6  8  10  9  7  5  3  1

sterlingpublishing.com

Design by Kevin Baier, KJWork Design Co.

Photo credits available on page 232

TO MOM AND DAD, WHO TAUGHT ME HOW TO WRITE
AND JUST ABOUT EVERYTHING ELSE, TOO.

# CONTENTS

INTRODUCTION . . . . . . . . . . . . . . . . . . . . . . . . . . . . . . 1

ELVIS PRESLEY "HOUND DOG"
(Big Mama Thornton cover) . . . . . . . . . . . . . . . . . . . . 10

THE BEATLES "TWIST AND SHOUT"
(Isley Brothers/Top Notes cover) . . . . . . . . . . . . . . . . 26

THE RIGHTEOUS BROTHERS "UNCHAINED MELODY"
(Todd Duncan cover) . . . . . . . . . . . . . . . . . . . . . . . . . 36

ARETHA FRANKLIN "RESPECT"
(Otis Redding cover) . . . . . . . . . . . . . . . . . . . . . . . . . . 44

JIMI HENDRIX "ALL ALONG THE WATCHTOWER"
(Bob Dylan cover) . . . . . . . . . . . . . . . . . . . . . . . . . . . . 56

JOE COCKER "WITH A LITTLE HELP FROM MY FRIENDS"
(The Beatles cover) . . . . . . . . . . . . . . . . . . . . . . . . . . . 68

THE WHO "SUMMERTIME BLUES"
(Eddie Cochran cover) . . . . . . . . . . . . . . . . . . . . . . . . 78

CREEDENCE CLEARWATER REVIVAL
"I HEARD IT THROUGH THE GRAPEVINE"
(Marvin Gaye cover) . . . . . . . . . . . . . . . . . . . . . . . . . . 86

GLADYS KNIGHT & THE PIPS
"MIDNIGHT TRAIN TO GEORGIA"
(Jim Weatherly cover) . . . . . . . . . . . . . . . . . . . . . . . . . 96

PATTI SMITH "GLORIA"
(Them cover) . . . . . . . . . . . . . . . . . . . . . . . . . . . . . . . 104

TALKING HEADS
"TAKE ME TO THE RIVER"
(Al Green cover) . . . . . . . . . . . . . . . . . . . . . . . . . . . . . 116

**DEVO "SATISFACTION"**
(The Rolling Stones cover) . . . . . . . . . . . . . . . . 128

**"WEIRD AL" YANKOVIC
"POLKAS ON 45"**
(various artists cover) . . . . . . . . . . . . . . . . 140

**PET SHOP BOYS
"ALWAYS ON MY MIND"**
(Elvis Presley/Brenda Lee cover) . . . . . . . . . . . 152

**WHITNEY HOUSTON
"I WILL ALWAYS LOVE YOU"**
(Dolly Parton cover) . . . . . . . . . . . . . . . . . 160

**FUGEES "KILLING ME SOFTLY"**
(Roberta Flack/Lori Lieberman cover) . . . . . . . . . . . . . 170

**THE GOURDS "GIN AND JUICE"**
(Snoop Doggy Dogg cover) . . . . . . . . . . . . . . . . . . . . . . 180

**JOHNNY CASH "HURT"**
(Nine Inch Nails cover) . . . . . . . . . . . . . . . . . . . . . . . . 192

**ADELE "MAKE YOU FEEL MY LOVE"**
(Bob Dylan cover) . . . . . . . . . . . . . . . . . . . . . . . . . . . . .208

**ACKNOWLEDGMENTS** . . . . . . . . . . . . . . . . . . . . . . . . . . . . .219

**BIBLIOGRAPHY** . . . . . . . . . . . . . . . . . . . . . . . . . . . . . . . .228

**INDEX** . . . . . . . . . . . . . . . . . . . . . . . . . . . . . . . . . . . . . . .232

**PHOTO CREDITS** . . . . . . . . . . . . . . . . . . . . . . . . . . . . . . .232

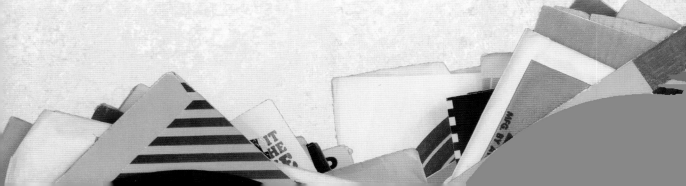

# INTRODUCTION

In a 2011 interview with George Lopez, Prince explained his feelings about cover songs: "I don't mind fans singing the songs, my problem is when the industry covers the music. You see, covering the music means your version doesn't exist anymore. There's only one version of *Law & Order*, but there are several versions of 'Kiss' and 'Purple Rain.'"

Put aside his poor choice of comparison—there are, at latest count, seven versions of *Law & Order*. Was he right about cover songs? Do covers somehow diminish the originals? Can you really have too many versions of "Purple Rain"?

This book is filled with examples of songwriters who thought exactly the opposite, from Mick Jagger dancing around the room when Devo played him their "Satisfaction" to the Beatles sending Joe Cocker a thank-you note for his take on "With a Little Help From My Friends." Jagger and the Beatles knew that these covers didn't diminish their legacy; they burnished it. Prince, of all people, should have known this, too—how many people would know his song "Nothing Compares 2 U" without Sinéad O'Connor's massively popular cover (ever an

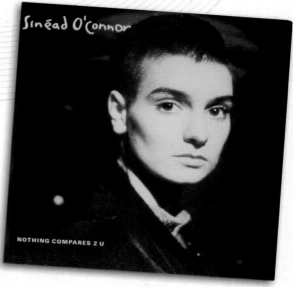

**OPPOSITE:** Prince lays down the solo for "Purple Rain" (the song) in *Purple Rain* (the movie). **RIGHT TOP:** Sinéad O'Connor's 1990 Prince cover was the biggest hit of her career. **RIGHT BOTTOM:** Willie Nelson wrote only two of the ten songs on his cover-heavy 1982 album.

enigma, Prince reportedly loved this cover—a fact hard to square with his 2011 complaints)?

A cover song doesn't mean, as Prince put it, that the original artist's "version doesn't exist anymore." Instead, a great cover adds to the song in a number of ways.

In some cases, a cover song can reveal new meaning in a songwriter's lyrics. The Pet Shop Boys said their electronic cover of "Always on My Mind" made the country standard's lyrics seem cynical and disturbing after the more traditional Elvis Presley and Willie Nelson versions. Presley himself took the sexual innuendo out of "Hound Dog," while Patti Smith added sex and danger to Van Morrison's bar-band staple "Gloria."

Some cover songs explore cultural avenues that the original song only hinted at. Otis Redding's "Respect" strictly addressed a relationship, but Aretha Franklin's cover became a generational anthem. Jimi Hendrix transformed the Bob Dylan deep cut "All Along the Watchtower" into a storming anthem for soldiers in Vietnam. Johnny Cash remade Nine Inch Nails' industrial-rock drug song "Hurt" into a song about old age and dying.

A well-done cover song can introduce a little-known song to a broader audience. "Unchained Melody" would have remained an obscure movie-soundtrack curio if the Righteous Brothers hadn't belted it. The Fugees translated "Killing Me Softly" for a hip-hop generation that might have never heard of Roberta Flack. Adele took a recent Dylan song and made it a modern-day songbook standard (no artist has benefited more from cover songs than Dylan).

> A well-done cover song can introduce a little-known song to a broader audience.

Though the cover song may seem like a niche category in today's music industry, when most musicians either write their own material or have it written specifically for them by teams of professional songwriters, the vast majority of musical compositions ever performed were on some level covers, from orchestras playing Mozart and Beethoven to farmers singing to each other in the fields. In fact, the first song ever recorded was a cover.

In 1860, a French printer and bookseller named Édouard-Léon Scott de Martinville sang the traditional folk song "Au clair de la lune" into a new invention he called the phonautograph. The phonautograph could only record sound, though, not play it back (scientists finally figured out how to play Martinville's primitive recording in 2008—it sounds like a warped transmission from another galaxy). The first recording someone could play back immediately came from Thomas Edison two decades later, and it was once again a cover song: "Mary Had a Little Lamb."

Of course, no one would have called these cover songs back then. Actually, up until the midpoint of the twentieth century, the "cover song" as a concept did not really exist. Before then, consumers had no expectations that singers would record songs they had written themselves. Moreover, the audience for recorded music often did not care who sang their favorite songs.

**OPPOSITE:** Thomas Edison with a phonograph, c. 1877. Edison claimed he was the one singing ("shouting" in his phrasing) on that historic early cover of "Mary Had a Little Lamb."

With a few big-name exceptions, listeners in the 1930s and '40s bought records by song title, not artist. They would go looking for a recording of "Some Enchanted Evening" and usually didn't know or care who had sung it as long as it roughly sounded like the version on the radio. This is a huge mental change from today's consumers. You don't want a record of just anyone singing "Someone Like You"; you want to hear Adele. But before the dawn of rock and roll, the *song* was paramount, not the singer.

The phrase "cover song" came out of this era, just after World War II. The first mention of the phrase in the leading music-industry magazine *Billboard* comes in 1949. In a discussion of current country-music hits, *Billboard* writes, "The original disking of *Why Don't You Haul Off and Love Me?*, cut for King by Wayne Raney, has hit 250,000, and versions are now available on all major labels." They then continue on to another song: "Another King disk, *Blues Stay 'Way From Me?*, by the Delmore Brothers, is close to 125,000 in six weeks, and the other companies have just begun to cover the tune."

What do they mean by "cover" here? It's not really what we mean today. We think of musicians, not companies, covering songs. The key comes in the preceding sentence: "versions are now available on all major labels." In the era when customers were more likely to request something they heard on the radio by song title rather than artist, labels would rush out sound-alike copies of popular hits. These labels tried to hoodwink a listener who heard a hit song on the radio into mistakenly buying a copycat version by their own artist. A "cover" back then was a trick, a con on the listener.

To stick with the *Billboard* example, within months of Raney releasing his wonderfully titled 1949 hit "Why Don't You Haul Off and Love Me?,"

his label's competitors had their own artists record similar versions. They rushed these "covers" onto shelves, and stores would sell whichever version they had in stock. Some big hits could earn the backhanded compliment of up to a dozen copycat covers hitting the market within weeks. The five-and-dime store chain Woolworth's even had its own record label churning out copycat covers to sell cheaply in its stores. A cover song only existed to ride the coattails of someone else's hit.

There are several theories behind why these copycat songs became known in the industry as "covers." Some sources say the word comes from a label "covering its bets" by releasing its own recording of a popular song. Others claim labels aimed to have their record literally "cover up" another version of the same song on a store's shelves. The third theory holds that when a label exec asked an artists and repertoire (A&R) man if his label had any recordings of a popular song to release, the A&R man would respond, "We've got it covered!"

Whatever the reason for the word entering music-biz jargon, a "cover" then was not what we now think of it as. The goal was not to raise the profile of the original song, but to bury it. Prince's critique would hold more merit had he made it in 1949. Cover songs were copycat recordings done quickly. Creativity was not the goal, just profit. "American Pie" songwriter Don McLean, whose song "Empty Chairs" later inspired the oft-covered "Killing Me Softly," complained on his website in 2004:

> The word "cover" is now used by music writers and music fans incorrectly. They use it to describe any attempt by an artist to perform old songs or previously recorded material. The use of this term gives them a bit of authority since it makes them sound like they are in the music business. They are

*in fact ignorant of what a cover version of a song really is.*

*Back in the days of black radio stations and white radio stations (i.e., segregation), if a black act had a hot record, the white kids would find out and want to hear it on "their" radio station. This would prompt the record company to bring a white act into the recording studio and cut an exact, but white, version of the song to give to the white radio stations to play and thus keep the black act where it belonged: on black radio. A "cover" version of a song is a racist tool. It is NOT a term intended to be used to describe a valid interpretation of an old song. . . .*

*Madonna did not "cover" American Pie; she just sang an old song and made an old songwriter mighty happy.*

Wayne Raney's country hit "Why Don't You Haul Off and Love Me?" was one of the first times the term "cover" was used, inspiring "covers" from early R&B star Bull Moose Jackson to Dolly Parton.

McLean's critique underscores another issue surrounding these early cover songs: racism. When the industry trend of cover songs emerged in the 1940s, any record by a black artist was confined to *Billboard*'s "Race Records" chart. Enterprising label executives would scan this chart for hits and then rerecord them with their white artists for the other, white charts. (This could go the other way, too: "Why Don't You Haul Off and Love Me?" by Raney, who was white, was promptly covered by Bull Moose Jackson for the "race" market.)

McLean is not wrong about the music history, but his definition of cover songs is out of date. Language changes, and the term "cover" has as well. As we mean it today, Madonna *did* cover "American Pie." None of the covers we explore in this book fit the Don McLean description—because, for the most part, those early copycat-covers he was discussing offered nothing creatively. The cover song only came into its own as a valid artistic expression with the dawn of rock and roll.

As the 1950s moved forward, the trend of the copycat-cover subsided. Performers became as important as the song they were performing. It's hard to pinpoint any single cause of such a broad shift in people's thinking, but the advent of television and its accompanying music-performance shows likely played a role. You knew if you bought "Hound Dog" after seeing it performed on TV that the label had better read "Elvis Presley." This was not entirely unprecedented; in the 1940s, so-called "bobby-soxers" (the precursors to teenyboppers) swooned for Frank Sinatra and wouldn't have accepted some sound-alike. This expectation became the norm rather than

## The Billboard MUSIC POPULARITY CHARTS   PART VI

### Race Records

Based on reports received last three days of Week Ending January 7

## BEST-SELLING RETAIL RACE RECORDS

Records listed are race records that sold best in stores according to The Billboard's special weekly survey among a selected group of retail stores, the majority of whose customers purchase race records.

| Weeks to date | Last Week | This Week | | |
|---|---|---|---|---|
| 8 | 2 | 1. | BEWILDERED ............R. Miller Trio..Bullet 295—ASCAP | |
| 8 | 1 | 2. | CHICKEN SHACK BOOGIE..A. Milburn..Aladdin 3014—ASCAP | |
| 8 | 3 | 3. | BEWILDERED .............A. Milburn..Aladdin 3018—ASCAP | |
| 10 | — | 4. | LONG ABOUT MIDNIGHT..R. Brown Mighty, Mighty Men..De Luxe 1154—ASCAP | |
| 4 | 7 | 5. | TEXAS HOP .............Pee Wee Crayton......Modern 643 | |
| 2 | — | 6. | UP ABOVE MY HEAD, I Sister Rosetta Tharpe-M. Knight-HEAR MUSIC IN THE AIR.. S. Price Trio....Decca 48090—BMI | |
| 5 | 3 | 7. | TREES ................A. Hibbler.......Miracle M-501—ASCAP | |
| 2 | — | 7. | WRAPPED UP IN A Do, Ray and Me.. DREAM ............Commodore C-7505—ASCAP | |
| 10 | 3 | 9. | A LITTLE BIRD TOLD ME..P. Watson.....Supreme S-1507—ASCAP | |
| 11 | — | 9. | BLUES FOR THE RED BOY..Todd Rhodes......King 4240 | |
| 11 | — | 9. | IT'S TOO SOON TO KNOW..D. Washington..Mercury 6107—ASCAP | |
| 1 | — | 9. | HOT BISCUITS ..........J. McShann......Downbeat 165 | |
| 2 | 10 | 13. | BOOGIE CHILLEN ........J. L. Hooker......Modern 627 | |
| 3 | 7 | 14. | PETTIN' AND POKIN'.....L. Jordan and His Tympany Five....Decca 24257—ASCAP | |
| 1 | — | 14. | SWEET GEORGIA BROWN..Brother Bones and His Shadows....Tempo 652—ASCAP | |

**WARNING!** In utilizing these charts for buying purposes readers are urged to pay particular attention to information listed which shows the length of time a record has been on the chart, and whether a record's popularity has increased or decreased. This data is shown in the left hand columns under the headings: "Weeks to Date," "Last Week" and "This Week." If a record has had an unusually long run, or if its current position "this week" versus "last week" shows a sharp drop, readers should buy with caution.

## MOST-PLAYED JUKE BOX RACE RECORDS

Records listed are race records most played in juke boxes according to The Billboard's special weekly survey among a selected group of juke box operators whose locations require race records.

| Weeks to date | Last Week | This Week | | |
|---|---|---|---|---|
| 9 | 2 | 1. | BEWILDERED ..............Red Miller Trio......Bullet 295—ASCAP | |
| 8 | 1 | 2. | CHICKEN SHACK BOOGIE..A. Milburn..Aladdin 3014—ASCAP | |
| 8 | — | 3. | A LITTLE BIRD TOLD ME..P. Watson......Supreme S-1507—ASCAP | |
| 11 | 7 | 4. | LONG ABOUT MIDNIGHT..R. Brown Mighty, Mighty Men...De Luxe 3154—BMI | |
| 5 | 3 | 5. | BEWILDERED .............A. Milburn..Aladdin 3018—ASCAP | |
| 8 | 9 | 6. | MY FAULT ..............Brownie McGhee....Savoy 5551 | |
| 2 | — | 7. | 'FORE DAY IN THE R. Brown....De Luxe 3198 MORNING ........... | |
| 1 | — | 8. | I'LL ALWAYS BE IN LOVE The X-Rays.....Savoy 681 WITH YOU ........... | |
| 20 | 9 | 9. | CORN BREAD ............Hal Singer Sextette....Savoy 671—BMI | |
| 2 | — | 9. | IT'S GONNA BE A LONELY The Orioles.....Jubilee 5001—ASCAP CHRISTMAS ........... | |
| 31 | — | 9. | LONG GONE ............Sonny Thompson....Miracle M-126—ASCAP | |
| 15 | 12 | 12. | IT'S TOO SOON TO KNOW..The Orioles......Natural 5000—ASCAP | |
| 2 | — | 13. | PETTIN' AND POKIN'.....L. Jordan and His Tympany Five....Decca 24257—ASCAP | |
| 9 | — | 14. | HOP, SKIP AND JUMP.....Roy Milton and His Solid Senders....Specialty SP-314—ASCAP | |
| 8 | — | 14. | PLEASING YOU ..........L. Johnson......King 4245—BMI | |
| 2 | 6 | 14. | WALKIN' AROUND ........P. Williams "35-30" Sextette....Savoy 680 | |

## ADVANCE RACE RECORD RELEASES

A Woman on Every Street
Forest City Joe (Memory of) Aristocrat 3101
After You've Gone
S. Jonah's Joy Boys (House Party) Capitol 15356
Behavin' Myself for You
M. Sullivan (The Story) MGM 10343
Don't Worry 'Bout Nothin'
E. Gorman (My Song) DeLuxe 3200
Free
H. Humes (I've Got) Mercury 8119
Gloomy Monday Blues
P. Brown (Mourning Blues) Apollo 402
Goodbye Dorothea
King Porter Ork (That Early) Imperial 5032
Hey Mama (He's Tryin' To Kiss Me)
V. Watkins (My Real Fine) MGM 10344
Hour After Hour
Cee Pee Johnson & Band (I'm So) Apollo 403
House Party Blues
S. Jonah's Joy Boys-H. Hooper (After You've) Capitol 15356
I'm So Lonesome
Cee Pee Johnson & Band (Hour After) Apollo 403
I've Got the Strangest Feeling
H. Humes (Free) Mercury 8119
Lay Right Down and Die
S. Parker (You Don't) Columbia 30151

Memory of Sonny Boy
Forest City Joe (A Woman) Aristocrat 3101
Mourning Blues
P. Brown (Gloomy Monday) Apollo 402
My Baby, My Baby
Sunnyland Slim (She Ain't) Aristocrat 1304
My Real Fine Man
V. Watkins (Hey Mama) MGM 10344
My Song While We Dance
P. Gayten-P. Gayten Trio (Don't Worry) DeLuxe 3200
(Instead of Breaking My Heart) Please Give My Heart a Break
O. Wilson & the Basin Street Boys (To Make) Mercury 820
She Ain't Nowhere
Sunnyland Slim (My Baby) Aristocrat 1304
That Early Morning Boogie
King Porter Ork (Goodbye Dorothea) Imperial 5032
The Story of Our Love Affair
M. Sullivan (Behavin' Myself) MGM 10343
To Make a Mistake Is Human
O. Wilson & the Basin Street Boys (Please Give) Mercury 8120
You Don't Know About Love
S. Parker (Lay Right) Columbia 30151

the exception. Consumers cared more about the performer than just the performance.

The cover song as we know it today evolved out of this cultural shift. This was the moment when the cover song as a unique creative expression was born. From this point forward, a musician had to bring something new to the table if he or she wanted to sing a song someone else had already recorded. The art of interpretation became worth celebrating. A cover was no longer ripping someone off but was rather an artist taking a song someone else performed and making it his or her own.

Unfortunately, listeners didn't always see it that way. As the 1960s moved toward the '70s, the "cover" once again found itself a dirty word, but for a different reason. After the Beatles and Dylan, a premium was placed on an artist writing his or her own songs. Singing someone else's songs was often seen as creative bankruptcy, particularly for pop or rock musicians. To this day, you occasionally hear a pop star criticized with "Well, I heard he/she doesn't even write their own songs!"—as if there is no art to interpreting a song someone else wrote (any number of great jazz singers would beg to differ).

When musicians did release a cover in the latter half of the twentieth century, they would often pick a deliberately obscure song so people did not know it wasn't an original—the exact reverse of the term's origins of covering only hits. For example, Joan Jett did not exactly advertise that her huge hit "I Love Rock and Roll" was a nearly identical cover of a song by the short-lived British trio the Arrows. Even "Hallelujah," today covered to the point of cliché after Jeff Buckley's revelatory rendition, was originally a track from an obscure Leonard Cohen album that his label hadn't even bothered to release in the United States. Unless you were friends with a record-store

OPPOSITE: *Billboard* categorized songs targeted at black audiences as "Race Records" from 1945 to 1949. **ABOVE:** Madonna's "American Pie" cover was recorded for the soundtrack to her mostly forgotten 2000 romantic comedy, *The Next Best Thing.*

clerk, how would you ever know that an obscure folk songwriter named Jake Holmes released "Dazed and Confused" two years before Led Zeppelin did?

Today, the Internet has erased the stigma. Cover songs have come out of the shadows. No one could get away with releasing a cover song without their fans finding out—any song's origins are only a Google search away.

So artists took back control of the cover. As avenues to release music have proliferated, artists have found freedom in being able to perform the songs they loved with lower stakes. Artists can still release covers on albums or singles just as they could in the 1960s, but now they can also post them on YouTube or Soundcloud, record them for a radio session, play them live and see fan-filmed videos soar through music blogs. In 2015, *Rolling Stone* magazine wrote over three hundred stories about new cover songs—that's almost one a day, just from A-list artists alone.

With this newfound freedom, musicians could easily turn fans on to their influences or surprise them by radically altering a song no one would expect them to like. This finally erased the cover song's stigma and led to its recent resurgence. To take just one example among many, in 2016 the indie-rock community released *Day of the Dead*, a tribute album to the Grateful Dead. This was not the first Dead tribute by any means, but tributes from decades past mainly contained contributions by the Dead's 1970s peers. *Day of the Dead*, though, included only the coolest of the cool bands, and not just a handful; this was a fifty-nine-track behemoth that included Wilco, the National, and the Flaming Lips. Seemingly every "hip" alternative musician of the past twenty years was lining up to cover that eternally unhip phenomenon: a jam band. Cover songs are cool again.

No site has tracked this trend more closely than the cover-songs blog *Cover Me*. But then again, I'm biased: it's my site. For ten years, my team and I have written news stories and features about cover songs new and old, big artists covering classic hits and under-the-radar artists digging up obscure gems. Ten years ago, it was a challenge to find something new to post every day. Now we can only post a small fraction of the stuff people send us.

The blog began in 2007, but its origins go back a year earlier, to July 2006. At the time, Bob Dylan hosted a syndicated radio show called *Theme Time Radio Hour*. He would play songs he loved on a particular theme—songs about the weather one week, songs about New York City the next. The tenth episode tackled summer songs, from Sly & the Family Stone's "Hot Fun in the Summertime" to Eddie Cochran's "Summertime Blues," which was later covered by the Who (we'll get there).

He began the show with one song more famous than even these: George Gershwin's standard "Summertime." This was one of those songs in the 1930s that saw hundreds of versions released in quick succession, most sounding roughly the same. And even since then, covers of it tend to follow a formula: languid and slow-moving, a hot summer day sitting in a porch's shade. Some are beautiful, no doubt, but to my ears they all sounded somber and subdued, in contrast to lyrics about fish jumpin' and wings spreadin'.

On *Theme Time Radio Hour*, Dylan played a different sort of "Summertime." "Time to open up the fire hydrants and have a party in the streets," he said by way of introduction, "'cause it's summertime." And "party in the streets" was right! After Dylan's intro, soul singer Billy Stewart leapt in with a rolled-*r* vocal blast. Drums crashed in behind him, followed by blaring horns. He starts shouting "huh!" and "yeah!" The tempo was about three times faster than any torch-song version I'd heard before, and it seemed like blasphemy. This was not how "Summertime" was supposed to sound.

Billy Stewart's "Summertime" opened my eyes to the expansive possibilities of cover songs. It took a song I thought I hadn't even liked that much (too slow, too maudlin) in an entirely irreverent, up-tempo direction. It brought new meaning to the lyrics, sounding more like what summertime actually is: fun.

Billy Stewart's radical reimagining of Gershwin's "Summertime" hit #10 on the charts in 1966—and partly inspired this book.

A college radio show started from there, and a year later came the *Cover Me* blog. Ever since then, readers have periodically suggested I write a book about cover songs. To which I invariably responded, "Dumb idea. That's like saying 'I'm going to write a book about original songs.'" (I phrased it more politely, I hope.) "Cover songs" is too broad a category. There are covers in all genres and all styles, covers that build on the originals and covers that bring nothing to the table, covers that soar and covers that flop. There's no unifying theory of cover songs to fit tidily between two book covers; it's too big and messy and wonderful a tent for that.

That explains the book you now hold in your hands. It's not a book "about cover songs." It's a book about nineteen *specific* cover songs. But through these nineteen, a cover-songs story emerges. It involves artistic triumphs and music-industry shenanigans. It touches on trends in record-making, music videos, and the Internet's impact on music (did you know the first viral song was a cover?). There are beautiful moments of unlikely artists coming together and some uglier instances of exploitation and racism. Every major change in the music industry since the advent of rock and roll finds some expression in the world of cover songs.

So no, someone covering "Purple Rain" doesn't mean Prince's version doesn't exist anymore. A great cover only makes a song stronger. It can make you think about a lyric in a way you never had before, or make you remember a favorite song from years ago. It can bring a great song to a wider audience, or bring a forgotten song to a younger audience. Here are nineteen such examples of covers that did all that and more. ◉

# ELVIS PRESLEY
## "HOUND DOG"

⚡ **BIG MAMA THORNTON COVER** ⚡

**SONG**
"HOUND DOG"
[BACKED WITH (B/W) "DON'T BE CRUEL"] (1956)

**WRITTEN BY**
JERRY LEIBER, MIKE STOLLER

**FIRST RECORDED BY**
BIG MAMA THORNTON (1952)

On July 25, 1956, songwriter Mike Stoller thought he was going to die. As he played poker on an Italian cruise liner, the *Andrea Doria*, it crashed into another boat outside of Nantucket. The cruise liner began to sink, and its 1,700 passengers scrambled to board limited lifeboats. Nearby ships eventually rescued those who made it. The refugees spent twelve long, cold, and shivering hours packed onto those rescue ships before disembarking at New York Harbor. Fifty-one passengers died that day, but Stoller was not among them. When he stepped out onto the dock, Stoller's songwriting partner Jerry Leiber greeted him. Leiber had some big news.

"Mike," Leiber said as soon as he saw him, "we got a smash hit on 'Hound Dog'!"

"Big Mama's record?" Stoller replied.

"No. Some white kid named Elvis Presley."

The "Big Mama" Stoller referred to was Big Mama Thornton (real name: Willie Mae), a three-hundred-pound blues belter with scars crossing her face. Dressed in overalls and combat boots, she aimed to appear as intimidating as possible. And by all accounts she succeeded.

Four years before their dockside reunion, Leiber and Stoller had been commissioned by producer Johnny Otis to write a hit for Thornton after her first two singles flopped. Leiber and Stoller were still teenagers at the time, white Jewish kids who loved rhythm and blues. After meeting Thornton, they knew they needed to write a low-down gritty blues to match what Leiber called her "monstrous" persona.

In the car on the way to the session, they wrote one on the dashboard in ten minutes.

"I was beating out a rhythm we called the 'buck dance' on the roof of the car" while scribbling down lyrics, Leiber told the website *Rock's Backpages* before his death. "We got to Johnny Otis's house and Mike went right to the piano . . . didn't even bother to sit down. He had a cigarette in his mouth that was burning his left eye, and he started to play the song. We took the song back to Big Mama and she snatched the paper out of my hand and said, 'Is this my big hit?' And I said, 'I hope so.'"

They titled the song "Hound Dog," but the lyrics had nothing to do with a dog, and certainly contained no lines about catching rabbits. The subject was a no-good man the narrator had caught stepping out. Stoller has said "hound dog" was actually a euphemism for a word you couldn't say on the radio: "motherfucker." Leiber and Stoller described it in their coauthored book (called, appropriately, *Hound Dog*) as a "deadly blues," but when Big Mama went to record it in Otis's garage, she didn't sing it that way. This massive blues belter sweetly crooned like Frank Sinatra.

"I'm looking at her, and I'm a little intimidated by the razor scars on her face, and I said, 'It don't go that way,'" Leiber said. "And she looked at me like looks could kill and said—and this was when I

They titled the song "Hound Dog," but the lyrics had nothing to do with a dog.

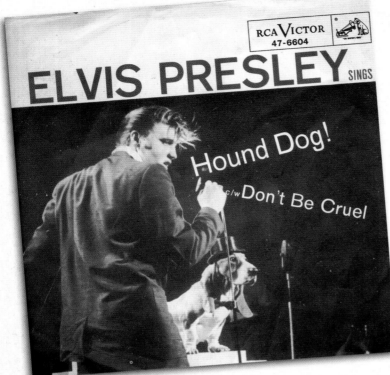

ELVIS PRESLEY SINGS
Hound Dog!
c/w Don't Be Cruel

RCA VICTOR
47-6604

The cover photo for Elvis's "Hound Dog"/"Don't Be Cruel" single came from the (in)famous Steve Allen performance, where he sang to an actual dog.

potent and could bust through quickly," and indeed it did. Within a month "Hound Dog" was a smash hit on the Rhythm & Blues chart. It stayed there for eleven weeks, seven of them at number one. After several misfires, Thornton finally had her hit.

Unfortunately, the charts, like so much of American culture, were still segregated in 1953. The "Rhythm and Blues Records" chart that "Hound Dog" topped had until just recently gone under another name: "Race Records." And though the name had changed, the stigma remained for any song that appeared on that chart. The other two major charts—"pop" and "country" (which itself had recently been renamed from "hillbilly")—might as well have hung a sign saying "Whites Only." Even a number one hit among African-American audiences stood little chance of crossing over to the white market.

found out I was white—'White boy, don't you be tellin' me how to sing the blues.'"

Leiber eventually prevailed, convincing Thornton to sing "Hound Dog" more aggressively while the two songwriters barked and howled in the background. The result was a tough, swaggering track, rawer than the era's typical R&B records, with only a guitar, bass, and drums played by Otis (who had to use a pseudonym as he was signed to a competing record label).

The single was released on the Texas R&B label Peacock Records in February of 1953. Industry magazine *Billboard* wrote that "this one is mighty

Some white artists tried to make the leap that Thornton couldn't. This was still the era of copycat covers. Within a month of "Hound Dog" topping the chart, six cover versions by white artists were rushed onto shelves. The threat of listener confusion appeared serious enough though that Thornton's label took out an ad in *Billboard* proclaiming it "The Original Version of 'Hound Dog' . . . Beware of Imitations." None of the covers were particularly distinctive, though, and for the most part vanished without a trace.

In addition to the knockoff covers, Peacock also had to contend with a phenomenon known as "answer songs." This was a short-lived phenomenon in which other artists would "answer" a hit single (a concept that sees some modern-day parallel in back-and-forth diss tracks in hip-hop). An artist would record a song that changed a hit's lyrics without changing the music, using his own words to somehow reply to the original singer's. The concept was similar to a cover, but one that only worked if you knew the original lyrics.

In this case, the upstart Memphis label Sun Records quickly got a local DJ named Rufus Thomas to record "Bear Cat (The Answer Song to Hound Dog)." Sun's Sam Phillips refashioned "Hound Dog"'s lyrics as the man's response to the woman's accusations and rush-released it for what *Billboard* called "the fastest answer song to hit the market." The magazine added, "It used to be that the answers to hits usually waited until the hit had started on the downward trail, but today the answers are ready a few days after records start moving upwards. This has led some to remark that the [manufacturers] soon may be bringing out the answers before the originals are even released."

"Bear Cat" became a surprise hit for Sun Records, the fledgling label's first. It rose to #3 on the same R&B chart that "Hound Dog" had topped. This started a run at Sun that within a few years would include Johnny Cash, Jerry Lee Lewis, and, of course, a young kid from Tupelo named Elvis.

The success of "Bear Cat," though, marked the end of the answer-song era. Because Phillips had replaced Leiber and Stoller's names with his own on the songwriting credits, the "Hound Dog" publishers sued and won to the tune of $35,000. In a strange twist of history, this began a financial decline for Sun that culminated in Phillips having to sell Elvis's contract shortly before he recorded his own "Hound Dog" cover.

Though there were no more answer songs to contend with, two years later another artist changed Leiber and Stoller's lyrics without permission. Freddie Bell led a musical-comedy band in Philadelphia called Freddie Bell and the Bellboys. As other artists had before them, Bell and his producer Bernie Lowe thought "Hound Dog" could be a hit among white audiences. They decided the reason that those previous attempts had failed was the song's salacious subject matter. To sanitize it, they would have to rewrite it.

Their solution? Make "Hound Dog" about an actual dog. They dropped double entendres like "You can wag your tail / But I ain't gonna feed you no more" and substituted "Well, you ain't never caught a rabbit / And you ain't no friend of mine." The fact that this rendered the other half of the song meaningless—how could a dog say he's high class?—didn't concern them (if one wants to get nitpicky, one could also note that hound dogs aren't supposed to catch rabbits at all, just point them out for their owner to shoot). Leiber himself would later complain that these rewritten lyrics made "no sense."

Regardless, Freddie Bell and the Bellboys released their rewritten "Hound Dog" on Lowe's small Teen Records label in 1955. It got some airplay in Philadelphia, but little traction nationally. It did, however, interest a concert promoter enough to book the band for a residency at the Sands in Las Vegas. "Hound Dog" soon became the band's showstopping closer. They added choreography and hammed it up for the older Vegas audiences, who chuckled at a novelty song that seemed to be sending up the rock-and-roll movement.

One night, though, Bell had a much younger man in his audience. This musician was playing his own Vegas residency and had heard good things about Bell's show.

In April of 1956, a twenty-year-old Elvis Presley was a rising star. After a string of successful Sun singles, his contract had been sold to RCA after a bidding war the previous fall. His debut album that spring had gone straight to #1.

But if he was a hit among teenagers, word had not reached the Las Vegas high-rollers more accustomed to a Judy Garland floor show. Like Bell, Presley had been booked for a residency in town, a two-week stand at the New Frontier Hotel. Unlike Bell, his was going poorly. He was billed alongside a saxophone-playing bandleader and the four songs Elvis performed each night—"Heartbreak Hotel," "Long Tall Sally," "Blue Suede Shoes," and "Money Honey"—went over like a strip show at the country club. He later said, "It was strictly an older group of people. They weren't my kind of audience, they didn't applaud, and I couldn't tell if they were dead or alive."

When he wasn't busy bombing onstage, Elvis had a lot of free time. He didn't drink or gamble, which limited one's options in Vegas, so he mostly went to movies and concerts. He attended Freddie

Bell's show and liked it so much he came back again and again. He was especially taken with Bell's closing number.

Sources differ on whether Presley had ever heard Big Mama Thornton's original "Hound Dog." As a fan of R&B records, he likely had, and it's hard to imagine he wouldn't know "Bear Cat," the big hit for Sun Records shortly before he joined the label. A childhood friend even said he remembered Elvis singing along to one of the crossover attempts by Bob Wills and the Texas Playboys (though presumably the friend meant former Texas Playboy Tommy Duncan, as Wills never covered the song himself). Regardless, the goofy novelty cover Freddie Bell and the Bellboys were performing struck Elvis in a way no other version had.

"When we heard them perform that night, we thought the song would be a good one for us to do as comic relief when we were onstage," Elvis's guitarist Scotty Moore wrote in his autobiography. "We loved the way they did it. They had a piano player who stood up and played—and the way he did his legs, they looked like rubber bands bending back and forth." In another interview, Moore was more succinct: "We stole it straight from them."

Presley asked Bell's permission to perform his arrangement live, and Bell agreed. According to one source, Elvis's manager Colonel Tom Parker promised Bell an opening slot in return, but if so it never materialized. Bell would later say onstage that he had given Elvis the tune to do. "He was proud that Elvis did what he did," says Bell's later musical director Gary Olds. "He was always the type of guy who would share the stage and go out of his way to help an up-and-comer like Elvis out."

"I didn't feel bad about that at all," Bell once told an interviewer, "He was an extraordinary talent but he didn't know how to sell rock 'n' roll in Vegas. We had choreography, while Elvis just stood and sang."

Elvis soon threw "Hound Dog" into his live set. "He came onstage one night and told us he was going to sing it," drummer D.J. Fontana said a few years later. "We just [held on tight], every man for himself."

Just as it had for Freddie Bell and the Bellboys, "Hound Dog" quickly became a crowd favorite for Elvis, and he too began closing his shows with it. "We were just looking on it as comic relief, if you will," guitarist Moore said, "just another number to do onstage."

The lackluster Vegas audiences had done nothing to slow Elvis's momentum, and the band was soon booked for their second appearance on the *Milton Berle Show* on June 5, 1956. The band had first played the show two months earlier to rave reviews, and, more importantly for Berle, huge viewership.

Getting ratings like that was a rarity for the fading TV star in those days. A series of poor business decisions and shifting audience tastes had seen his show's formerly huge audience dwindle. Shortly before Elvis's appearance, NBC told Berle his show would be canceled. June 5 would be its final episode. Berle wanted to go out with a bang, and a return from Elvis was the just the way to do it.

Plus, unlike his rival, Ed Sullivan, Berle actually *liked* this new music called rock and roll. Backstage before the show, Berle suggested Presley perform without a guitar, saying "Let 'em see you, son."

For the first time on TV, Elvis was unencumbered by an instrument, free to move around. And move he did. He performed two songs: his current hit single "I Want You, I Love You, I Need You" and his live showstopper "Hound Dog," which few viewers would have known.

For the first half of "Hound Dog," Presley stood still, save for a few toe shuffles. But then a cymbal crash moved the song into a half-speed knock-'em-dead ending the band had honed on the road. Elvis began hamming it up in an exaggerated bump-and-grind, jerking his hips about and dragging the microphone. The teenage girls in the audience cheered, but you can also hear some laughs at the jokey theatrics. It was sexy, sure, but also goofy, a bit of physical comedy. When Berle came out after Elvis finished, he began imitating the movements in a slapstick routine while Elvis grinned. Berle asked, "If I did that thing the same way you did, do you think I could get all the girls like you?" Elvis replied, "Well it might not get you girls, but it will sure keep your blood circulating."

The next day, though, the press didn't see the humor. Critics blasted his supposedly offensive "Hound Dog" performance (totally ignoring the other song he did with a tame barbershop quartet) and branded him "Elvis the Pelvis." The *New York Times* called him "a rock-and-roll version of one of the most standard acts in show business: the virtuoso of the hootchy-kootchy" and compared him to a burlesque dancer. The *New York Journal-American* lamented "a display of primitive physical movement difficult to describe in terms suitable to a family newspaper."

This polite Southern boy suddenly epitomized everything older generations feared about rock and roll's corrupting influence. Elvis was forced to defend himself in interviews. "I'm not trying to be sexy," he told one reporter. "It's just my way of expressing how I feel when I move around." He called his new nickname "one of the most childish expressions I've ever heard coming from an adult."

**This polite Southern boy suddenly epitomized everything older generations feared about rock and roll's corrupting influence.**

Despite outrage with "Hound Dog" in the highbrow media, the ratings told a different story. Berle got the out-with-a-bang finale he wanted. Twenty-two million people reportedly tuned in, and Elvis's office was deluged with thousands of letters containing money for fan club photos ("I got so much money I can't bring it in," Elvis's PR man told the bank). The attention gave an Elvis song that no one had known a week before a massive launch.

Four weeks later, Elvis appeared on TV again, this time on NBC's Sunday night program *The Steve Allen Show*. While Berle's show was at its end, Allen's was brand-new, launched only the week earlier to try to compete with Ed Sullivan's juggernaut over at CBS. Unlike Berle, Allen was not a fan of rock and roll and had only booked Elvis opportunistically. After the "Hound Dog"

**RIGHT:** Elvis's August 1956 Tampa concert was the town's second rock-and-roll show ever, after Bill Haley & His Comets came through that May.

fracas, Sullivan had publicly vowed never to book Elvis, and Allen made a ratings play. Still, NBC put out a statement saying the show "won't stand for bad taste under any circumstances."

The question on everyone's mind: Would Elvis repeat his "Hound Dog" performance? One *New York Daily Mirror* columnist even penned a poem about it:

> *Will Elvis rock and wiggle on Steve Allen's show tonight???? While thirty million teenage fans applaud in wild delight??? And will he shake his torso like a trotter with the heaves??? While pear-shaped notes of purest gold tell how his poor heart grieves??? Will Presley's fans all rally at the nearest TV set??? While mom and pop retire just as far as they can get??? Will maidens swoon and lads grow faint when Elvis starts to squeal??? And who can Sullivan dig up to fight such (ugh) appeal???*

As it happened, the answer to most of those questions was "no." Elvis did not wiggle and maidens did not swoon. Not wanting to court controversy so early in his show's run, Allen reined in Presley. "I had no interest in . . . letting him do his spot as he might in concert," he said later. Instead, he dressed Elvis up in a tuxedo and made him sing "Hound Dog" to an uninterested basset hound in a top hat. Elvis gamely played along, throwing baleful looks to the audience when the dog refused to cooperate, but despite his best efforts it was a castrated display devoid of the energy and excitement of his *Milton Berle* appearance. Moore said it must have been "one of the most excruciating performances of his career."

Despite—or because of—the efforts to make "Hound Dog" tamer, the press hated it. In a dramatic 180, they now decried Allen for preventing a repeat of the display that four weeks earlier had

so appalled them. And once again, ratings shot through the roof. Allen won his sought-after victory over Sullivan, with a whopping 55 percent of the television viewing audience tuning in to the (even) goofier version of "Hound Dog."

The day after the Allen show, July 2, 1956, Elvis had a recording session booked at New York's RCA Studio A. He arrived at the studio in the early afternoon. Outside, a couple girls were carrying picket signs that proclaimed "We Want the Real Elvis" and "We Want the Gyratin' Elvis."

After the exposure "Hound Dog" had gotten on TV, it would seem natural to release it as his next single, but Elvis initially resisted recording it. He saw the tune as a live novelty not worth putting to disc. Cooler heads eventually prevailed, among them RCA's Steve Sholes, the legendary A&R man responsible for poaching Elvis from Sun, who produced the session. Elvis eventually consented, but protested that it was the silliest song he'd ever done and he thought he would sell ten or twelve copies to his parents' neighbors.

After warming up with a couple spirituals, Elvis kicked off the "Hound Dog" session with the whole band recording live, as was still required at the time. He used his regular road band: Scotty Moore on guitar, Bill Black on bass, and newcomer D.J. Fontana on drums. To this he added his backup singers the Jordanaires, for what would be their first of many recordings with Presley: Gordon Stoker (first tenor), Neal Matthews (second tenor), Hoyt Hawkins (baritone), and Hugh Jarrett (bass).

The band played through the song once. Photographer Al Wertheimer described what happened when they went to listen: "Everyone sat on the floor around the one speaker in the room. Elvis held his forehead in his hand and concentrated on the sound. Steve Sholes stood by, shirtsleeves rolled up, his hands in his pockets, waiting for the reaction. At the end of the playback, Elvis looked up preoccupied and discontent. The engineer was concerned the drums were too loud. Elvis thought they were all right, he wanted more guitar and another run-through."

They played through the song again. And again. And again. The band had been confident that "Hound Dog" would be a snap to record, having been honed over two months of live performances and a pair of TV appearances, but it proved just the opposite. Over the next two hours they did thirty-one takes. Some lasted only a few seconds before someone messed up. On some, Elvis's bouncing around took him too far from the microphone. On others, one player or another flubbed their part, knocked into a mic, or missed a beat.

For the first dozen takes or so, the band joked around about their mistakes. When Fontana missed a drum beat, he turned it into a long drumroll. When Moore flubbed a note, he began loudly playing another song entirely. As time went on and they couldn't seem to get through the song right, though, tensions rose.

"The humor that had started the session was fading and people began glancing at Elvis to check his mood," Wertheimer wrote. "He wasn't happy." Surely exacerbating his grumpiness was that, despite the 83-degree temperature outside, the building's air-conditioner had been turned off

> **They played through the song again. And again. And again.**

due to the noise interfering with recording. The session went on for so long that pianist Shorty Long had to leave for another appointment and was replaced by Gordon Stoker of the Jordanaires. That meant the entire backing vocal needed to be rearranged, since they all needed to sing around one microphone and he couldn't reach it sitting at the piano. Stoker later said, "That's one of the worst sounds we ever got on any record."

As frustrations grew, the band began playing more aggressively. Fontana pounded his drums harder and harder, distorting the recording so much that the engineers gave up trying to keep the needle out of the red. On the end result, the only drum even audible in the mix is the snare. Rolling Stones drummer Charlie Watts called it "one of the great drum tracks of all time." Moore's guitar solo also grew increasingly unhinged, "the result of frustration" he wrote, later labeling it "ancient psychedelia." Keith Richards said that it sounded like Moore had gotten that raw sound by taking off his guitar and dropping it on the floor (he meant this as a compliment).

Elvis's vocals too got rougher and rougher. He had already made the decision to lop off the slow outro they had been doing live in favor of a harder-hitting version that raced to the finish. He traded any remaining nuance for high-decibel shouting, and the result was a far cry from the crooning Elvis of "I Want You, I Need You, I Love You" or "Heartbreak Hotel."

After thirty-one exhausting takes, Elvis and Sholes thought they might finally have it. Everyone slumped around the speaker to hear the recordings. As Wertheimer describes it, "Elvis combed his hair, drank the Coke offered by [an assistant] and shrugged in reply to comments about how good the music was. Steve trod lightly: 'Elvis, you ready to hear a playback?' As if bad news never had good timing, he said, 'Now's as good a time as any.'

"Elvis sat cross-legged on the floor in front of the speaker. The engineer announced the take over the PA and let the tape roll. Elvis winced, chewed his fingernails, and looked at the floor. At the end of the first playback, he looked like he didn't know whether it was a good take or not. Steve called for take eighteen."

This went on for take after take, until eventually Elvis settled on take thirty-one. He asked if a copy could be brought to his hotel the next morning. Then, after two stressful hours, they moved on to the next song.

RCA knew they had a hit on their hands and rushed out the single to capitalize on all the TV attention. Less than two weeks after it was recorded, "Hound Dog" started hitting store shelves, jukeboxes, and radio. It was backed with another song recorded in New York, the Otis Blackwell–penned ballad "Don't Be Cruel." In a sign that any bad feelings had been forgotten, the cover featured an image of Presley on the *Steve Allen Show*, singing to that basset hound.

The double-sided single was a huge hit, the best-selling of Presley's entire career. Within a week it had sold almost one million copies, and by September the pair of songs was #1 on all three major charts (Pop, Country, and R&B). "Hound Dog" had finally crossed over. Technically B-side "Don't Be Cruel" reached #1 and "Hound Dog" topped out at #2, but because of the confusing

way charts were then calculated, that didn't necessarily mean the former was actually more popular. It just meant it did better on radio, the only place two sides of the same single could be tabulated independently (whereas a sale from "Hound Dog" in stores would count equally for both sides). *Variety* reported that this single at one point amounted to a full two thirds of the discs RCA Records was manufacturing.

Just as the TV performances had earlier that summer, the "Hound Dog" single divided listeners along generational lines. Perry Como said, "When I hear 'Hound Dog' I have to vomit a little." Frank Sinatra sarcastically called it "a masterpiece" when he joined a campaign against "inferior music."

The next generation of musicians, though, had a different reaction. Over in Britain, a nine-year-old named Davy Jones was listening. "I saw a cousin of mine dance when I was very young," the boy said years later, when he had rechristened himself David Bowie. "She was dancing to Elvis's 'Hound Dog' and I have never seen her get up and be moved so much by anything. It really impressed me." Up in a Minnesota, a fifteen-year-old Robert Zimmerman, soon to be called Bob Dylan, was equally impressed. "When 'Hound Dog' came across the radio, there was nothing in my mind that said, 'Wow, what a great song, I wonder who wrote that?' It didn't really concern me who wrote it. It was just there."

Very few people, it seemed, wondered who wrote it. Few reviews mentioned the Big Mama Thornton original, and none mentioned the Freddie Bell arrangement Elvis had lifted. No one buying the disc would be any the wiser, either, as neither of their names appeared anywhere on it. As far as the public was concerned, "Hound Dog" belonged to Elvis.

This irked those involved with the original. Leiber and Stoller famously hated Presley's cover, though in later interviews they often added "until the checks started coming in!" He "ruined the song," Leiber told a TV interviewer. "It was a song that had to do with obliterated romance. In effect, she was saying, 'Get out of my house.' And 'You ain't caught a rabbit, and you ain't no friend of mine' is inane. It doesn't mean anything to me." "It sounded too nervous," Stoller said. "The original record is insinuating and funky and this was some kind of fast, nervous, rockabilly version."

Despite his gracious words initially, Freddie Bell did later sue Elvis for a share of the profits. It wasn't a matter of ego, Bell's music director Gary Olds says. He just needed the cash as bookings dried up. Bell lost the suit, though, because he hadn't ever gotten permission to alter the lyrics. So while credited songwriters Leiber and Stoller made millions off Elvis's hit, Bell never saw a penny.

Thornton, who never had another hit and whose hard living led to a long downward spiral (by her death in 1984, the woman known as "Big Mama" had wasted away to ninety-five pounds), was not pleased, either. "I never got a dime" when he recorded it, Thornton told an interviewer later. "I didn't even get a box of nothing. He refused to play with me when he first came out and got famous. They wanted a big thing with Big Mama Thornton and Elvis Presley. He refused."

Though it's hard to know to what exactly she's referring—she never elaborates and no one else ever mentioned a possible collaboration—her story is plausible. Though Elvis would regularly acknowledge his musical influences generally, neither he nor his people were ever very overt about mentioning when particular songs they did were

covers. Indeed, not long after "Hound Dog," they made it a practice to demand Elvis be added as a co-writer to any songs he recorded, despite him never writing a note.

Big Mama's accusations contribute to a reputation that plagues Elvis to this day, one not uncommon in the world of early cover songs: racism.

In 1989, twelve years after Elvis had died, Public Enemy had a #1 rap song with the incendiary title "Fight the Power." At the beginning of the third verse, Chuck D raps "Elvis was a hero to most but he never meant shit to me / Straight-up racist, that sucker was."

This was a reasonably common sentiment by this time, particularly in the African-American community. One oft-cited piece of evidence was—and still is—"Hound Dog." Elvis took a song sung by a black woman and had a huge hit, giving her neither credit nor money. A few years before Public Enemy's song, acclaimed *Color Purple* author Alice Walker helped popularize this narrative with a short story in which a fictional black blues singer named Gracie Mae (a stand-in for Thornton's real name of Willie Mae) gives a song she wrote to a "womanish-looking" white boy. He has a hit and becomes the "Emperor of Rock and Roll" while Gracie Mae is relegated to history's dustbin.

The accusation that Elvis earned far more money and fame for "Hound Dog" than Big Mama did is, of course, true. But how much blame should be assigned to him and how much to the culture that surrounded him? Was Elvis really, to quote Chuck D, a "straight-up racist"?

What does someone covering a song owe to that song's original performer?

Racial appropriation has long been a dark undercurrent in the history of cover songs. The copycat covers of the '40s and '50s often used white performers to "cross over" black hits. One famous example was Pat Boone having a bigger hit with his carbon-copy "Tutti Frutti" cover than Little Richard. Boone's producers thought Richard's R&B hit could cross over if a white face sang it, and Richard loudly and publicly called them out for whitewashing his song. Another example was Bill Haley changing the lyrics to Big Joe Turner's "Shake, Rattle, and Roll" to remove any references that might scan as black.

There are many instances of white covers cashing in on black creativity, and the music industry, like so much else, was inarguably racist at the time. Indeed, a number of white performers had tried to copy Big Mama Thornton's "Hound Dog" for white audiences. But the picture with Elvis's "Hound Dog" is a little more complicated than "Tutti Frutti" or "Shake, Rattle, and Roll." For one, in this case the songwriters were also white. And, perhaps even more importantly, the musician Elvis took his version from wasn't Big Mama Thornton, but Freddie Bell, a lounge singer as white as they come. If anyone had a bone to pick, it was Bell.

This doesn't clear Elvis of some blame in how he handled "Hound Dog." He certainly could have made it more of a point to credit Thornton in interviews, acknowledging her song specifically, rather than just his appreciation of black musicians in general. And there's no question that a white

**Elvis grew frustrated with the "Hound Dog" albatross hanging around his neck.**

face had an easier time getting on the charts in 1956 than a black one. But any mistakes he made recording and promoting this song were born more out of naïveté than racism. The fact that he had the bigger hit than Thornton is an indictment of the system as much as anything.

Fifteen years after "Fight the Power," even Chuck D would change his tune. "He was a bad-ass white boy," he said in a documentary. "Elvis had a great respect for black folk at a time when black folks were considered niggers, and who gave a damn about nigger music?"

Elvis had many other hits over the years, but according to guitarist Scotty Moore, "Hound Dog" remained their most requested song right up until Presley's death in 1977. It would be "a riot every time" they played it, Moore wrote. And dutifully, Elvis continued to deliver the hit live and on TV.

Despite initially claiming he would never book Presley ("He is not my cup of tea"), Ed Sullivan couldn't ignore his rivals' ratings forever and booked Presley three times in '56 and '57. Elvis played "Hound Dog" each time, in one instance famously being filmed from the waist up to avoid the camera catching any untoward hip movements. In what was becoming a pattern, once again people were outraged, only solidifying the song as an iconic part of any Elvis performance.

Over the years, though, it would appear Elvis grew frustrated with the "Hound Dog" albatross hanging around his neck. As his music grew richer and more orchestrated, he showed increasing reluctance to perform the rudimentary number with the nonsense lyrics. He never spoke about it—interviews grew increasingly rare, supposedly because his manager wanted to hide the fact that he was an "idiot savant"—but he expressed his feelings onstage.

After performing "Hound Dog" as his showstopping closer for a decade, in the '60s he moved it to the middle of the set. He began racing through the song faster and faster; in 1973's famous *Aloha in Hawaii* concert, he finished "Hound Dog" in all of forty-four seconds. Clearly bored with the song, over the years he tried a number of changes to spice it up, including adding funk guitar, syncopating scatting ("you ain't nothing but a hound dog . . . chicka . . . bom bom . . . "), and a half-speed opening in the vein of his old closing bump-and-grind.

The song gradually became comic relief again, an in-joke with the audience. Once he rolled around onstage with a statue of the RCA dog. Another time his band sent out a live basset hound as a birthday gag. Oftentimes in later years, he would strike a sexy pose before he began the song, legs akimbo and hips thrust, just as he had on TV twenty years earlier. As the audience cheered, he would give them a knowing look and say, "Here we go again . . . " ⬤

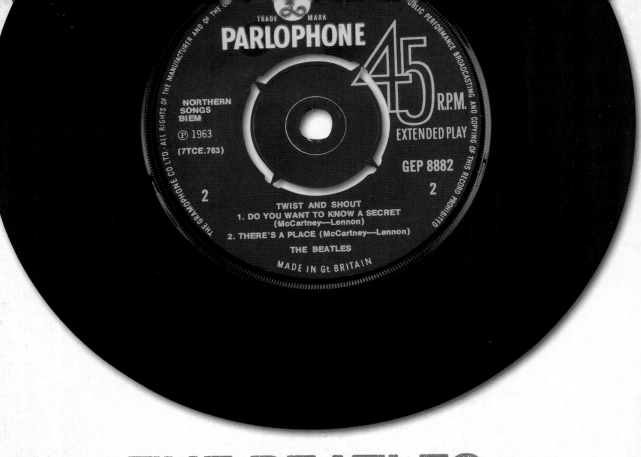

# THE BEATLES
# "TWIST AND SHOUT"

⚡ ISLEY BROTHERS/TOP NOTES COVER ⚡

SONG
"TWIST AND SHOUT"
[B/W] "THERE'S A PLACE" (1963)
————
WRITTEN BY
BURT BERNS, PHIL MEDLEY
————
FIRST RECORDED BY
THE TOP NOTES (1961)

Before "Yesterday," "Let It Be," and "Hey Jude"—before even "Love Me Do" and "Please Please Me"—the Beatles were a covers band. Every night they played Top 40 hits to inebriated patrons in Liverpool and Hamburg bars. They catered to their audiences, and their audiences did not want to hear songs a bar band had written themselves.

They didn't even always want rock and roll, so the covers the Beatles played branched beyond the obvious Elvis and Buddy Holly tunes. "We had these fat old businessmen coming in . . . and saying 'Play us a mambo or a rumba' or something," Paul

PREVIOUS: The adorable mop-tops in February 1963, five months before "Twist and Shout" (below) blew everybody's hair back.

McCartney said later. "So we had to get into this kind of stuff."

The pre-fame Beatles covered Johnny Mercer's schmaltzy big-band song "Dream." They covered Irving Berlin's classic ballad "Blue Skies." They covered a Leiber and Stoller song much more obscure than "Hound Dog," "Some Other Guy." And they covered songs from the era's dance craze: the twist.

Joey Dee and the Starliters's "Peppermint Twist" and Gene Vincent's "Twist in the Street" (rewritten from "Dance in the Street" to capitalize on the fad) both found their way into the band's repertoire. McCartney even wrote an original twist song called "Pinwheel Twist" (a friend who heard it described it as "fucking awful"). One twist song really got the crowd dancing, though: a cover of the Isley Brothers' new single, "Twist and Shout."

It's a testament to the Beatles' love of American rhythm and blues that they knew this song at all. As first recorded by the Top Notes, "Twist and Shout" had flopped. The Isley Brothers' subsequent cover did slightly better, but still had not reached the chart heights of "Peppermint Twist," Sam Cooke's "Twistin' the Night Away," or any of Chubby Checker's *three* twist songs. Not only that, but what success it had was in America, where it

The Isley Brothers performing on the British show *Ready Steady Go!* on November 27, 1964; ironically, one of their fellow performers on that episode was the Beatles.

was still orders of magnitude more popular than it was England. But among Liverpool's few superfans of American R&B were John, Paul, George, and Ringo.

"If the Beatles ever wanted a sound, it was R&B," McCartney said. "That's what we used to listen to, what we used to like and what we wanted to be like. Black, that was basically it."

But the Beatles weren't black, and they weren't an R&B band. They played rock and roll. So over the course of hundreds of concerts, they adapted "Twist and Shout" to fit their abilities. They amped up the guitars. They ditched the original's prominent horn part. They added a second crescendo (the "Ahh-ahh-ahh" bit) to drag out the audience ecstasy that much longer. They adored the Isley Brothers, but their cover didn't sound much like them.

Being such fans of the original, they felt a little guilty about their inauthentic cover. "I always hate singing the song 'Twist and Shout' when there's a colored artist on the bill with us," John Lennon said at the time. "It doesn't seem right, you know. I feel sort of embarrassed . . . It makes me curl up. I always feel they could do the song much better than me."

But the crowds loved it, so the band began to make it their sure-fire show closer. It wouldn't have been as familiar as many of the other covers they did, but crowds never failed to erupt. When Bruce Springsteen closed his own shows with the song, he called it his "stadium-wrecker" for the way it made the building go wild (years later). It served the same purpose for the Beatles—though then in small, sweaty clubs rather than stadiums.

Fast-forward a couple years and hundreds of concerts. By February 1963, the Beatles were no longer a covers band, reportedly boasting over a hundred original compositions even then. Both the singles they had released in their fledgling recording career—"Love Me Do/PS I Love You" the previous October and "Please Please Me/Ask Me Why" in January—had raced up the British charts. They needed to record an album, and fast, to capitalize on their early success. Then called *Off the Beatles Track* (a title thankfully abandoned), the album needed ten more songs to surround these hit singles. A day

**But the Beatles weren't black, and they weren't an R&B band. They played rock and roll.**

was booked at EMI Studios—later to be known as Abbey Road—to bang out some tracks. They had four songs done and only one day to record the rest of the album. It's become known as the most productive day in the history of recording studios.

"They realized this was quite a different technique than standing in front of a stage with screaming girls," remembers studio engineer Richard Langham of the recording process. "They were so used to singing and playing on top of each other with everything spilling over into all of the microphones. Our main challenge was to get isolation so you could control them. They were quite amenable [to taking more care to get the sound right]."

Despite their years playing covers, the band members now considered themselves primarily songwriters, and wanted their first album to be entirely original material. "We want to try to make the LP something different," Lennon said in an interview at the time. "You know, not just all somebody else's songs."

However, things got off to a slow start. The first half of the day was spent recording two original songs, "I Saw Her Standing There" and "There's a Place," and in neither case did they deliver a satisfactory take after hours of trying. They'd used up half of the only day they had to record the album.

To speed things along, they began recording some of the crowd-pleasing covers they'd honed on club stages, songs they knew backwards and forwards. Whatever notions they'd held of an all-originals album vanished. In short order the band recorded Lenny Welch's chirpy pop rarity "A Taste of Honey," Arthur Alexander's soul weeper "Anna (Go to Him)," and girl group songs by the Cookies ("Chains") and Shirelles ("Baby It's You" and "Boys," Ringo's singing debut).

They banged out the covers quickly, trying to re-create their stage show within the cold confines of the studio. "That record tried to capture us live, and was the nearest thing to what we might have sounded like in Hamburg and Liverpool," Lennon said in 1975. "It's the nearest you can get to knowing what we sounded like before we became the 'clever' Beatles."

The covers required only one or two takes, having been refined over so many shows. Despite the late start, by the time night fell they'd recorded nine complete songs—five originals and four covers. It was late and they were exhausted. But they still needed one more song.

Most people think the Isley Brothers' 1961 "Twist and Shout" (shown here) was the first recorded version of this song, but the Top Notes actually got there first, in 1956.

Like so many things in the Beatles' world, their eleventh-hour decision to record "Twist and Shout" has taken on near-mythic status among fans. Multiple people have claimed credit for suggesting the song that night. The most-told story finds the band hosting a late-night summit in the studio's cafeteria, exhausted and unsure how to finish the album until a visiting reporter makes the crucial suggestion.

It's a good story, but that and most of the others are bogus, says studio engineer Langham. "If everybody was there who says they were there, there wouldn't have been any room for me to get in there and work," he says. "Basically we recorded their stage show, what songs they knew already. 'Twist and Shout' was just one more at the end. [Producer] George Martin said to John, 'Shall we give it a go and see if your voice will take it?'"

Not only did they plan on recording "Twist and Shout," but they planned on recording it last. Lennon's only other lead vocals that day—"Anna" and "Baby It's You"—were midtempo ballads that demanded little vocally. "Twist and Shout" was different. John knew from closing so many concerts with it that performing the song would shred his vocal cords. And that was on a good day. On this day he was sick.

## You can hear the sickness in Lennon's voice, scratchy and cracking repeatedly like a pubescent teen's.

"John's voice was pretty shot," first engineer Norman Smith remembered. "They had a whole tin of throat lozenges plus cartons of cigarettes on the piano. John had to do the last track ['Twist and Shout'] on that first album, so he swallowed two or three of the lozenges before we attacked it. It's not an easy number for any vocalist to sing, but we had to get it in one take."

Lozenges downed, Lennon stepped up to the microphone. Despite being sick and exhausted— one report says he was so overheated he took off his shirt, but Langham can't confirm whether that's true—he pulled himself together and delivered one of the greatest vocal performances of his career. The Beatles rarely recorded covers as dynamically as they did their own songs. But their performance of "Twist and Shout"

**RIGHT:** In 1966, the Beatles returned to their old stomping ground of Hamburg, Germany—only this time, they weren't playing in a grotty beer hall but a 5,600-seat arena.

proved transcendent, not in spite of the trying circumstances but because of them.

You can hear the sickness in Lennon's voice, scratchy and cracking repeatedly like a pubescent teen's. The rawness is what makes the song stand out, grittier and more passionate than the clean and polished pop nuggets they were doing elsewhere. They tried a second take, but his voice was already gone. If Lennon hadn't gotten it right that first time, "Twist and Shout" might never have been heard outside the beer halls of Hamburg.

"There's a power in John's voice there that certainly hasn't been equaled since," McCartney said years later. "And I know exactly why—it's because he worked his bollocks off that day. We left 'Twist and Shout' until the very last thing because we knew there was one take."

"The last song nearly killed me," Lennon remembered a few years before his death in 1980. "My voice wasn't the same for a long time after— every time I swallowed it was like sandpaper. I was always bitterly ashamed of it because I could sing it better than that, but now it doesn't bother me. You can hear I'm just a frantic guy doing his best."

The album—retitled *Please Please Me*—was released a month later, with their "Twist and Shout" cover as the final track. You know what happened next.

Ed Sullivan. Screaming girls. The movies. India.

As opposed to "Hound Dog" or many other iconic cover songs, "Twist and Shout" didn't dramatically change the band's career arc. They had enough other hit songs in their arsenal, most of them originals. They didn't need "Twist and Shout." But it remains important for a reason. Though they continued to include covers on their next few albums, "Twist and Shout" remains the best showcase of the Beatles' ability as first-rate song interpreters.

It also offers an early example about how a band can learn enough covering other people's songs to eventually write their own. "Twist and Shout" illustrates

the transition happening for cover songs in the mid-'60s. It was the moment when cover songs really came into their own.

Look at any hit from the first half of the twentieth century, and the performer's name will rarely be the same as the songwriter. From Frank Sinatra through Elvis, performers were not expected to write their own material. As a result, few singers or fans thought of the cover song as a separate category. For the first half of the twentieth century, *everything* was a cover song for all intents and purposes. Musicians were expected to interpret songs other people wrote, not write anything themselves. Singer and performer were two separate career paths.

But by the mid-sixties, singer-songwriters were on the rise. Fans began placing a premium

["Twist and Shout"] was the moment when cover songs really came into their own.

on singers writing their own material. The three most enduring rock artists of the decade—the Beatles, the Rolling Stones, and Bob Dylan—all followed a similar trajectory: each of them started their career covering other people's songs, but within a few years began writing their own material. In doing so, they raised the bar for their peers and flipped the pattern. Original songs became the norm; covers the exception.

"Twist and Shout" marks the end of the era where a band could record covers as a matter of course. "Real" musicians were now expected to write their own stuff. That meant that if you were going to buck the trends and do a cover, you'd better be damn sure it was worth it. ◉

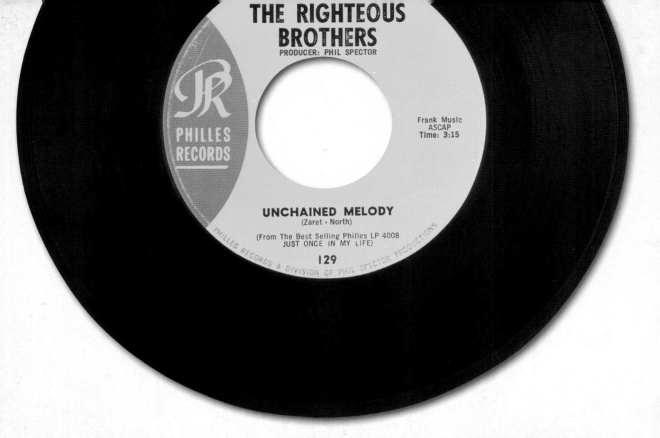

THE RIGHTEOUS BROTHERS
"UNCHAINED MELODY"

⚡ TODD DUNCAN COVER ⚡

SONG
"UNCHAINED MELODY"
[B/W "HUNG ON YOU"] (1965)

WRITTEN BY
ALEX NORTH, HY ZARET

FIRST RECORDED BY
TODD DUNCAN (1955)

The scene: a medium-security prison in California. A dozen inmates sit around their cell. One strums a guitar. Another, lying in his bunk, begins to sing: "Oh . . . my love . . . my darling . . . I've hungered for your touch."

The movie was *Unchained,* an otherwise unmemorable 1955 prison-escape film. The singer was Todd Duncan, an opera star assigned a minor role just so he could sing this song. The song was unimaginatively titled after the movie: "Unchained Melody."

**PREVIOUS:** Bobby Hatfield and Bill Medley make righteous melodies, 1965. **BELOW:** *Unchained*'s only other claim to fame might be a poster referencing "the searing pages of Reader's Digest!"

The melody dated back to the 1930s, when composer Alex North wrote it and put it on the shelf. It sat there for two decades until North was hired to score *Unchained* and gave lyricist Hy Zaret four days to put words to his tune. Zaret reluctantly agreed, but refused the producers' request to use "unchained" in the lyrics or tie the song lines to the film's plot.

This proved a blessing, making the song universal. It was nominated for an Academy Award for Best Song, the only Oscar nomination *Unchained* received. The movie was quickly forgotten. Its theme song was not.

Before the Righteous Brothers got to it a decade later, several artists had already covered "Unchained Melody." Orchestral bandleader Les Baxter recorded a saccharine instrumental. Children's quartet the Lennon Sisters performed a chipper *Sound of Music*–style version on *The Lawrence Welk Show*. Doo-wop group Vito & the Salutations sped it way up, like the Four Seasons at a sprint.

The most important of those early covers proved to be Roy Hamilton's. The Jersey soul singer's take was soaring but subtle, with strings and his beautiful voice adding a passion and emotion missing from many of the early covers. It brought some listeners to tears. Two listeners in particular.

"Bobby and I loved Roy's version," Righteous Brothers singer Bill Medley remembers. "I can't remember if we'd ever seen the movie, but Roy was our inspiration. We sang a bunch of stuff he did."

Medley's partner Bobby Hatfield (they were not, in fact, brothers), who died in 2003, had sung Hamilton's version in his pre–Righteous Brothers group, the Variations. When the Righteous Brothers formed in the early 1960s, though, Hatfield did not bring the song with him. He and Medley needed duets to sing, and "Unchained Melody" was unequivocally a solo performance.

Within their first couple years, the two made hits of several such duets: first the Medley-penned "Little Latin Lupe Lu" in 1963, and the following year the chart-topping "You've Lost That Lovin' Feelin'." A local DJ coined the term "blue-eyed soul" to describe the white singers, and soon they were opening for the Beatles on the band's first U.S. tour. Music-producing legend Phil Spector signed the pair, the first white act on his new soul label Philles Records.

The Spector signing came with a caveat, though. Phil cared about singles, not albums. He would produce all their singles in his famous "Wall of Sound" style, but the band was on their own to produce B-sides and album filler tracks. No one would listen beyond the single anyway, Spector reasoned, so his time was better spent elsewhere. He had even been known to deliberately put a subpar track on the flip side of a record to ensure DJs played the correct A-side single.

And Spector knew just what the Righteous Brothers' next single would be. He was sure the song he'd picked would become a guaranteed classic: "Hung on You."

"Unchained Melody" began as a soundtrack song and was used in later movies as varied as *Goodfellas* and *Ghost*.

"Hung on You" did indeed bear the markings of a surefire hit, being written by the dynamite team of Carole King and Gerry Goffin. In the past couple years alone, the duo had written "Will You Still Love Me Tomorrow" for the Shirelles, "The Loco-Motion" for Little Eva, and dozens more. Spector recorded the Righteous Brothers singing it and assigned Medley and Hatfield to come up with something—anything—for the single's B-side. He didn't care what. No one would be playing that side anyway.

Hatfield told his partner that he used to sing "Unchained Melody" in his old show. Medley

Bill Medley (left) and Bobby Hatfield (right) working in the studio with a seemingly spooked Phil Spector (center), 1967.

knew the song and was also a huge fan of Roy Hamilton's version. Though Hatfield's was a solo performance—not what Righteous Brothers fans were looking for—Medley didn't mind. Medley sung the more prominent part on "Hung on You," and, besides, "Unchained Melody" was only a B-side.

"There are only so many songs that work as good duets," Medley says. "So we would use those as the singles but then use other songs to fill out the albums. I had sung more of a lead role on our earlier hits like 'You've Lost That Lovin' Feelin'' anyway, so I was happy for Bobby to take this one."

Since "Unchained Melody" was not a potential single, Spector was not involved in the production. He turned it over to Medley, who had produced the duo himself before Spector signed them. "Bill took

**"It was just one more track among many."**

his production cues from Phil," remembers Art Munson, one of the band's guitarists at the time. "He would do things like bring in two or three piano players, we'd have both electric bass and upright bass, a couple of drummers. He was going for that same kind of sound."

Medley modeled the music after his beloved version by Roy Hamilton: a simple rhythm track (including Medley himself on piano) overdubbed with soaring strings and horns. "I wasn't trying to imitate Roy's production exactly," Medley says. "I just wanted a good, dynamic bed for Bobby to sing over. When the song is written that well, you don't need any studio tricks."

Recording the instrumental track took little time; it was knocked out alongside several other B-sides and album tracks in one afternoon.

"There was no sense this might be a hit," Munson remembers of the session. "It was just one more track among many."

When Bobby Hatfield came in to record his vocals, he already knew the song cold from singing it with the Variations so many times. He sang his version over the music Medley had recorded and nailed it in two takes.

Hatfield left the studio to go home. Medley was getting ready to leave himself when Hatfield suddenly walked back in. "I thought we were done, but he said he wanted to punch in one new part," Medley says. "It was risky because with the equipment we had, to do another take you had to tape right over the previous one. But I agreed and cued up the tape to the right moment. He steps up and he starts singing these new high notes, the 'I *neeeeeed* your love' part, which he had never done before. It was spur-of-the moment inspiration."

Hatfield would later complain that he wished he'd sung the song better, but to everyone else's ears his vocals on the recording were perfect. "I heard him sing it even better later, like on *The Andy Williams Show* and *Shindig!*, but this was ideal for the recording," Medley says. "It's a powerful performance with a lot of emotion, but it's not totally overwhelming. It's a track you can listen to again and again."

Perfect or not, they had no expectations that "Unchained Melody" would reach an audience. It was a B-side, after all; the most they could hope for was a few fans of "Hung on You" eventually flipping the single over. Which is basically what happened—except instead of fans, it was radio DJs, and instead of a few, it was a lot.

When the "Hung on You" single started landing at radio stations, it didn't receive the rave response that Spector had anticipated. Local disc jockeys soon discovered that they got more calls after playing the track on the record's other side. The much-hyped new Righteous Brothers single was a stiff, but the B-side was on its way to becoming an unexpected smash.

**"I had an accidental hit."**

"I had an accidental hit," Hatfield said in a *Rolling Stone* interview before his death. "It was kind of cool because Bill was singing lead on all of the songs then, so it was like, 'Wow, who's that little shit with the high voice?'"

This infuriated the hot-tempered Spector, who started calling radio stations to demand that they stop playing "Unchained Melody." For all his industry sway, he was ignored. Spector changed tactics and began sending out new singles with "Unchained Melody" listed on the A-side alongside a prominent credit: "Producer: Phil Spector."

"I wasn't really annoyed when Spector started taking the credit," Medley says. "I was never paid for all the sessions I was producing anyway. That was just how it went."

The next year, Medley and Hatfield split from Spector and signed with a new label, where they would continue to produce hits. "Unchained Melody" faded from the charts as all hits eventually do, settling into what looked like a quiet retirement on oldies radio. But then, twenty-five years later, Patrick Swayze came along to give the song its second coming.

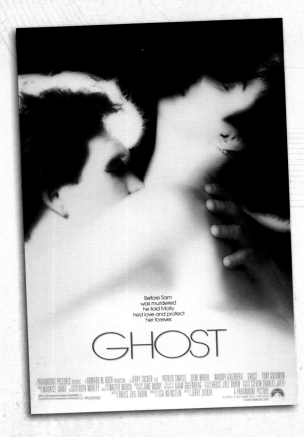

After receiving new life via the movie *Ghost*, the Righteous Brothers' "Unchained Melody" was inducted into the Grammy Hall of Fame in 2000.

Fittingly, the song's afterlife came about thanks to a movie called *Ghost*. By the time the 1990 movie was being made, the Righteous Brothers were mostly through, occasionally performing together but decades past their last hit. Medley had a burgeoning solo career demanding his time, even scoring his own hit with "(I've Had) The Time of My Life" in 1987's *Dirty Dancing*.

That movie's star, Patrick Swayze, was a Righteous Brothers fan, but Medley says "Unchained Melody" unexpectedly turning up a few years later in *Ghost* was not Swayze's doing. "Some producer was just driving in his car one day on the way to the movie set," he says, "and 'Unchained Melody' came on the oldies station. Apparently, he immediately said 'That's it, that's the song we've been looking for.'"

At the time, though, Medley and Hatfield knew none of this. They were not even told the song would be in the movie. "A friend called me up one day and said, 'Have you seen this new movie *Ghost*? Because your song's in it,'" Medley says. "I'm not even sure I'd heard of the movie, but once I saw it, I knew this would be big."

"Our tour manager called me up and said *USA Today* wanted to do an interview," Hatfield recalled during an interview for the Righteous Brothers' website shortly before his death in 2003. "And I said why, and he said because of this new movie *Ghost*. I said well, I'm not even in it. And they said yeah, but your recording of 'Unchained Melody' is."

Medley knew from his own recent experience that this movie could give the song a second life. Not only had he become a star in his own right from *Dirty Dancing,* but a year before that, Tom Cruise had memorably serenaded Kelly McGillis with "You've Lost That Lovin' Feelin'" in *Top Gun.* When Medley had asked the label back then to rerelease that song to capitalize on the new attention, they'd refused. Medley still felt burned.

"I knew we had lost out on a lot of play after *Top Gun* when the label didn't rerelease 'Lovin' Feelin',' and I wasn't going to let it happen again," he says. "I asked the label to rerelease 'Unchained Melody' after I saw *Ghost,* but once again they said it wasn't really necessary."

So Medley and Hatfield took it upon themselves to rerecord "Unchained Melody" so they could push the single themselves. "We tried to get the rerecord as close as we could," Medley says, "but you can never get it exactly the same—the magic of the first one, how mics bleed into each other, how Bobby was feeling that day."

Their new version shot up the charts, and the movie was so popular that the old one did as well—even without the label promoting it. The Righteous Brothers became the first act to have two versions of the same song in the Top 20 simultaneously. A movie had started the winding story of "Unchained Melody," and another movie thirty-five years later gave it a new life. To younger listeners hearing the cover for the first time, it might as well have been called *"Ghost* Melody."

> **The Righteous Brothers became the first act to have two versions of the same song in the Top 20 simultaneously.**

Since the Righteous Brothers had their two-time hit cover, the song has become a go-to track for hundreds of other performers who want to show off their pipes, whether it's U2 or a wannabe star on a singing competition. But the only other cover to compete with the Righteous Brothers' version comes from someone who had reached the point where he could barely sing at all but still had one more great cover left in him.

On June 21, 1977, Elvis Presley was two decades and a lot of miles removed from his "Hound Dog" youth. At a concert in South Dakota, he looked like a parody of "washed-up Elvis": puffy, sweaty, bedazzled in a rhinestone jumpsuit that went two steps beyond flashy into ridiculous. Yet against all odds, two months before his death, he delivered one of the best performances of his entire career.

Near the end of the evening's concert, Elvis threw a curveball. He'd already delivered the hits: "That's All Right," "Jailhouse Rock," and a half-assed mumble through "Hound Dog." Next up on the set list was his standard closer, "Can't Help Falling in Love." But as the band was about to start, he waved them off. "I'm going to do this first," he said and sat down alone at the piano.

The piano didn't have a mic stand, so Elvis made a stagehand stand there holding the microphone up to his mouth. "I don't know all the chords," he muttered, "so if you hear me getting my fingers caught in the keys back here, you know what it is."

Then he began to sing a song that was not a part of his usual set: "Unchained Melody." Elvis's shaky vocals couldn't come close to Hatfield's; he would have been laughed right out of an *American Idol* audition. But the power comes in the effort, a raw and vulnerable performance, showing a commitment long absent in his work. He'd come a long way since he covered "Hound Dog." But after all the excess, the movies, the drugs, and the rhinestones, Elvis's ability to take someone else's song and make it his own shone through one last time. It couldn't have been further from the Righteous Brothers' cover, but, as Medley says, a song that good can soar in any number of interpretations. ◉

# ARETHA FRANKLIN
## "RESPECT"

⚡ OTIS REDDING COVER ⚡

SONG
"RESPECT"
[B/W "DR. FEELGOOD"] (1967)

WRITTEN BY
OTIS REDDING

FIRST RECORDED BY
OTIS REDDING (1965)

One February evening in 1968, Aretha Franklin walked onto a Detroit arena stage in front of twelve thousand screaming fans. This was new to her. Not going onstage—she'd been a singer for a dozen years already—but having crowds waiting to see her when she got there. That night, in fact, was a celebration of her finally becoming a star.

Various music-industry publications presented her with awards that night: *Billboard, Cash Box, Record World*. The most meaningful award to her, though, was the Drum Beat Award for Musicians from the Southern Christian Leadership Council. The Council's president had even flown in to present it: Dr. Martin Luther King Jr.

When King handed Franklin the award, he didn't say a word. He couldn't, since he had come down with laryngitis. Instead he silently congratulated her as those twelve thousand rose to their feet. "It was like the ceiling was coming down," she said later. And it had all started with one cover song.

A year before that concert, Aretha Franklin did not have thousands of fans greeting her. Though she was only twenty-four years old, her career—which had begun with her first album at age fourteen—was already floundering. She'd released nine albums on Columbia Records, and despite being shepherded by the legendary producer John Hammond, each had flopped. She was supposed to be Columbia's next big R&B star, but she'd only had one song crack the Top 40 (and barely at that, at #37).

When her Columbia contract came up in January 1967, she chose not to renew it. She felt the light jazz they had made her sing didn't draw on her strengths: her gospel background, her big voice, her swagger. After a brief bidding war, she signed with Atlantic Records. "I did some nice things," she told Atlantic's famed producer Jerry Wexler about the Columbia experience, "but now I want hits."

"She was my personal project," Wexler told the *Detroit Free Press* the year before his death in 2008. Her records at Columbia flopped because "they tried to make her everything from Edith Piaf to Judy Garland to Peggy Lee. They tried this, they tried that. Nothing happened."

Wexler had earned his reputation producing hits for Ray Charles and Wilson Pickett. The man knew rhythm and blues; heck, he'd *coined* the term. Atlantic's soul music was loud, raucous, and, above all, danceable—a far cry from the polished, respectable cocktail-lounge music Franklin had recorded at Columbia. "The soul sound of Atlantic in the '60s depended on some tightly played horns and a great rhythm section, playing danceable and hard rhythmic patterns" was how in-house arranger Arif Martin described it. In Franklin, Wexler saw the label's next big success. Unlike the suits at Columbia, though, he would let her do it her way.

Wexler's first idea was to draw Franklin out of her geographic comfort zone, and he wasted no time in doing so. Within weeks of her Columbia contract's expiring, Wexler brought her from New York down to Muscle Shoals, Alabama, to record at FAME Studios with its now-legendary house musicians. Despite being in their early twenties, the "Swampers," as they were known, had already backed Wilson Pickett on recent hits like "Mustang Sally" and "Land of 1000

**PREVIOUS:** Aretha Franklin performing in 1965. **ABOVE:** The moment it all changed: Aretha Franklin signs her Atlantic contract, 1966, with producer Jerry Wexler (seated) and her husband and manager, Ted White (standing).

Dances." "We were the groovingest, funkiest players happening at the time in the South," tenor saxophone player Charlie Chalmers says now. By setting her up in Muscle Shoals with these hot session guys, Wexler hoped to encourage Franklin to make bolder music.

The experiment didn't last long. Near the end of the first day, an argument broke out between one of the horn players and Franklin's manager/husband Ted White. It began at the studio with White objecting to something the horn player did (they'd both been drinking), then escalated into blows when FAME boss Rick Hall showed up later at White and

> **Wexler had been right about one thing: Franklin and the Swampers did have chemistry.**

Franklin's hotel room. By the next morning, Franklin and White had hopped a plane back to New York.

Though that was the end of the Muscle Shoals excursion, Wexler had been right about one thing: Franklin and the Swampers did have chemistry. When Wexler gave the one song they'd recorded there to a few radio DJs, it was clear that they had a major hit on their hands—Franklin's first.

Titled "I Never Loved a Man (The Way I Love You)," the song was everything her earlier Columbia material wasn't: loose, sassy, dripping with personality. They sent the song to some influential radio stations, and the response was immediate. As it gained momentum on radio, though, the label panicked. Atlantic couldn't release a physical single to stores because they had no song to place on the B-side. Franklin had only completed that one song before the Alabama sessions fell apart. A hit's not much use if no one can buy it. Atlantic needed more songs from Franklin, and fast.

But Franklin had made one thing very clear: she would not return to Alabama under any circumstances. She would, however, be happy to continue working with the same musicians (minus the troublemaking horn player) in New York. So two weeks after the Alabama sessions, the Muscle Shoals Swampers got on a plane to the big city. They had to tell Rick Hall that they were recording with sax player King Curtis, though; Wexler knew

Hall would be irate if he learned his guys were still recording with Franklin at another studio. The Swampers landed in New York and waited to see what songs Franklin would bring in.

"I remember arriving in New York with Aretha and feeling like we were all on a mission," Aretha's sister and backup singer Carolyn Franklin said. "We realized that our sister was on the brink of letting the world know what we had always known—that she was, hands down, the scariest singer in the world."

Two years earlier, another scary singer was down in Memphis recording his third album for Stax (a subsidiary of Atlantic). Named Otis Ray Redding Jr., the twenty-three-year-old had already had several hits with "These Arms of Mine" and "Mr. Pitiful." Though the new album would be mostly covers, he'd written one song he was particularly proud of. Drummer Al Jackson, a founding member of Booker T. & the M.G.'s, said this song came out of a conversation the two had had. Redding was complaining about the difficulties of touring, to which Jackson responded: "What are you griping about? You're on the road all the time. All you can look for is a little respect when you come home." Redding quickly turned that line into the song "Respect." Unlike Aretha's version, which came to symbolize respect on a grand scale, Redding's request remained a literal one, asking for respect from a girlfriend when he returns from work.

Redding's "Respect" didn't feature many of the trademarks that would become

Otis Redding's original "Respect" was recorded in July 1965 with a star Stax lineup (Steve Cropper produced and Booker T. & the M.G.'s backed) and released the following month.

Otis Redding performing in 1967.

associated with the song: no "R-E-S-P-E-C-T," no "just a little bit," not even the opening guitar line. There was no chorus or bridge; the verses just shuffled along. Redding's charisma and a hard-hitting horn section gave it some power, but it would end up on few people's top tier of Redding recordings.

Stax released the Redding single in August 1965, and it became a moderate hit, reaching #35 on the charts—his second biggest yet, after the album's previous single "I've Been Loving You Too Long." If it didn't reach the heights of later hits, like "Try a Little Tenderness" or the posthumous "(Sittin' On) The Dock of the Bay," it certainly paved the way for them. Redding thought "Respect" deserved to be in those songs' company. "That's one of my favorite songs because it has a

better groove than any of my records," Redding said in 1967, not long before his death. "The song lines are great. The band track is beautiful. It took me a whole day to write it and about twenty minutes to arrange it. We cut it once, and that was it. Everybody wants respect, you know."

When she signed with Atlantic, Franklin had just begun covering the song in her live act in a new arrangement, one very different from Redding's. She'd first heard it on the radio; "I had just moved out of my father's home and had my own little apartment," she said. "I was cleaning the place, and I had a good radio station on. I loved it. I *loved* it!"

She had written some new lyrics with her sisters and backup singers Carolyn and Erma during a long night at her New York apartment. "Obviously, Otis wrote the song from a man's point of view, but when Erma and Aretha and I worked it over, we had to rearrange the perspective," Carolyn said. "We saw it as something earthier—a woman having no problem discussing her needs."

Their additions included many of the song's now-iconic parts. They added the "R-E-S-P-E-C-T" chorus ("I thought I should spell it out," Franklin said simply in a TV interview decades later). They came up with the "sock it to me" line, popularizing a phrase Carolyn had heard on the streets ("There was nothing sexual about that," Franklin claimed, though Wexler argued "What else could 'sock it to me' mean?"). They even added the backing part "Re-Re-Re-Re," which, in addition to echoing the first syllable of "respect," was a play on Aretha's nickname "Ree."

Manager/husband White mentioned to Wexler that Franklin's "Respect" might be a good song to record. "Long as she changes it up from the original," Wexler responded. "You don't gotta worry about that, Wex," said White. "She changes it up, all right."

When Franklin brought the song in to the reconvened sessions in New York on Valentine's Day 1967, none of the musicians had heard her live version. "She walked in with this [song]," Wexler recalled later. "I didn't know what she had in mind. Aretha was terrific at setting up a song the way she wanted it to go. Many of the songs she would bring in—basically the cake was in the oven; all you had to do was bake it. She would work out the rhythm part, the piano arrangement, she worked out her vocals, she'd bring in her backup singers. When they came in singing 'Respect,' they had the whole template. They had everything."

Even recording engineer Tom Dowd didn't know she'd be singing "Respect" that day—and he'd also recorded Redding's original. "I walked out into the studio and said 'What's the next song?'" he said. "Aretha starts singing it to me; I said 'I know that song, I made it with Otis Redding like three years ago.'" But they treated it like a totally new song—which, in many ways, it was.

One key decision Wexler had made early on was to put Franklin back on piano. She was a gifted piano player, but this talent had been underutilized at Columbia. With her on piano, she could be more than a singer; she could be a bandleader. "Putting me back on piano helped Aretha-ize the new music," Franklin wrote in her autobiography.

While Franklin and her sisters had already worked out the vocal arrangements, the instrumental parts were a collaborative process done in the studio. "I would be out there in the studio, pencil and music paper in hand, trying to ascertain what Aretha would be playing on the piano," said arranger Arif Martin. "I would write down chord changes. The guitar player would look at her right hand and find out what position she was using; the bass player would listen to her left hand and try to come up with a bass line. This all stemmed from her piano. And then, like cooks, we would make the soup and everybody would add an ingredient."

"Many of the arrangements were done on the spot, in what we called head sessions," Franklin

**OPPOSITE:** Aretha Franklin at the piano in the Atlantic recording studio in New York, 1967, backed by Spooner Oldham.

wrote in her book. "This was worlds away from how I had worked at Columbia, far more spontaneous and free-flowing, with so much more room to be creative."

Anchored by Franklin's barrelhouse piano, the music played by the Swampers' rhythm section had far more attitude than her older albums. "If you listen to Otis's original and then Aretha's cover, the first thing you notice is that her groove is more dramatic," said Wexler. "That stop-and-stutter syncopation was something she invented. She showed the rhythm section I had shipped up from Alabama—[guitarist] Jimmy Johnson, [bassist] Tommy Cogbill, and [drummer] Roger Hawkins—how to do it."

"Everyone was very happy, and we were laughing and carrying on," says sax player Chalmers about the session. "She started playing the song and singing on the piano in the studio and then we all started falling in and putting our thing together as well. We would suggest a change here and there. It took us about an hour to get it structured the way it was."

The musicians felt like something was missing, though. The whole song was the same three chords repeated over and over. Despite Franklin's rewritten vocal parts, her version still felt a little one-note. They decided it needed an instrumental bridge to break things up. The horn section led by Chalmers was tasked with creating that bridge.

"When we got serious about recording that song, we took a look at it and realized there was no bridge," Wexler said. "It's something you'd never notice with Otis because of his incredible projection and magnitude. We came up with using the chord changes of Sam and Dave's 'When Something Is Wrong with My Baby.' They're very jazzy, a very advanced chord progression."

## "Putting me back on piano helped Aretha-ize the new music."

The musicians had recorded a cover of that Sam and Dave song earlier that week with sax player King Curtis (the session they'd used as their excuse to go to New York). The decision was made to borrow those chords and let King Curtis take a short solo over it.

"We thought, how could we lift this song up?" arranger Martin remembered. "'Respect' is in C. But that bridge, Curtis's saxophone solo is in F sharp—a totally unrelated key, but we liked it! So we put it in. It was a very interesting solo construction and we did it right there."

The four new horn parts—two tenor saxes performed by Chalmers and Curtis, plus a baritone sax and a cornet (a variation on a trumpet)—were arranged on the spot. "We were embellishing the groove in the empty holes where they needed to be," says Chalmers. "The horn players could all read each other's minds in a way, and so when I would come up with a line, the other guys would fall in and add the harmonies and so forth. Then, if we didn't like somebody's part, well, I might say you take the third up on top, and we'd talk it out. We were kind of competitive. The first one to come out with a killer part, well, then everybody would fall into that."

Franklin would sing along at the piano while the band recorded, but only to help them follow her vision. A perfectionist, she knew a vocal sung amid such noise would not suffice. Once the instruments were recorded to her satisfaction, she turned her attention to getting a proper vocal.

"The method she'd begun in Muscle Shoals was continuing in New York," said engineer Dowd. "She played the instruments with the band while singing a scratch vocal to help the musicians understand exactly how she was going to tell the story. We'd then throw away the scratch vocal, and, with an instrumental take that was acceptable to her, she went into the studio to sing the lead to track. That was the moment of truth. She was out there alone on the other side of the glass; I was behind the board in the control booth with Wexler hovering over me and all the musicians gathered around."

"The floors rumbled and the walls shook" when Franklin sang, organ player Spooner Oldham recalled. "It was magic in the studio. We all felt we were on to something new, from the perspective that she was bridging a gap in a way that hadn't been done before, bringing rhythm and blues into pop and into the mainstream. It just crossed all boundaries, all genres."

But Franklin was a perfectionist. Even when everyone in the control room listening thought it couldn't possibly get better, she'd request another take.

"We'd very often redo her vocals at her request," Wexler said, "because she could envision . . . a better way to go. As a producer, I would ask a singer sometimes: Give me another one, and I'd tell them what I wanted. I couldn't tell her what I wanted—I didn't know. But *she* knew. And she'd lay down a vocal, and I'd say 'Hey, that's great—we're done.' And she'd say, 'Oh, wait, I've got something else.' And she'd go some other place with it."

The result took the bigger-bolder-louder template of "I Never Loved a Man" and pushed it even further. Franklin used her gospel training to unleash the full power in her lungs. Anyone familiar with her tepid Dinah Washington covers would be little prepared for the rawness of her voice near-cracking as she belted "All I want you to do for me" and shout-vamping "Whoa!"s over the background singers in the outro.

Eventually, Franklin, Wexler, and the musicians judged the track complete. They moved on to another song, completing four that day. Atlantic now had plenty of music to release to stores.

"Everybody was really, really excited," Franklin remembered, "but Jerry said, 'Wait until tomorrow. If we feel the same way about it as we do tonight, then maybe we have a hit.'"

They did feel the same way the next day. Less than a month later, on March 10, 1967, the full album *I Never Loved a Man the Way I Love You* was released. The title track was still climbing the charts, so "Respect" was not released as a single until the following month. It entered at #50 on April 29, in between the Young Rascals' "Groovin'" and James & Bobby Purify's "Shake a Tail Feather," and moved up quickly. It finally hit #1 on June 3, replacing "Groovin'," which had moved up even quicker. In all, though, "Respect" incredibly spent only two weeks atop the chart—a hit certainly, but hardly a sensation (for comparison's sake, a few weeks earlier the featherweight California band the Association lasted twice as long at #1 with the justly forgotten "Windy").

The chart performance hardly tells the whole story, though. More than just a hit, "Respect" was a cultural sensation, an anthem for a turbulent summer. A breezy number like "Groovin'" made a good soundtrack for the Summer of Love out West. But Franklin's "Respect" cover soundtracked the *other* summer of '67, the summer of violent race riots in Newark, Chicago, Buffalo, and Franklin's hometown, Detroit. *Ebony* termed that season the "Summer of 'Retha, Rap, and Revolt" ("Rap" referring to civil rights activist H. Rap Brown).

**The fact that "Respect" became a civil-rights anthem was a bit of a surprise even to Franklin.**

After *I Never Loved a Man the Way I Love You* was released, the *New York Times* said that "Seated at the piano, surrounded by the band, her voice filled with mysterious sorrow, Franklin effectively reshaped popular music."

That the song would become a civil-rights anthem might not be apparent from a literal reading of the lyrics. Unlike James Brown's hit "Say It Loud (I'm Black and Proud)" the following year, Franklin's words have little to do with race. Like Redding's version, her call for respect is strictly in the context of a man-woman relationship. Her album even closed with a more obvious candidate for a civil-rights anthem: her cover of Sam Cooke's "A Change Is Gonna Come" (though she left out the song's most overtly political verse). But "Respect" had the advantage of ubiquity. "[I] could hear Aretha in the '60s three or four times an hour," civil-rights activist and comedian Dick Gregory said, "where I never heard King except on the news."

"We always sang songs about things we didn't have," said Ben Chavis, a civil-rights activist who worked with King and the former CEO of the NAACP. "We said 'We shall overcome.' We hadn't overcome, but we sang 'We shall overcome.' And when Aretha came out with 'Respect,' we weren't getting any respect. Black folks were being disrespected, being beat down, killed trying to get the right to vote. Being beat down and killed trying to get . . . civil rights. And so when she came out with this song, 'Respect,' it was like she was fulfilling not only an urgency of the movement of that time, but she made known through her song that we were going to get respect."

The fact that "Respect" became a civil-rights anthem was a bit of surprise even to Franklin. "I'm not a politician or political theorist," she said later. "I don't make it a practice to put my politics into my music or social commentary. But the fact that 'Respect' naturally became a battle cry and an anthem for a nation shows me something." Though the words said she wanted respect for herself, her voice said she wanted respect for her people.

The song also became an anthem for the burgeoning feminist movement. The trio of powerful female voices—for though labeled "background singers," Carolyn and Erma's parts joined Aretha's center stage—lent the song a feeling of sisterhood (literally in this case), of women demanding respect now rather than waiting around for it to be offered later. Bonnie Raitt once said, "I learned way more about being a woman from listening to her sing 'Respect' than I ever did from any man."

If you believe Franklin, the song's becoming a feminist anthem was just as much a surprise as its becoming a black-pride anthem. "I think that's Gloria Steinem's role," she told *Rolling Stone* when asked about feminism. "I don't think I was a catalyst for the women's movement. Sorry. But if I were? So much the better!"

Steinem, however, thinks Franklin does not give herself enough credit: "I always felt that nothing too bad could happen in the world while I was listening to Aretha Franklin. Everything was good, including that I could dance with nobody around. True, there was a line in 'Respect' that made me anxious for both of us: something like 'I'm about to give you all my money.' But I figured Aretha knew what she was doing, and nobody was going to mess with her. With us."

> **"The girl has taken that song from me."**

Decades later, Franklin's cover of "Respect" still regularly ranks on lists as one of the best cover songs of all time. *Rolling Stone* even ranked it the fifth-best song, *period* (Redding made that same list three times himself, though not with "Respect"). Alicia Keys called it the "first anthem of gender equality," and Christina Aguilera said, "From the moment you hear the letters being spelled out in that sultry, soulful voice, you can't help but pay attention and give the respect the song calls for and deserves." Despite many subsequent hits, Franklin herself still lists the song as her favorite.

"So many people identified with and related to 'Respect,'" she wrote in her autobiography, *Aretha: From These Roots*, in 1999. "It was the need of a nation, the need of the average man and woman in the street, businessman, the mother, the fireman, the teacher—everyone wanted respect. It was also one of the battle cries of the civil-rights movement. The song took on monumental significance. It became the 'Respect' women expected from men and men expected from women, the inherent right of all human beings. Three decades later, I am unable to give a concert without my fans demanding that same 'Respect' from me. 'Respect' was—and is—an ongoing blessing in my life."

Redding tragically died in a plane crash just a few months after Franklin's "Respect" became a hit. But before he passed, Wexler played him Aretha's cover. "He broke out into this wide smile," Wexler recounted, "and said 'The girl has taken that song from me. Ain't no longer my song. From now on, it belongs to her.' And then he asked me [to] play it again, and then a third time. The smile never left his face." ◉

REPRISE RECORDS

JIMI
HENDRIX
EXPERIENCE

Produced by
Jimi Hendrix

0767
(L 5424)

ALL ALONG THE WATCHTOWER
(Bob Dylan)
Dwarf Music
BMI - 4:01

MADE IN U.S.A. · REPRISE RECORDS, A DIVISION OF WARNER BROS.-SEVEN ARTS RECORDS, INC.

# JIMI HENDRIX
## "ALL ALONG THE WATCHTOWER"

⚡ BOB DYLAN COVER ⚡

SONG
"ALL ALONG THE WATCHTOWER"
[B/W "BURNING OF THE MIDNIGHT LAMP"] (1968)

WRITTEN BY
BOB DYLAN

FIRST RECORDED BY
BOB DYLAN (1967)

**B**rian Jones was in bad shape. The Rolling Stone had staggered into London's Olympic Studios one chilly January day when Jimi Hendrix was trying to record a new Bob Dylan song. Though Jones could barely stand upright, he demanded to play on the track. Hendrix's band had already recorded many takes and the arrangement was finally starting to come together. But Jimi, ever accommodating to his friends, sat Jones down at a piano. Jones proceeded to botch take after take. With his offbeat clunks and clangs, he sounded like he was playing with his elbows.

Things in the studio were already rocky, and now the whole song was on the brink of collapse.

**PREVIOUS:** Jimi Hendrix in August 1967. **BELOW:** "All Along the Watchtower" was one of the most-loved songs from the 1967 instant-classic album *John Wesley Harding*.

Where Hendrix first heard "All Along the Watchtower" is a matter of some debate. His publicist at the time, Michael Goldstein, says he played it for him at a Greenwich Village party before Dylan's album *John Wesley Harding* was even released.

"I went to dinner with [Dylan's manager] Albert Grossman in an awful Mexican restaurant around 46th Street," he says. "He gave me this cassette and said 'Here's a sample of Dylan's latest songs.' I had a party a week or so later and Jimi was there. I said 'How would anybody like to hear something from Dylan that you haven't heard?' and I played the tape. Jimi came up to me and said, 'Hey, Mike, can I take that home with me? I really want to listen to that again.' I said 'Sure, you can have it, what the hell do I care?'"

Hendrix's girlfriend Kathy Etchingham, whom he was living with in London at the time, says she first heard the song the way any other Dylan fan would have: he bought a copy of the new album. "It was soon after he came back [from touring the States]," she recalls. "I remember him having the album when he came back, along with a bottle of duty-free American whiskey. We played it over and over again. He just loved it."

There are other stories as well. Dave Mason of Traffic claims a party he threw in London was Hendrix's introduction to the song. And in the reissue liner notes to Hendrix's album *Electric Ladyland,* music journalist Michael Fairchild points to a session Hendrix played in with Paul McCartney's brother Mike McGear as a possible first exposure.

Hendrix listening to records at his London home—in his hand is *Lenny Bruce is Out Again*. Bob Dylan's *Blonde on Blonde* is facing the floor.

In a way, though, where he heard it doesn't matter. Because there was no way Hendrix was *not* going to hear a new Dylan song sooner or later. He was the type of superfan who carried a Dylan songbook in his travel bag, who once almost started a fight in a Harlem club after making the DJ play "Blowin' in the Wind" (not surprisingly, it cleared the dance floor), and who pestered Dylan's guitarist Robbie Robertson with questions about how Bob wrote his songs (Robertson's curt reply: "Usually on a typewriter"). He once even used lyrics from Dylan's brutal kiss-off song "Most Likely You Go Your Way (And I'll Go Mine)" to dump a girlfriend.

Hendrix first professionally covered a Dylan song in 1965 as a session player for Curtis Knight's "Like a Rolling Stone" ripoff "How Would You Feel." The actual "Like a Rolling Stone" became a staple of Hendrix's early live shows. It was after hearing one such performance that his manager Chas Chandler, bassist for the Animals—who had recently had their own hit with a song they first heard on a Dylan record ("House of the Rising Sun")—decided to sign him.

Hendrix would record a handful of Dylan songs in his career—"Can You Please Crawl Out Your Window," "Drifter's Escape," "Tears of Rage"—and toyed around with others. A *Rolling Stone* interviewer in 1969 described him idly strumming along to "The Ballad of Frankie Lee and Judas Priest" while

A young Dylan in Greenwich Village, 1961.

answering questions. "It's not a wonder to me that he recorded my songs," Dylan wrote of Hendrix in 1988, "but rather that he recorded so few of them because they were all his."

Hendrix met Dylan at least once, but the interactions they had were by all accounts inconsequential. In that same *Rolling Stone* interview, Hendrix reported: "I only met him once, about three years ago, back at the Kettle of Fish [a folk-rock era hangout] on Macdougal Street. That was before I went to England. I think both of us were pretty drunk at the time, so he probably doesn't remember it."

For his part, Dylan recalls another meeting, equally inauspicious. "First time I saw him, he was playing with John Hammond," he wrote in the liner notes to his career retrospective *Biograph*. "He was incredible then." Dylan added that he saw him again shortly before Hendrix's death. "He was slouched down in the back of a limousine. I was riding by on a bicycle. I remember saying something about that song 'Wind Cries Mary,' it was a long way from playing behind John Hammond. . . . Both of us were a little lost for words, he'd gone through like a fireball without knowing it, I'd done the same thing like being shot out of cannon."

Perhaps the best story—though one confirmed by neither party—was told by Hendrix's friend

Deering Howe in Charles R. Cross's biography *Room Full of Mirrors*. Cross writes:

> One day that fall [Howe] was walking down Eighth Street in New York City with Jimi when they spied a figure on the other side of the road. "Hey, that's Dylan," Jimi said excitedly. "I've never met him before; let's go talk to him." Jimi darted into traffic, yelling "Hey, Bob" as he approached. Deering followed, though he felt uneasy about Jimi's zeal. "I think Dylan was a little concerned at first, hearing someone shouting his name and racing across the street toward him," Deering recalled. Once Dylan recognized Jimi, he relaxed. Hendrix's introduction was modest enough to be comic. "Bob, uh, I'm a singer, you know, called, uh, Jimi Hendrix, and . . ." Dylan said he knew who Jimi was and loved his covers of "All Along the Watchtower" and "Like a Rolling Stone." "I don't know if anyone has done my songs better," Dylan said. Dylan hurried off but left Jimi beaming. "Jimi was on cloud nine," Deering said, "if only because Bob Dylan knew who he was. It seemed very clear to me that the two had never met before."

Back in London, Hendrix and Etchingham played *John Wesley Harding* over and over, and Hendrix knew immediately which song he wanted to cover: "I Dreamed I Saw St. Augustine."

Then he had second thoughts. "He thought it was too personal," Etchingham says. "It was Bob Dylan's dream, so he wasn't going to take that, because he didn't dream it himself." (As John Perry notes in his book on *Electric Ladyland*, it also would have been an odd song musically for Hendrix to cover. The 3/4 waltz of "St. Augustine" was a meter Hendrix rarely attempted in his career.)

## [Hendrix] used lyrics . . . from "Most Likely You Go Your Way (And I'll Go Mine)" to dump a girlfriend.

After he got cold feet on "Augustine," someone, probably Etchingham (she can't remember for sure), nudged him toward "Watchtower." "Sometimes I do a Dylan song and it seems to fit me so right that I figure maybe I wrote it," Hendrix recalled later. "I felt like 'Watchtower' was something I'd written but could never get together. I often feel like that about Dylan."

Song decided upon, he set his mind to recording it.

At the time Hendrix began recording "Watchtower," his career was in a strange place. The Seattle native had scored three Top 10 hits in Britain, but he remained all but unknown in his home country. Some reasons were unique to his situation—he was managed by a Brit, for one—but others spoke to larger industry trends. Despite the much-hyped British Invasion of America a few years earlier, it remained common for bands to become huge in Britain and then fail to translate that success stateside. Some did eventually cross over after years of trying—the Kinks, the Rolling Stones—but many stayed household names in Britain and nobodies in the States—Cliff Richards, the Move, and a million other names most American readers won't recognize. Hendrix needed something that would move him from that second group to the first, something to make America sit up and take notice of its native son making it big across the pond.

Throughout the 1960s, Dylan covers had proven as good a way as any to make a play for the U.S. charts. It was no secret to those in the industry that Bob Dylan songs had the potential to be huge hits—when sung by someone other than Bob Dylan. In the preceding few years alone, the Turtles, the Byrds, and Peter, Paul and Mary had all had hits with songs Dylan himself hadn't managed to get on the charts at all (a trend that continues to this day, with people like Adele making hits of more recent Dylan songs).

By this point in the late '60s, though, cover songs were on the verge of being uncool. The Beatles had stopped doing covers, the Rolling Stones

### Dylan covers were an exception.

were doing far fewer, and the folk movement had put a premium on the singer-songwriter. Someone like Elvis, who never wrote a line, would have had a hard go of it had he come along ten years later. In the late '60s and early '70s, covers started to be seen as an indication that you couldn't write your own material. But even at this most marginalized period in music history for cover songs, Dylan covers were an exception. A well-chosen Dylan cover could make the difference for a career without being a knock on the singer's credibility.

**RIGHT:** Hendrix performing at the Golden Bear Raceway in Sacramento, CA, 1970.

Unlike the later New York *Electric Ladyland* sessions—which featured such a large crew of leeches and hangers-on that manager Chandler quit in frustration—the January 21 recording of "All Along the Watchtower" was relatively calm. In the studio were Hendrix, Traffic's Dave Mason on twelve-string guitar, and Jimi Hendrix Experience drummer Mitch Mitchell. Brian Jones played piano for as long as he could be tolerated, then was switched to percussion, where he could do less damage.

The song was so new that many people in the room had never heard Dylan's original. Hendrix had no patience for rehearsal, either; he just shouted out the chord changes as they played. "When he was doing his own arrangement, he did it very quietly, without being plugged into an amplifier, so nobody knew what he was doing because only he could hear it," Etchingham recalls.

Though uncredited on the final LP due to tension with the manager who replaced him, Chandler produced the track, while Hendrix's trusted engineer Eddie Kramer rolled the tape. With credits including the Beatles, the Rolling Stones, and the Kinks, Kramer was Hendrix's right-hand man behind the boards. "Jimi really felt he had an ally in Eddie, because he would always listen to his ideas," drummer Buddy Miles said in the reissue liner notes. "Nothing was more important to Jimi than his music, and Eddie was always pushing him."

Hendrix's bassist Noel Redding was there, too—briefly. After an argument with Hendrix, he stormed off to the Red Lion pub across the street. "We were having a few problems with the band already, and I said I didn't like the tune," Redding said in a BBC documentary years later. "I prefer Dylan's version."

"Initially there was no bass," Kramer told recording magazine *Sound on Sound* in 2005. "Jimi just played a six-string acoustic guitar while Traffic's Dave Mason played twelve-string and Mitch was on drums. That's how Jimi wanted to cut it, and as a result the track had a marvelous, light feel, thanks to the acoustic guitars that were driving it. Jimi not only loved the lyrics but also the chord sequences of 'All Along the Watchtower,' and he just gave them a terrific bed to do a nice solo."

**Hendrix had laid down the basic "Watchtower" track in one day.**

Leaked outtakes of that day in the studio confirm Kramer's memory, offering an unusual way to hear the song—no electric guitar and no vocals, just a gentle rhythm jam. Hendrix was particularly concerned about getting the dynamics right. "Dave, make it more distinctive between the loud part and the soft part, okay?" he instructs Mason at one point with what sounds like growing frustration (this is not the first time on the tapes you can hear him bring the issue up).

The fourteenth take is the first with Jones on the piano, and even in the twenty-three seconds they manage before Hendrix cuts it off, you can hear this was a bad addition. "He was completely out of his brain," Kramer recalled. "Poor Brian, he was a good mate of Jimi's and we all loved him. Jimi could never say no to his mates, and Brian was so sweet. He came in and said 'Oh, let me play,' and he got on the piano . . . and we could just hear '*clang, clang, clang, clang, clang. . . .*' It was all bloody horrible and out of time, and Jimi said, 'Uh, I don't think so.' Brian was gone after two takes. He practically fell on the floor in the control room."

Jones was eventually switched to percussion—that's him playing the *thwack* at the end of each bar in the intro, on an instrument called a vibraslap—and the session wound down after twenty-seven takes. The song did not yet have vocals or most of the electric guitar parts, but the basic rhythm track was in the can for Hendrix to tinker with and overdub later.

And overdub he did. Endlessly.

After a lengthy break for a slate of tour dates, by the summer of 1968 the *Electric Ladyland* sessions had moved to New York's Record Plant, where most of the album was cut (the only other songs with London roots were "Crosstown Traffic" and "Burning of the Midnight Lamp"). Hendrix tinkered for months, upgrading the master tape from the original four-track offered at the London studio to take advantage of the state-of-the-art twelve-track machine at the Record Plant. Then, when sixteen-track entered the picture, he upgraded again, adding more parts each time. What had started as an impromptu jam session with some friends became an obsessive endeavor.

"Hendrix would stop the tape, pick up his guitar or the bass, and go back out and start re-overdubbing stuff," said Record Plant engineer Tony Bongiovi. "Recording these new ideas meant that he would have to erase something. In the weeks prior to the mixing, we had already recorded a number of overdubs, wiping track after track—and I don't mean once or twice. He would overdub the bass and guitar parts all over, until he

was satisfied. He would say, 'I think I hear it a bit differently.'"

The sessions continued throughout the summer of 1968, six months after Hendrix had laid down the basic "Watchtower" track in one day. At some point, he decided he could do a better bass track than Dave Mason had and swapped it out. "Jimi was a fine bass player," drummer Mitchell said in the reissue liner notes, "one of the best, very Motown-style. . . . Even being left-handed, he had no problem picking up a right-handed bass—he just had that touch."

During that time, Hendrix also laid down the song's most iconic section: the guitar solo. And he didn't just record one solo; he tried out many. Eddie Kramer said by the end he had seven great guitar parts to choose from, not counting the many others that got taped over.

Hendrix divided his main solo into four discrete sections. The first he plays straight, flashing up and down the neck of the guitar for thrilling waterfalls of notes. Second comes the slide guitar, which was apparently so spur-of-the moment that he didn't even have a slide with him. "I saw Jimi, frustrated, running around, trying to get a sound out that he had in his head, but not being able to do it," his friend Velvert Turner said in the BBC documentary. "[He grabbed] beer bottles, soda bottles, knives, and everything trying to get the middle section, where there's a Hawaiian guitar sound." He ended up using a cigarette lighter. Eddie Van Halen has called this section one of his favorite guitar solos ever.

After a yell of "Hey!" the psychedelic wah-wah section begins. Hendrix was in fact one of the pioneers of the wah-wah, with *Electric Ladyland* marking one of the pedal's first appearances on a major record. Then for the last eight bars, Hendrix reins it back in slightly for what might be thought of as the "rhythm solo," mirroring and embellishing on the chords more directly before wrapping with a quick ascension up the guitar's neck.

Hendrix also recorded his vocals at the Record Plant. As always, he hated this part. Many friends and collaborators have detailed his terrible insecurity about his singing voice. "He'd always face the other way," Kramer said. "He hated to be looked at. He was very shy about his vocals."

In fact, according to his father, Al Hendrix, Bob Dylan inspired the guitar ace to try singing in the first place, a sort of "If he can succeed sounding like that, why not me?" outlook. "I thought you must admire that guy for having that much nerve to sing so out of key," Jimi once said. He would in fact frequently defend Dylan's voice in interviews, attacking those who accused him of sounding like a "broken-leg dog."

After the endless overdubs and rerecordings of guitars, vocals, and bass, it came time to mix the record. By this point, Chas Chandler, who had produced the original London sessions, was long gone. His original mix had been relatively subdued, focusing heavily on the acoustic guitars and giving even the loud solos plenty of room to breathe.

The new version that Hendrix mixed with Eddie Kramer went in the opposite direction. "It was a case of Jimi and I [sic] doing it together and just making it sound as commercial as we possibly could," Kramer said. With sixteen tracks at their disposal, they had plenty of room to add compression, reverb, chorusing, and other studio tricks to make the entire thing louder and more

aggressive. With many other tracks on the album too long or too far-out to ever be played on radio, the goal for "Watchtower" grew increasingly clear: hit single. Everyone hoped this would finally make Hendrix a star in America like he was in Britain.

It worked. Released as a single in the U.S. on September 21, 1968, and backed with "Burning of the Midnight Lamp," "All Along the Watchtower" became Hendrix's first and only Top 40 single on the American *Billboard* charts, climbing from #66 on its debut to a peak of #20 (it made #5 in the UK, where he was already famous). In fact, it sold more in the States than the group's previous four singles combined—and that includes "Purple Haze" and "Foxy Lady."

One group of Americans who loved the cover wasn't even in America: troops in Vietnam. The army's official radio broadcasts were tightly controlled, but GIs overseas had made a regular practice of setting up pirate radio stations in the field. "Watchtower" began to get heavy airplay on those stations. One veteran recalled in Stephen Roby's *Black Gold,* "I just spun the dials . . . lo and behold, there's Midnight Jack broadcasting: 'Midnight Jack, man, I'm deep in the jungle. . . . What can I play for you, man?' He's gone for about thirty seconds and I imagine he's putting a reel-to-reel tape on, and here comes Jimi Hendrix. . . ."

Perhaps most importantly to Jimi, Bob Dylan loved it, too—though it's not clear that Hendrix ever knew this, as all Dylan's public comments occurred after Hendrix's death. "It overwhelmed me, really," Dylan told the *Florida Sun-Sentinel* in 1995. "He had such talent, he could find things inside a song and vigorously develop them. He found things that other people wouldn't think of finding in there. He probably improved upon it by the spaces he was using. I took license with the song from his version, actually, and continue to do it to this day."

For his part, Hendrix seemed pleased that people liked his Dylan cover but, true to his reclusive nature, didn't say much about it. When asked if Hendrix ever commented on how he felt about the song's success, Kathy Etchingham answers with a resounding no. "Jimi never sat down and talked about his music," she says. "He just did it. He didn't sit down and pick his music to pieces. He might have done it in his head privately, but he certainly didn't do it [to others]."

Three months later, he had already moved on, dropping "Watchtower" from his set lists and ignoring or declining audience requests. "We recorded that a year ago and, if you heard it, we are very glad," he told a Frankfurt crowd. "But tonight, we're trying to do a musical thing, okay? That's a single, and we released it as a single. Thank you very much for thinking about it, but I forgot the words. That's what I'm trying to say." ◉

# JOE COCKER
## "WITH A LITTLE HELP FROM MY FRIENDS"

⚡ THE BEATLES COVER ⚡

SONG
"WITH A LITTLE HELP FROM MY FRIENDS"
[B/W "SOMETHING'S COMING ON"] (1968)

WRITTEN BY
JOHN LENNON, PAUL McCARTNEY

FIRST RECORDED BY
THE BEATLES (1967)

When moviegoers filed in to see the 1970 documentary *Woodstock,* any number of top-tier names might have drawn them there: the Who, Janis Joplin, Jefferson Airplane, Jimi Hendrix. But the lasting image many took away from the theater was none of these. Rather, the film's unforgettable performance came from a flailing mutton-chopped man in dirty tie-dye hollering through an unhinged Beatles cover (though at times the only evidence that it was a Beatles song was the backing vocals, as his yelps and whoops were otherwise indecipherable).

"Almost nobody in the crowd had heard of this wild man," recalled an attendee in *Back to the*

**Cocker's performance instantly became iconic—and ripe for parody.**

*Garden,* Pete Fornatale's book about Woodstock. "His spastic body movements and screaming vocals would eventually prove intoxicating, but right now, it was a bit shocking."

Joe Cocker, the wild man, looks out of his mind in the movie. Some viewers assumed he was on drugs (not a bad guess for a Woodstock performer). Ironically, he was the only one in his band sober that day. This was just how he performed.

"The rest of us were all on acid," remembers Cocker's bandleader and right-hand man Chris Stainton today. "I had taken what they called orange sunshine acid tabs, and I vomited on the helicopter they flew the band in on. It was terrible. When we came to do the actual set, I looked at the keyboards and everything looked like it was all wavy and wobbly. But Joe never did anything nasty in those days."

Though the Beatles cover he performed had already been released, its inclusion in the movie made Cocker a star. "I'm told by people that they play that song over and over and over again as a stand-alone experience because he's just so interesting to watch," said the movie's director Michael Wadleigh. "Playing his air guitar, he's pigeon-toed, nearly falling over, staggering everywhere, sweat just flying off of him. . . . It's a phenomenally genuine performance." In his original review, Roger Ebert called Cocker's performance the best of the movie. "Some kind of strange sensation inhabits our spine," he wrote, "when Joe Cocker and everybody else in the whole Woodstock nation sings 'With a Little Help from My Friends.'"

**PREVIOUS:** Cocker leaves it all on the stage at Woodstock, August 1969. **BELOW:** The cover of *Sgt. Pepper's Lonely Hearts Club Band* featured a roll call of the Beatles' heroes, from Alfred Einstein to Sonny Liston and Bob Dylan.

Cocker's "With a Little Help from My Friends" performance instantly became iconic—and ripe for parody. On the third episode of *Saturday Night Live,* a young John Belushi re-created Joe's performance, tie-dye and all; Cocker said Belushi (who had honed the impression at his pre-*SNL* stint at Chicago's Second City improv comedy theater) sounded so much like him, he thought he was lip-syncing. More recently, a YouTube video has earned millions of views humorously captioning what it sounds like Joe was singing (i.e., instead of "I need someone to love": "I did some Wonder loaf").

But on that stage in 1969, the "With a Little Help from My Friends" performance didn't feel iconic for its singer. To Joe Cocker, it was just another gig.

"Were we epic? I dunno," he told website Team Rock in 2013 shortly before his death. "We got some nice footage for memories. I was wearing a tie-dyed shirt, and when I took it off after, the colors had stained my chest in the exact same pattern."

Just a few years before Woodstock, Joe Cocker had been a struggling musician gigging around his native Sheffield, England, trying to pay the rent. Ever since he'd turned sixteen, Cocker had led a variety of bands, playing shows constantly with little to show for it except an electric stage act. One evening, Cocker and his friends were goofing around backstage when someone brought out a Ouija board. The story goes that Cocker asked it, "How will I ever get famous?" The board answered—and this was before the Beatles had even written the song—"With a little help from your friends."

It's hard to prove a story like that, but Stainton believes it. "He was quietly ambitious," he says. "He always said he wanted to have his name in lights."

What is certainly true is that when the Beatles released their album *Sgt. Pepper's Lonely Hearts Club Band* in 1967, it was all Cocker listened to. "We played *Sgt. Pepper's* wall to wall, like all night," says Stainton. Cocker had already tried covering Beatles songs—"I'll Cry Instead" was his first, failed single—and perhaps he connected that Ouija proclamation to the new Ringo-sung track on the Beatles' album. Soon after that, he thought up a way to sing the song his way.

"We used to have an outdoor toilet in Sheffield when I was growing up," Cocker said. "I used to go there and sort of meditate once in a while. I just remember sitting in there, and I was looking for a vehicle, as we call songs sometimes, to do a waltz with. I suddenly got this concept in my mind of doing ['With a Little Help from My Friends'] with a chorus of black girls." Stainton says that the toilet still stands and that there is a plaque on the door commemorating Cocker's bathroom brainstorm.

Cocker took inspiration from his favorite singers Ray Charles and Aretha Franklin, imagining a massive soulful cover of the pop ditty backed by powerful gospel singers in the style of Charles's Raelettes. While Ringo sang lead on the original, Cocker envisioned more of a call-and-response duet between him and the gospel singers. Just as in Franklin's cover of "Respect" two years earlier, the so-called backup singers would be almost as important as the lead.

Cocker and Stainton developed such an arrangement and taught it to the band one afternoon a few months after the album came out at their rehearsal space, an old movie theater procured

by Cocker's manager Chris Blackwell (soon to go on to fame of his own, founding Island Records and discovering Bob Marley). However, the band's version didn't live up to Joe's vision. They didn't have any "chorus of black girls," so his white male band did their best imitation. "It was terrible, because none of us could sing," Stainton says.

The song still became a regular feature of the band's constant gigs. Then Cocker got the call he'd been waiting for. The demos he had been quietly sending around to producers had paid off. Someone wanted to record him.

The first song Cocker recorded actually wasn't "With a Little Help," but rather his original song "Marjorine." He'd sent it blindly to producer Denny Cordell and his protégé Tony Visconti, who would later become best known as David Bowie's go-to producer. "Joe and Chris sent us a little demo on four-inch reel-to-reel tape," remembers Visconti. "We flipped out; we couldn't even believe it was a home recording."

They brought Cocker down to London to record the song. Despite all his stage charisma, he was nervous in a studio environment. "Joe was extremely shy," says Visconti. "He looked honestly a bit frightened. He certainly had the look of someone who had never been to London before. I had a hard time understanding his accent. It was very, very thick. Chris Stainton had to act as his translator."

**ABOVE:** Cocker's 1969 debut album went gold in the U.S. at a time when singers were increasingly expected to write their own material.

Cocker having a drink on the cusp of stardom, 1968.

Cocker, Cordell, and Visconti put everything they had into recording and promoting "Marjorine," but the single flopped—this even despite the valiant intervention of famous British actor Terence Stamp, who personally called the BBC while stoned to request it. Undeterred, Cordell and Visconti decided to record a full album with Cocker anyway. They were still convinced Cocker was a star, even if the public didn't know it yet.

Though Cocker had written that first single, everyone at that point—Joe included—knew he was as much a song *interpreter* as a songwriter. And one of the songs he wanted to interpret on his first album was "With a Little Help from My Friends."

As soon as Cordell and Visconti heard Cocker perform it live, they knew this topped their earlier effort. "This was a very different record, and it was great," Visconti says. "'Marjorine,' on the other hand, was a cool recording, but it wasn't that different than what else you'd be hearing on the radio. A cover of a Beatles song is usually the kiss of death, but radio was craving for something different, and they respected creativity back in those days. I knew it was either going to be a massive hit or a massive flop."

In the spring of 1968, they decided to record "With a Little Help" as the first single on his debut album. Cocker and his band had their live arrangement down. But Cocker's onstage confidence did not extend to his offstage interactions. In the studio, he remained quiet and shy with those he didn't know well, spending long periods of time sitting off to the side when it wasn't his turn to sing.

"Joe was often a bit bedraggled in the studio," says Visconti. "Everything always took time and, since Joe didn't play any instruments, he'd often just sit in the corner looking like a marionette whose strings were cut. Just waiting to be called. But the transformation when he got up to sing was amazing. That shaking of his hands, all the quirky facial expressions—he would do all that in the studio, because he had been doing it for years in concert."

That high-voltage performance style did not make him easy to record, though. His body would jerk around so much he'd miss the mic, or his vocals would spill over onto the drum track. What was so dynamic live became a nuisance in the studio. "He always performed like that," says Stainton. "He was like full-on in the studio, no holding back. He wasn't capable of rehearsing a song; he would just perform it fully every time."

> **Joe was often a bit bedraggled in the studio.**

Though it was difficult to capture his vocals, Cordell didn't want to sacrifice an ounce of Cocker's passion. To really sell the song, Cordell wanted the most intense and unhinged performance of Cocker's life, and he pushed the singer to his limit to get it. Watching Cocker at Woodstock, it seems amazing that he can get through the song once without collapsing; but in the studio he sang the song over and over again for two straight hours, going full-throttle every time. But it still wasn't good enough.

"Then Denny thought, Joe will sing better if he tilts his head back," recalls Visconti about what happened next. "So he moved the mic about a foot and a half above Joe's head. Joe proceeded to sing in the third hour straight up in the air—which I know is a bad singing technique. He was in agony. But people would do anything Denny would tell them to, unquestionably. And sure enough, Joe finally hit all the notes. You can hear it on the recording: his throat is absolutely raw. I wouldn't want to go down there with an X-ray to see what shreds his vocal cords were in."

Cocker's work was done, but Cordell was far from finished. For months he kept tinkering and trying to enhance the recording. The intricate layering on *Sgt. Pepper's* had affected him as much as it had Cocker; the old studio mode of knocking songs out live didn't seem enough anymore. "[Cordell] spent a lot of money recording this song," Visconti

**OPPOSITE:** Joe Cocker contorts his way into music history at Woodstock.

says. "He was so crazy that he couldn't fail on this one. 'Marjorine' failed, and he took it very, very personally."

In trying to get a Stax sound, Visconti arranged and recorded an entire horn section that barely got used (they fade in thirty seconds from the song's end). They brought in studio ringers to record the parts: BJ Wilson from Procol Harum on drums, and a young session guitarist named Jimmy Page, shortly before he formed Led Zeppelin. ("I didn't even know who he was," says Stainton, "just another musician playing with the band.") And they recorded the "chorus of black girls" Cocker had dreamed up on the toilet.

The problem, in Cordell's mind, was that the singers he recorded in London weren't black *enough*. The fact that two of them were British-Indian, he thought, meant that they weren't sufficiently soulful.

"He went manic about the backing vocal girls," says Visconti. "So he went to America. He went to the South, West Coast, East Coast, and he recorded five different sets of black ladies doing the backing vocals. He kept sending mixes back. Each one was awful. He just couldn't do better than the singers we'd recorded in London. Everyone had put their heart and soul into this first recording. Whereas when he was running around America with his eight-track tape, they just didn't feel it."

This continued for a month. Cordell would travel somewhere else in America, record a new group of women, send the tape back to London, then repeat. Eventually, David Platz, Cordell's partner in the studio—the businessman supplying all the money Cordell was wasting in America—intervened.

"David thought Denny had lost his mind," says Visconti. "David said to me 'The things Denny's sending back are *horrible*. Can you find the best mix that you and he did and let's just put it out? We're wasting time; this record's got to be out on the market.'"

Visconti did a quick mix—with the original backing singers—and they released it as a single. No one told Cordell, who was still in America recording more singers. Cordell must have heard it on the radio and realized what had happened, though, because his dispatches back to London suddenly stopped.

"We had two weeks where we didn't hear from him," Visconti says. "I honestly thought I was going to be fired. I was on tenterhooks, waiting for his return. When he finally came back to England, though, he wasn't angry. He was relieved that we had taken matters out of his hands."

> **Just as the Ouija board had predicted, Cocker had become famous.**

The single was an immediate smash, topping the charts in the UK in October 1968. In 2012, *Rolling Stone* readers voted Cocker's agonized howls one of the ten best vocal performances in history. In 2014, BBC listeners voted "With a Little Help from My Friends" the seventh-best cover song ever.

Just as the Ouija board had predicted, Cocker had become famous. He started getting fan letters. One in particular stood out. It read: "Thanks. You are far too much. John and Paul."

No one had consulted the Beatles before recording "With a Little Help" (they wouldn't have known who Cocker was then anyway), but it turned out they adored his version. They quickly became Cocker's biggest champions, even giving him new unreleased compositions to sing on his next album. Cocker once told the story of his first visit to the Beatles' studio:

*They stuck me in a room for an hour with nothing to look at but carpet. Eventually Paul turned up. He played me the medley from* Abbey Road: *"Golden Slumbers" and "Carry That Weight." I was all ears until he said: "You can't have 'em. You can have this, though." He played me "She Came in Through the Bathroom Window." I was floating on the ceiling when George Harrison walked in shortly after. He played me "Old Brown Shoe." By now I was getting a bit fussy, so I said: "I can't see myself singing that." George played me three other songs and seemed a bit miffed. [He said:] "The Beatles will never use these. I've got this one called 'Something.' I wrote it for Jackie Lomax, and I wanted Ray Charles to sing it. You might as well have it." He actually played and sang it for me. I was gobsmacked.*

Cocker recorded both "She Came in Through the Bathroom Window" and "Something" for his next album, before the Beatles had even released their own versions. Throughout his career he often went back to that well, recording numerous other Beatles songs and even some solo Beatles compositions (Lennon's "Jealous Guy" and "Isolation," McCartney's "Maybe I'm Amazed").

"In a lot of these songs I'm not trying to top the original, 'cause you can't," Cocker said. "I'm just trying to give them some new life."

But he never topped his first hit, "With a Little Help from My Friends." It got a second life in the *Woodstock* documentary, and then a third when it was used as the theme song for the hit TV show *The Wonder Years* in 1988. That one song started Cocker down the path to a fifty-year career.

When Cocker died in 2014, McCartney put out a statement:

"He was a lovely northern lad who I loved a lot and, like many people, I loved his singing. I was especially pleased when he decided to cover 'With a Little Help from My Friends,' and I remember him and Denny Cordell coming round to the studio in Savile Row and playing me what they'd recorded, and it was just mind-blowing, totally turned the song into a soul anthem, and I was forever grateful to him for doing that." ◉

# THE WHO
# "SUMMERTIME BLUES"

⚡ EDDIE COCHRAN COVER ⚡

SONG
"SUMMERTIME BLUES"
[B/W "HEAVEN AND HELL"] (1970)

WRITTEN BY
EDDIE COCHRAN, JERRY CAPEHART

FIRST RECORDED BY
EDDIE COCHRAN (1958)

Roger Daltrey remembers when he first heard Eddie Cochran's 1958 hit "Summertime Blues." "I was in school the year it came out," he says today. "It was him, Buddy Holly, the Everly Brothers—they were the people that we idolized. I was a year older than [my bandmates], so I was probably influenced by those people more. But where Buddy Holly's songs were male–female, Eddie's were more male derivative, which later was reflected in the Who's audience. We were much more of a blokes' band than a girls' band. We weren't very good at love songs."

Still a teenager himself when he cowrote "Summertime Blues" with his manager Jerry Capehart, Cochran expressed a quintessentially high school dilemma in his lyrics: the singer has to work to afford summer vacation, but he can't enjoy that vacation because he's so busy working. Daltrey was only fourteen years old himself when Cochran's song came out, so he could relate to Cochran's frustration.

As Daltrey entered his twenties and left his years of summer vacations behind, he held on to "Summertime Blues" as the perfect distillation of school-age angst. As he began to develop his new band—first called the Detours, then, when they discovered another group with that name, renamed the Who—he suggested they cover the song.

His three bandmates did not take much convincing. Pete Townshend had learned to play the guitar in part from listening to Eddie Cochran records, and drummer Keith Moon had in fact already been playing "Summertime Blues" in his previous band, the Beachcombers. Cochran may have had only one big hit (he died in a car crash a few years after it, only twenty-one years old), but that hit became a rock-and-roll-band staple. Like "Gloria" or "Louie Louie,"

it required only a few chords and a lot of attitude, perfect for budding rock-and-roll musicians.

The Who, though, did not play the same kind of straight cover that was in every bar-band's repertoire. They made the song angrier, casting aside the original instrumental parts for a more wild and slashing arrangement. "We just did it onstage one day," Daltrey says. "The way Eddie did it, it wasn't very easy to cover it. So I said to Pete, just play it as power chords, and he did."

Where Cochran's delivery was bouncy and light-footed to match the silly lyrics, the Who's version took on an aggression and a power—not to mention a volume—absent in the original. Early live videos show Townshend slashing furiously at his guitar while Moon seems to pursue a record for drums-hit-per-second. This wasn't the performance where they would famously smash all their instruments onstage, but it might as well have been.

"The Who was music to fight to," Daltrey says of their aggressive arrangement. "We'd taken the song from being in kind of a swing rhythm on the off-beat to a rock rhythm on the one. You leave the holes and that makes it more punchy."

Despite the volume, they did bring in a little of their Everly Brothers influence on the chorus line "There ain't no cure for the summertime blues," pausing the assault for a moment for a quick three-part harmony. For the song's punch lines—like the congressman saying, "I'd like to help you, son, but you're too young to vote"—they turned vocals over to comically low-voiced bassist John Entwistle.

**PREVIOUS:** The Who's mod look took on more color as the hippie era approached, 1966. **OPPOSITE:** Eddie Cochran playing at Wembley in 1960, when Roger Daltrey was still playing with the Detours.

Though loud and powerful, the song still didn't take itself too seriously.

"Summertime Blues" quickly became a crowd favorite when they played it in concert, even though they hadn't recorded it. It wasn't the only Eddie Cochran cover the Who played—they had also worked up versions of "C'mon Everybody" and "My Way"—but it stayed in the band's set list much longer. When asked if the fans' enthusiastic response kept "Summertime Blues" in the band's set, Daltrey bristles.

"I didn't really give a fuck whether they liked it or not," he replies. "We always used to play music that we liked. You should never, ever ask the fans what they think of anything. If they didn't throw bottles, they must have thought it was all right."

Since their fans didn't throw bottles, the next obvious step was for the Who to record "Summertime Blues" in the studio. Which they did in the late 1960s—but no one quite remembers what for. Some sources say the song was recorded for their commercialism-lampooning concept album *The Who Sell Out,* complete with fake radio-jingle intro, or even a covers record that never happened. Their longtime engineer Bob Pridden thinks maybe they planned to make it a stand-alone single. Daltrey doesn't remember recording a studio version at all ("We used to do loads of silly little things in the studio and they'd get forgotten").

This studio version was eventually released on a 1998 rarities collection. Whatever it was recorded for, it's clear why it was not used. In the recording, the band goes through the motions, but the song presents nowhere near the energy or excitement it did live. Removed from the fervor they worked themselves into in front of screaming fans, the band could muster only a halfhearted cover, not a classic.

From their earliest tours, the Who had earned a reputation among people who had seen them as one of the best—maybe *the* best—live rock-and-roll band of their day. The *San Francisco Examiner* reviewed a show this way: "[Concertgoers] had just heard the finest two-hour concert of their lives. They knew it. The Who knew it. . . . Exaggeration? I can't exaggerate perfection." And that was just a typical night.

But as one can hear on the recorded "Summertime Blues," capturing that live power in a studio setting was nearly impossible. So they rarely tried, instead either recording ambitious "rock operas" like *Tommy* or tight pop singles. They were like two different bands in the studio and onstage—and the latter was a whole lot louder.

"It was very difficult to capture the dynamics of the Who in the studio," engineer Pridden says, "because onstage the dynamics were just unbelievable. It was just like fire. To bring that into a studio is very difficult."

Though Daltrey doesn't remember recording "Summertime Blues" specifically, he agrees that they rarely captured their high-voltage live sound on records. "We were always a very different band onstage than we were on record," he says. "Our records were almost in some ways a demo for what it would become onstage. The only album we ever kind of knew what we were doing before we recorded it was *Who's Next.* All the rest we were learning in the studio. When we got the songs onstage, they became more and more developed and became totally different in a lot of ways. A lot more power, that's for sure."

If you can't bring the live show into the studio, why not bring the studio to the live show? Live albums had grown increasingly prominent in the rock world by the late 1960s, from the Rolling Stones' *Got Live If You Want It!* to Cream's *Wheels of Fire*. This offered a way to capture the power of "Summertime Blues." In those early days, though, live albums were hit-or-miss—mostly miss. Many, like the Rolling Stones' album, sounded like they'd been recorded inside a tin can. Others weren't really live at all, but rather recorded in a studio somewhere, with canned applause added after the fact.

Despite the audio obstacles, in 1969 the Who decided a live album needed to be the next stage in their career. Their fame had just hit new heights with the phenomenal success of *Tommy,* and they weren't

**ABOVE TOP:** The Who featuring the aerodynamic Pete Townshend, 1973. **ABOVE:** *Live at Leeds* is generally considered one of, if not *the*, greatest rock concert albums of all time.

sure what to do next. "I'm sure the Beatles were faced with it after . . . *Sgt. Pepper's*," Townshend said in a *Rolling Stone* interview at the time. "It would be very, very difficult to follow up *Tommy*, and I don't want to do it, and I don't think people really want it anyway."

So this proposed live album would serve two purposes: it would finally find a way to showcase the Who's power as a true rock-and-roll band (rather than just an arty group that made faux operas), and it would buy Townshend some time to figure out what was next. "It was filler between *Tommy* and something else that Pete was working on that became *Who's Next,*" Daltrey says. "We wanted to get it out there to remind people that we are a rock-and-roll band, and we're still alive."

To ensure that this live album contained their absolute best performance, the band recorded every show on their 1969 U.S. tour. This seemed like a smart idea until it came time to listen to all those tapes. "Suddenly someone realizes there are 240 hours of tape to be listened to," Townshend said in that *Rolling Stone* interview. "You know, now who's going to do this? So I said, well, fuck that, I'm not gonna sit through and listen, you'd get brainwashed, let's face it! So we just fucking scrapped the lot."

The tapes weren't just scrapped. To eliminate the risk of unauthorized bootlegs circulating (another quickly growing trend in the late 1960s), Townshend instructed Pridden to burn the recordings. He scorched the lot in his back garden while Pete looked on. "We put them all into an oil drum, bent over, and put a match to them," Pridden says.

> **Townshend instructed Pridden to set the recordings afire.**

With all their live recordings smoldering in a heap of melted plastic, the band and Pridden came up with a Plan B for their live album: they would schedule two more shows, record those, and just use whichever of the two sounded better. They booked college gigs in Leeds and Hull—"university audiences were always crazy," Pridden says, "and more into the music than most other places"—and brought along their recording equipment.

Mobile recording trucks—a full studio on four wheels—abound now but did not exist back then. So Pridden and his crew had to set up all their recording gear in the university's kitchen to tape the band playing in the dining hall two floors up.

Luckily, the crew had a lot of practice. Despite the earlier live tapes' fiery end, all that work around the U.S. paid off in one way. "It helped that we had experimented by recording all the other shows," Pridden says. "We had a lot of rehearsals for the real thing." Even then, accidents did happen—the bass on the second show in Hull did not get properly recorded, so Leeds won as the concert to release by default.

Leeds was an extraordinary show, even by the Who's standards. Taking place on Valentine's Day 1970, the concert featured the band at their most wild and frenetic. They did a long *Tommy* medley and a few well-honed covers, including "Summertime Blues." Shortly after, Townshend called it "one of the best and most enjoyable gigs we've ever done." And despite being confined to a cafeteria kitchen two floors below, Pridden was able to capture that excitement in his recording.

"We were trying to capture the rawness, not trying to smooth it out," Pridden says. "Live albums then weren't very good." He says too many so-called live albums weren't entirely live, but rather basic live recordings that the musicians then added to in the studio. "If you're going to start adding more instruments to things, you might as well not bother. We wanted to put the Who up there among the top two or three live bands in England, if not the world."

The Leeds tape showed everything the band was in concert: ragged, loud, sweaty, passionate. It abandoned any whiff of pretention or high-mindedness and showcased the band stripped back to their core. Whereas in the *Tommy* era, the Who occasionally seemed more like Pete Townshend and Associates—he wrote almost all the songs, and came up with the entire opera concept—the Leeds tape showed the band as an unstoppable foursome. "Summertime Blues" served as the pinnacle, letting each band member shine. Roger hollers the lyrics, Pete windmills furiously, John delivers the laugh lines, and Keith pounds away at his most manic.

Though he's since changed his tune, at the time the perfectionist Townshend wasn't thrilled about just how raw the recording was. "People wouldn't rave about us so much if they could just hear that tape," he said before it was released. "There's all kinds of bits where sticks are obviously in the air when they're supposed to be on the drums and arms are spinning when they're supposed to be playing solos. They did a terrible job on the recording. They fucked it up incredibly. They got crackles all the way through, horrible crackles. But I'm just going to put it out anyway."

They did put it out, on May 16, 1970, and quickly Townshend was proven wrong. People heard the tape and raved about the band more than ever. Though it was meant mostly as a stopgap, *Live at Leeds* became another hit for the band. The *New York Times* called it "the best live rock album ever made" in its review.

Though the band played thirty-three songs in that Leeds university dining hall, the final album was cut down to just six. "We've just gone for the hard stuff," Townshend said by way of explanation. They avoided most of the *Tommy* opera songs in favor of the huge, powerful live tracks, the band's ultimate room-shakers. Three of those six tracks were covers: Johnny Kidd's 1960 hit "Shakin' All Over"; an unlikely interpretation of Mose Allison's jazz song "Young Man Blues"; and, of course, their live favorite "Summertime Blues" were finally put on a record for people to hear in the comfort of their own living rooms.

"I was glad people could buy a record that reflected what we were onstage," Daltrey says. "I always felt that how the band sounded live was never on the record. There wasn't a studio big enough to capture our sound. When we put the live one out, there it was in its full glory, bum notes and all, and I love it. It's how we are. We are much rawer. The sound of the Who live was more primitive than it really ever was in the studio."

The label released "Summertime Blues" as the album's first and only single, and it hit the Top 40 in both the UK and the U.S., becoming one of their biggest hits to date stateside. It also holds the distinction of being the Who's only hit not written by Pete Townshend. Which, ironically, is why the Who doesn't play their most famous live song in concert today.

"We don't play 'Summertime Blues' anymore because it's not a Who song; it's an Eddie Cochran song," Daltrey says. "Pete doesn't really want to play our covers, I don't know why. I've given up asking him." ◉

Fantasy

LC 0720

GEMA

**BF 18405**
(BZ 1675) 3'58
Stone Agate
Music

45 UpM
STEREO
A
℗ 1970

Alle Urheber und Leistungsschutzrechte vorbehalten. Kein Verleih!

Keine unerlaubte Vervielfältigung, Vermietung, Aufführung und Sendung!

**I Heard It Through The Grapevine**
(Whitfield/Strong)
**Creedence Clearwater Revival**
Arranged & Produced by John C. Fogerty
Featuring John Fogerty

bellaphon

# CREEDENCE CLEARWATER REVIVAL
# "I HEARD IT THROUGH THE GRAPEVINE"

⚡ MARVIN GAYE COVER ⚡

SONG
"I HEARD IT THROUGH THE GRAPEVINE" (1970)

WRITTEN BY
NORMAN WHITFIELD, BARRETT STRONG

FIRST RECORDED BY
MARVIN GAYE (1968)

"I Heard It Through the Grapevine" had already been on quite a journey before it ever reached the ears of Creedence Clearwater Revival. Though destined to become a classic, the powers that be at Motown Records initially thought the song was a dud.

Motown's in-house songwriters Barrett Strong and Norman Whitfield had first written the song for Smokey Robinson, but his recording of it was shelved. Legendary Motown boss Berry Gordy thought the song was a stiff. His usual test of a song's worthiness was to ask people "If you had only enough money for this record or a sandwich, which would you buy?" Apparently, "Grapevine" didn't beat the sandwich.

PREVIOUS: John Fogerty in a typically wild and unrestrained moment, recording in San Francisco, 1970. **BELOW:** The Creedence cover of "I Heard It Through the Grapevine" ran eleven minutes long—almost four times the length of the original.

CREEDENCE CLEARWATER REVIVAL
Featuring John Fogerty

I HEARD IT THROUGH THE GRAPEVINE
Good Golly Miss Molly

bellaphon
BF 18405
STEREO

Fantasy

Strong and Whitfield remained undeterred. They tried again with Marvin Gaye, but his recording was also deemed not worth releasing. Rumor has it that the Isley Brothers cut a version, too, but no recording has ever surfaced. The two songwriters kept trying the song on new artists. "Norman believed in it so strongly, he almost lost his job," Strong remembered. "Berry finally said, 'Get out my face. Mention that fucking record again and you're fired.'"

The third (or, if the Isleys did record it, fourth) attempt came with Gladys Knight & the Pips, whose more upbeat arrangement finally got Gordy's seal of approval. The recording was an instant hit, going to #2. This encouraged Gordy enough to belatedly include Gaye's version on his new album, whereupon DJs immediately began spinning it, even though it wasn't the single. It soon topped even the Pips' version, reaching all the way to #1.

The usually prescient Gordy had been proven wrong. By the time John Fogerty encountered the song, "Grapevine" was a beloved hit twice over. And Fogerty heard it at a moment when his band Creedence Clearwater Revival really needed to prove itself.

Like New York in the 1970s or Seattle in the '90s, San Francisco in the late '60s was one of those legendary hives of music and creativity. The Grateful Dead were playing regular shows and happenings around town. Jefferson Airplane combined folk music and psychedelia for adoring crowds. Carlos Santana was woodshedding with his new band while washing dishes at a drive-in.

One thing San Francisco musicians and most other artists on scene had in common was an embrace of live improvisation, otherwise known as "jamming," which brought the spontaneity of jazz performance into rock clubs. Unlike their rock-and-roll predecessors like Elvis or the Beatles—who only a year earlier in 1966 had played their final concert there with the same eleven songs they'd played at every other date—San Francisco bands were mixing up set lists and incorporating songs from all across the genre map. Artists would pull not only from their own material but would also incorporate disparate cover songs—and jam those out, too. The Dead's cover of Bobby Bland's "Turn on Your Love Light" alone could stretch to thirty minutes or more.

However, one of the most popular San Francisco bands did not fit the mold. Creedence Clearwater Revival was not loose and freewheeling like their peers; they rehearsed endlessly and played songs that were tight and concise. They differed in another way, too: they had actual hits. In just their first year of recording, they had five Top 5 songs, including "Proud Mary," "Bad Moon Rising," and "Fortunate Son." By any objective standard, they were doing far better than most of their competition in 1969. But they still felt like pariahs in their hometown.

"Our peers in the Bay Area called us a Top 40 band," drummer Doug "Cosmo" Clifford remembers. "I talked to guys in the Dead later who said they hated us because we just popped singles out. Of course, as it turned out, they were really jealous because none of them could put a single

together. They would never admit that at the time, but that's what they aspired to do."

The members of Creedence began getting sick of other, "cooler" bands looking down their noses at them. They were never going to be a real jam band—for one, they had little interest in the drugs fueling so much of that scene (Fogerty called drugs "a threat to a career")—but they wanted a song in that vein, a song to show their peers they weren't just pop-radio lightweights.

"The other bands were telling us to do longer tracks, be more creative," Clifford says. "So we wanted to have a long song to show our peers we could stretch out. It was us saying, 'Hey, we don't particularly care to do this, but we can if we want to! We'll do it this one time, then we'll close the case and move on.'"

They holed up in their rehearsal space, trying to craft a long epic to impress the Grateful Deads of the world. Known as the Factory, the rehearsal space earned its nickname after guitarist Tom Fogerty, John's brother, commented, when an especially thick cloud of cigarette smoke permeated the unventilated room, that is was still better than working in a factory. This quip would soon give their album *Cosmo's Factory* its title.

"We were practicing in Tom Fogerty's garage a lot, and the neighbors were calling the cops," Clifford says. "The final time, they said the next time you come here we're arresting you. So we needed a new place to practice—otherwise we were going to jail, and we didn't want to do that. I had a rented house with a gardener's shack in the back yard, a place to store your lawn mower and that sort of thing. It was a very tight spot, you get a drum set and amps in there and it was ridiculous; but we couldn't afford anything else. I tacked rugs on the walls to soak up the sound."

The band rehearsed at the Factory daily, treating music-making like any other job. The drug-induced spontaneity of their peers was not for them; they exuded a blue-collar ethic of hard work and seriousness. Good as that mind-set was for their career, it was also causing them trouble crafting the sort of lengthy, freewheeling jam their more hippie-minded competitors delivered so effortlessly.

"The idea of jamming was cool to me—challenging—but the point was that it had to be great, not one-note meandering, and none of that nobody-knows-what's-going-to-happen-next philosophy," John Fogerty wrote in his book *Fortunate Son*. "It was organized. There were parameters for how far out the song could go. . . . I didn't want people falling asleep—the audience or the band. The difference between our jams and, say, the Dead's? In my band, there was an arrangement."

The four band members diligently worked every day at the Factory on an instrumental piece. Jamming without drugs required perseverance and effort, meticulously plotting out every section of the arrangement by playing it over and over again.

"We'd start with the rhythm section," bassist Stu Cook says. "Cosmo and I would lay down a groove, then the melody or the solo would be on top of it. There'd be accents, motifs, ideas that are stated and repeated and changed a little bit, in the tradition of classical music. Theme and variation. Then that inspires your playing different, sort of like follow-the-leader. Cosmo and I always felt our primary job

was to keep it solid underneath, so that all that other activity could take place on top. After all, it still had to be danceable and it had to groove, as opposed to a more free-form approach like the Dead."

"In typical Creedence fashion, even though it was supposed to be a jam, it was a rehearsed jam," Clifford adds. "We had parts. Most of the solo stuff is between me and John. I'm drumming against what he's playing, we're doing stuff back and forth. Sometimes I'm playing with him and sometimes against him. When we broke it down in the chorus, it sounded like a Native American war dance."

Though Fogerty's searing lead guitar was most prominent throughout the instrumental's eight minutes, he didn't aim to do a traditional guitar solo. Like everything else, it was meticulously plotted. This was not a solo in the style of his contemporary Jimmy Page, the hotshot gunslinger whose virtuosic playing soared away into the stratosphere. They aimed for grooves, not pyrotechnics.

"None of us were technical whizbangs," Fogerty told *Premier Guitar* magazine. "But since Booker T. & the M.G.'s were our idols, I didn't really think of them that way, either. The sound they made together was a really good groove, and I thought then—and for the most part I still think this way—that was much better than seeing some flashy guy playing nine million notes, with the band behind him just for backup. I always thought the idea of a band grooving was a far more powerful statement."

Eventually, they completed an epic instrumental jam. The piece sounded enough like a free-form improvisation (though it was anything but) to stand next to any San Francisco hippie band. But it was still untethered, with no actual song attached to it. Even the most far-out Dead song had *some* lyrics. All the band's focus had been on creating this far-out instrumental, but now they didn't know what to do with it.

The song that they used as a vehicle for that instrumental wasn't an obvious choice. Just as the Dead's marathon "Turn on Your Love Light" came from a two-minute, thirty-eight-second Bobby Bland song, Creedence's most epic track started as someone else's three minutes and thirteen seconds. In his autobiography, Fogerty remembers when he first heard "Grapevine":

> One day I was down in Los Angeles, maybe Sunset Boulevard, in a hippie clothing shop where they had a lot of leather, vests, and hats. They had an FM radio on and the speakers were really far apart—one was in the front of the store, another way in the back. I liked Marvin, especially his early stuff, but I really hadn't paid attention to his recent, very produced recordings, and "I Heard It Through the Grapevine" came on. Motown always had all that production and echo covering everything up. But because I was back there near one speaker, I was mostly hearing his voice—clear as a bell, with all his cool gospel inflections. Suddenly I was smiling—I was hearing Marvin really sing. I heard a guy really cutting it, singing his rear end off, and I was knocked out. I took it as a challenge, a throwdown—"That's kind of my territory. I could do that song."

And he did—but at first it didn't sound much like the Creedence version that would become famous. In those early days, the band still needed popular hits

to augment their own songs in concerts. They began performing "Grapevine" live, as they did so many other covers, sticking close to the original arrangement. "We played it the way it was played on the radio," Clifford says.

Eventually, though, someone—no one quite remembers who—had the idea to take the short "I Heard It Through the Grapevine" cover they'd been doing live and splice it onto the lengthy instrumental piece they'd written. It was a Frankenstein combination of two entirely different songs: the band plays a swampy cover of the Gaye song, then switches over into this epic instrumental section. But,

Gaye's "I Heard It Through the Grapevine" spent seven weeks at #1.

coming from four San Francisco longhairs, it made this Smokey Robinson/Gladys Knight/Marvin Gaye tune into something that worked. The combination both lifted their "Grapevine" beyond a simple cover and gave that instrumental some reason to exist.

Creedence were never afraid to have covers on their albums—their very first single, "Suzie Q," was a cover, though not a particularly successful one—but this seemed different than a quick run at a Roy Orbison or Ray Charles song. "Deciding to record ['Grapevine'] was kind of chancy," Cook says. "There had been

> **Creedence worked more like the early Beatles, banging out their latest dozen songs and calling it an album.**

two huge crossover R&B hits with it already. The song was not unfamiliar to the masses. But we did not go after the Motown feel at all. Our version was definitely for white kids."

They brought the song into their June 1970 sessions at Wally Heider Studios, the San Francisco music mecca that in its first year had already recorded soon-to-be-classic albums by Neil Young, Jefferson Airplane, and the Grateful Dead. By this point in Creedence's career, they were churning out albums at a rapid pace; they'd released three in 1969 alone, each going platinum several times over. This was not Jimi Hendrix laboring over each album track. Creedence worked more like the early Beatles, banging out their latest dozen songs and calling it an album.

"All of our recordings were quick," Cook says. "Most of the albums were recorded as a bunch of singles first. I think six of the eleven songs on *Cosmo's Factory* were singles. John had a horrible fear— unfounded, I believe—that if we didn't have a song on the charts all the time, we would disappear."

As a result, when it came time to record "Grapevine," it was one of just a half dozen songs they were recording to flesh out the album. Creedence still recorded just like the early Beatles had done with "Twist and Shout": surrounding their latest hit

Gladys Knight & the Pips released "I Heard It Through the Grapevine" in 1967, a year before Gaye's single.

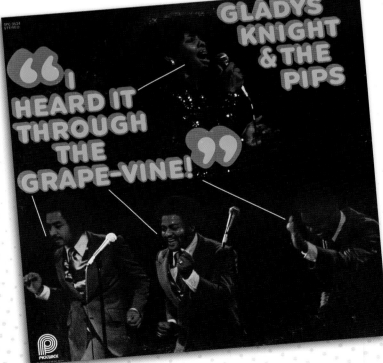

singles with filler tracks. Creedence had already recorded and released "Who'll Stop the Rain," "Travelin' Band," "Run Through the Jungle," and "Up Around the Bend" in the previous few months and needed some album cuts to pack around these hits.

"Even though we were always a well-rehearsed band who knew what we were doing when we went into the studio, because 'Grapevine' went so long, things came out spontaneously," Clifford says. "It was one of the few times where it was okay with John Fogerty to improvise, because it was supposed to be in the spirit of a jam. There are a lot of things in there that were created on the spot."

They knocked the song out quickly (or as quickly as one can play an eleven-minute song). They recorded it live in two takes, then overdubbed Fogerty's vocals and a little percussion. This was not unusual for Creedence. All the hard work had been done in those long Factory hours, so by the time they arrived at an actual studio they were ready to play. In the case of "Grapevine," this proficiency proved especially fortuitous. As Cook says, "I mean, how many times can you play an eleven-minute song before it starts to get stale?"

The length of "I Heard It Through the Grapevine" precluded its being a single, so there are no notable chart numbers to speak of (years later, the band's label did package it as a single without the band's permission, even remixing it for the disco market). It seemed destined to remain what it was recorded to be: a deep cut, something few would remember.

But radio DJs began playing the song anyway, spinning the full eleven minutes on air. Clifford and Cook say it became the most-played album track in AM radio history. It also became one of the band's show stopping live performances. It still is, in its own way.

In the decades since the band's 1972 breakup, the band members have had a famously acrimonious relationship, communicating primarily in lawsuits back and forth. But the music lasts. Notably, all three surviving Creedence members still make "Grapevine" a centerpiece of every show they play with their respective groups (Fogerty solo, Cook and Clifford as "Creedence Clearwater Revisited").

"I still love playing that song live," Cook says. "Most of the songs you play straight since the people came to hear them. You play them, you honor them, you go on to the next one. But 'Grapevine' stands alone. We still do like a twelve-, sometimes fifteen-minute version of it. We try to make it the musical performance of the evening."

> # "'Grapevine' stands alone."

A year after they recorded "Grapevine," Creedence learned what it felt like to be on the other side of a hit cover. At the time, they were touring with a young R&B duo they loved, Ike and Tina Turner.

"We'd been fans of them from the very beginning when they were on the Chitlin' Circuit," says Cook. "That's the kind of music we liked to listen to when we were kids, much to the chagrin of our parents."

"Every time we played with them, we made sure we were in the wings watching them," Clifford

says. "I remember one time we were in Utah, right in the middle of Mormon country. Tina comes out and does this thing with the microphone like she's giving it a blow job. It was very sexual. Her dress was short and she knew how to shake her moneymaker, to quote James Brown. You could see these guys with their suits on and their faces were just beet red."

Ike and Tina began covering one of Creedence's first hits, "Proud Mary." They borrowed elements from recent covers by Solomon Burke and the Checkmates, but made it all their own. Where on "Grapevine" Creedence had taken a soul song and turned it into rock, Ike and Tina took "Proud Mary" in the opposite direction. It was the biggest hit of their career together.

"They did a really interesting take, they took it in a completely different direction," says Cook. "They were smart enough to take a chance, and it worked big-time. I don't think a whole lot of inner-city people were aware of Creedence before then—but now they all know 'Proud Mary'!" ◉

**LEFT:** Tina Turner performing in Amsterdam, 1971; Ike Turner faces the drummer.

Side 1
STEREO
610.131
610.131-A
STEMRA
45 T
Time 3:55
℗ 1973

MIDNIGHT TRAIN TO GEORGIA
(J. Weatherly)
GLADYS KNIGHT AND THE PIPS
Produced and arranged by Tony Camillo
Co-produced by Gladys Knight and the Pips

BUDDAH RECORDS

# GLADYS KNIGHT & THE PIPS
## "MIDNIGHT TRAIN TO GEORGIA"

⚡ JIM WEATHERLY COVER ⚡

SONG
"MIDNIGHT TRAIN TO GEORGIA"
[B/W "WINDOW RAISIN' GRANNY"] (1973)

WRITTEN BY
JIM WEATHERLY

FIRST RECORDED BY
JIM WEATHERLY
[AS "MIDNIGHT PLANE TO HOUSTON"] (1972)

The phone rang in Farrah Fawcett's L.A. apartment. She answered—she wasn't yet famous enough to have someone taking her calls—but the call wasn't for her. The caller wanted to speak with her new boyfriend, budding TV star Lee Majors (soon to be known as the "Six Million Dollar Man"). Majors was out, though, and Fawcett got to chatting. She was packing for a flight to visit her family that night. She was leaving, she told the caller, on a midnight plane to Houston.

The caller was a young songwriter named Jim Weatherly, a flag-football teammate of Majors's. He forgot why he'd called Lee the moment he heard that phrase: "midnight plane to Houston." It was so evocative, he thought, four words that said a lot more.

"After I got off the phone, I sat down and wrote the song, probably in about thirty to forty-five minutes," Weatherly said. "It didn't take me long at all, 'cause I actually used Farrah and Lee as characters. A girl [who] comes to L.A. to make it and doesn't make it and leaves to go back home. The guy goes back with her. Pretty simple little story, but it felt real to me."

He wrote the song with the Fawcett-inspired title "Midnight Plane to Houston." In keeping with the Texas reference, he envisioned it as a country-rock ballad, something he might try to get Glen Campbell to record.

Campbell might have been a stretch for Weatherly, though. When he made that fateful phone call in 1970, Weatherly's biggest successes were songs placed on Peggy Lee and Dean Martin albums—deep cuts by two stars of yesteryear. He and his publisher wanted to go further. The publisher suggested that Weatherly

PREVIOUS: Gladys Knight, separated from her Pips by a wall of blue confetti, 1974. **ABOVE:** Farrah Fawcett and Lee Majors.

record his own album, not as a bid for solo success, but to get better recordings of his songs to send around.

A couple of years later, Weatherly released the unimaginatively titled album *Weatherly*. It includes his version of "Midnight Plane to Houston," a simpering, overwrought, country-pop recording dripping with strings. Listening to it now, it's really only notable for how far it had to go to become a hit. But somewhere buried in the gloss, Weatherly's publisher thought, lay a classic song. He dutifully began sending it around to country and R&B singers, including a young Motown Records star named Gladys Knight.

She ignored it.

Knight has never said why she initially rejected "Midnight Plane to Houston," but she perhaps thought—correctly—that the song sounded nothing like her. Whatever the reason, Weatherly's publisher didn't hear back and moved on to an R&B singer who *did* hear the song's potential: Cissy Houston.

A prominent backing vocalist for everyone from Otis Redding to Elvis Presley, Cissy Houston, mother of Whitney, had released her first solo record a few years earlier to moderate chart success (early singles misspelled her name "Sissie"). That 1970 debut album had included songs by Burt Bacharach, Bobby Darin, and Jimmy Webb, and she was looking for equally strong material for a follow-up.

Houston loved "Midnight Plane to Houston" when her producer played it for her. She only had one reservation: the title. "My people are originally from Georgia and they didn't take planes to Houston or anywhere else," she said later. "They took trains." She was surely also cognizant that singing about Houston could sound odd when your *name* is Houston (is she talking about herself in the third person?). Weatherly readily signed off on the name change she suggested, and with little fanfare "Midnight Plane to Houston" became "Midnight Train to Georgia." Houston and her producer released her cover in February 1973.

The title wasn't the only change from Weatherly's original. Houston's starts out in a similar country-rock vein; but once the first chorus hits, a notable addition enters: a backing

Jim Weatherly, whose songs "Neither One of Us (Wants to Be the First to Say Goodbye)" and "Best Thing That Ever Happened to Me" were also made into hits by Gladys Knight & the Pips.

**Somewhere buried in the gloss . . . lay a classic song.**

chorus. This introduces a side of soul into the mix; not nearly to the extent Gladys Knight & the Pips would incorporate it (the most prominent instrument in Houston's is still a harmonica), but an obvious step in that direction.

The other major change she made was switching the lyric's genders. Now it's not the woman failing professionally and returning home; it's the man. That gives this love story a lightly feminist shimmer. The woman succeeded where her man failed, but she will selflessly sacrifice her career to support him as he goes home, tail between his legs.

Houston's "Midnight Train" briefly hit the R&B chart and earned a small plug in *Billboard* magazine, but otherwise made barely a blip. Houston later complained that her label had not

sufficiently promoted it. In the end, few heard the first "Midnight Train to Georgia." But one of those few was the only person who mattered.

In 1973, Gladys Knight and her backing singers the Pips were at a major transition point. After a decade of hits at Motown, they had left for Buddah Records that February—the same month Cissy Houston's "Midnight Train" came out. Home to everyone from the Isley Brothers to Captain Beefheart, Buddah's roster was far broader than Motown's and offered artists more potential for creative freedom. Knight had begun to feel pigeonholed by the lush and polished Motown sound. She wanted more control picking her own songs and was looking for the track that could take her career to the next level.

As soon as Houston's "Midnight Train to Georgia" came out in 1973, Weatherly's publisher sent the recording to Knight just as he had Weatherly's. This time, Knight got it. She always chose her songs based on lyrics first, and she related to the new title more. She was from Georgia herself, and her people weren't taking planes any more than Cissy's were.

For Knight's cover of a cover, however, she wanted to complete the song's transition from country to soul. "I wanted an Al Green thing," she told the *Wall Street Journal* in 2013, "something moody with a little ride to it. I've always liked my tracks full—horns, keyboards, and other instruments—to create texture and spark something in me." Good-bye, harmonica; hello, horns.

**OPPOSITE:** An undated glamour shot of Cissy Houston.

Tasked with creating that track for her were producer Tony Camillo and engineer Ed Stasium. A Motown alum himself, Camillo had returned home to build his own studio in rural New Jersey. For one of his first projects there, he tasked Stasium with recording the instrumental backing tracks for Knight's next album. "Midnight Train to Georgia" was one of the last songs they tackled.

Due to his years at Motown, Camillo specialized in the very lush soul sound Knight was trying to shed. Giving her a track with a little more space—less Motown, more Muscle Shoals—proved a challenge. He and the band first recorded a big, splashy track: multiple guitarists, keyboardists, strings, what Stasium calls "the usual Tony Camillo kitchen sink method." They mailed it off to Knight in Detroit and a few weeks later her answer arrived: No. It's too much. Try again.

Reconvening the full band for a second attempt went no better. Knight still wasn't happy. She told Camillo she wanted a more Southern feel, suggesting a few specific Al Green recordings as examples.

Camillo grew frustrated. He had recorded plenty of top-selling artists in Detroit and never heard so many complaints. He felt the two versions they'd recorded were it. He dutifully began work on a third try, but did so halfheartedly. He was certain she'd come to her senses soon enough.

For this third attempt Camillo didn't even bother calling most of the band back. He and Stasium just assembled the three players who happened to be free on short notice one Sunday afternoon: guitarist Jeff Mironov, bassist Bob Babbitt, and drummer Andrew Smith, plus Camillo himself on piano. "[Camillo] treated [that session] as more 'Well, I'll give it a go, but I really think I have it already,'" Mironov recalls. "He was almost approaching it like it was just a demo."

As a guide, Camillo played the band the Al Green tracks that Knight had provided after the failed second attempt. "When we listened to the cuts that he played us, it was all pretty obvious that it was less busy than the Motown style of recording," Mironov says. "It had a more roots-oriented groove to it. The versions that we cut prior to that had a lot more activity to them, and now we were playing in a much simpler context."

The small band banged out this new version in an hour. Camillo sent it off to Detroit, still figuring this less polished approach would make Knight realize the first two recordings were the keepers. Then word came back: she loved it. She and the Pips were ready to sing. Camillo and Stasium hopped a flight to Detroit.

At Artie Fields studio near downtown Detroit, Knight sipped hot water and sucked on a lemon. That was how she prepared to sing. No vocal warm-ups, no rehearsing or run-throughs or sound checks. Just hot water and a lemon.

"Usually back then, I would do what's called a rundown [with the singer] to get the vocal level," engineer Stasium says. "You go through the song once or twice so I could figure what sounded good, microphone levels and that sort of thing. With Gladys, she was like no, I'm not doing that. We're going to record this right now."

Stasium cued up the backing track they had recorded in New Jersey. Knight stepped up to the microphone and delivered what would be the final version in a single take. She'd been practicing with the instrumental track and gave her vocals sass, attitude, and punch. Luckily, Stasium says, despite the lack of prep time, he was able to get it on tape. It took all of four minutes.

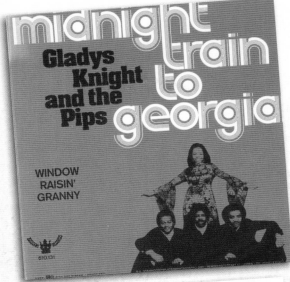

**LEFT:** "Midnight Train to Georgia" (single at top) was the first song on *Imagination*, their first post-Motown album.

The only part Knight did not record in that single take was the song's ending. For the last minute or so, the idea was to have her vamp, throwing out exclamations, lyric fragments, whatever came to mind as the mood struck. This semi-improvised "scatting" was a classic technique in soul music, but it had never been a part of the tightly orchestrated Motown records approach.

"I'm not a scatter or an ad-libber," she told the *Wall Street Journal.* "I had this mental block about doing that freely. [But] my brother [Merald] "Bubba" Knight, who led the Pips, said I had to put in some ad-libs. So Bubba went into the booth and fed them to me through my headset. So we did another take, with Bubba feeding me lines—things like 'Gonna board, gotta board, the midnight train' and 'My world, his world, our world' and 'I've got to go, I've got to go' . . . at the fade. Well, it worked."

After Gladys and Bubba completed their repeat-after-me routine, the Pips stepped up to their microphones. Typically on a song, backing vocals are just that—in the back. But everyone knew from the start that these would have to play a much bigger role than the rather timid backup singers Cissy Houston used. This version incorporated the call and response of the gospel tradition as much as Aretha Franklin did on "Respect," with the Pips sassily commenting on Knight's own lines. When she'd sing, "I'll be with him," they'd reply "I know you will!" When she'd sing about the man wanting to be a star, they'd chime in: "But he didn't get far!" They even added train-whistle noises. (Their parts became so iconic that a few years later, they sang just those backing vocals—without Knight— on Richard Pryor's NBC comedy show for a performance billed as just "And the Pips.")

Unlike Knight's vocals, though, the Pips' took many takes to perfect. Though finished singing herself, she stuck around to coach them through take after take. Eventually, with one final "I've got to go!" the track was complete.

Despite the unremarkable precedent set by Cissy Houston's single, Knight's new label knew this cover was a potential hit. In August 1973, not long after Knight recorded it, the song appeared on store shelves and the radio. Its impact was immediate. It entered the pop charts at #71 and two months later had risen to #1 (knocking off the Rolling Stones' "Angie"). The following year, it won the Grammy for Best R&B Vocal Performance.

*Imagination,* the album containing "Midnight Train," was released in October and produced two more Top 10 hits for Knight: "I've Got to Use My Imagination" and "Best Thing That Ever Happened to Me." But "Midnight Train" was the only chart-topper she ever had, and within a few years her songs had fallen off the charts completely.

Though it wasn't a harbinger of more #1 hits, "Midnight Train to Georgia" did prove prophetic for Knight in another way. Soon after its release, she and her husband divorced. "He was unhappy [that] we didn't have a more traditional marriage because I was often on the road or recording," she said. "Ultimately it proved too much for him, like the song said. I was going through the exact same thing that I was singing about when recording— which is probably why it sounds so personal." ◉

# PATTI SMITH
## "GLORIA"

⚡ THEM COVER ⚡

SONG
**"GLORIA"**
[B/W "MY GENERATION"] (1975)

WRITTEN BY
**VAN MORRISON**

FIRST RECORDED BY
**THEM (1964)**

In 1970, a young music journalist and guitarist named Lenny Kaye wrote an article for *Jazz & Pop* magazine. The subject was a cappella doo-wop, a music scene built around street-corner harmonizing and barbershop quartets. The genre's fan base was small but devoted, mostly people who had grown up listening to doo-wop during its 1950s heyday. One such fan who read the article cold-called Kaye at the record store where he worked.

"The article touched her because she had listened to much of the same music when she was growing up in South Jersey," Kaye remembers today. "She called me up and told me how much she appreciated this piece of writing and then came to visit me at the record store down on Bleecker Street. I put on our favorite records and we danced around."

Though he couldn't have known it at the time, Kaye and that doo-wop fan would go on to have a forty-year-and-counting working relationship. The woman was a young poet named Patti Smith. She and Kaye shared many of the same musical passions—garage rock, the Rolling Stones, the Doors—and also the same poetic passions.

Before long, Smith began preparing to read her poetry in public. As she practiced, she realized she needed something to distinguish herself. So she called Kaye again.

This time, she asked if he would accompany her on guitar while she read her poems. He agreed. Though his roots were in punchy garage rock, the versatile guitarist would improvise ambient guitar noises and squalls of feedback to punctuate her abstract, confrontational, and at times profane poems.

"I was just mostly trying to follow the dynamics of Patti's chants and musicality within her delivery of her poems," Kaye says. "It was just a very simple frame around what she did. It was never intended to be anything more than that one night."

> "It was never intended to be anything more than that one night."

One of the poems Smith performed at her very first reading in February 1971—in front of an audience of cutting-edge poetry luminaries including Allen Ginsberg, Jim Carroll, and Sam Shepard—was titled "Oath." "Oath" opened with a line that wouldn't become famous for five more years: "Christ died for somebody's sins but not mine." A giant kiss-off to Smith's Jehovah's Witness upbringing, the poem rattled off lines like, "Christ, I'm giving you the good-bye, firing you tonight" and "Adam placed no hex on me." The hostility toward religion that later shocked so many in the song "Gloria" pales in comparison to the text of the poem from which it emerged.

Though she kept performing "Oath" for the next few years, Smith must have sensed that it was missing something. When she released her first book of poems, 1972's *Seventh Heaven,* she left "Oath" out. Her second poetry book the following year, *Witt,* didn't include it, either. People would never know that "Oath" existed unless they came to see a reading in person—and even then they might have missed it, since it usually took all of sixty seconds to perform.

**PREVIOUS:** Patti Smith performing, with a neck brace.

It wasn't until 1975 that "Oath" would get any sort of release—and by then it had changed rather dramatically.

That first poetry reading became several, Kaye says, and over time the readings became more musical. "Even when we started performing more regularly at the end of 1973, we let it develop of its own accord," Kaye says. "We were dealing with something outside the framework of a traditional rock-and-roll band. We were able to follow its improvisations and its growth, especially when [pianist] Richard Sohl joined us."

The trio began a practice of segueing from one of Smith's poems into a cover of a popular song. Smith would recite a poem that climaxed in "tick tock, fuck the clock," then go into "Time Is on My Side," a Kai Winding song that Smith knew from the hit cover by the Rolling Stones. Or she would read a poem about the violence around Patty Hearst, and then the group would transition into a fiery cover of the murder ballad "Hey Joe." "It was a context in which to blend these worlds of music and poetry together so they would illuminate each other," says Kaye.

In 1974, Smith released her "Hey Joe" poem-cover as her debut single. Her musical ambitions were growing, and the trio began the transition from poetic accompaniment to a real rock-and-roll band.

**RIGHT:** The front and back of the "Gloria" single, featuring a much grubbier rock-and-roll look than the stark Mapplethorpe photography of the *Horses* album.

"In the beginning, it was just Lenny and I, and then we brought in a piano player," Smith told *Fresh Air*'s Terry Gross in 1996. "So it was just the three of us . . . and we did very simple songs, because the configuration was so simple. We just chose songs that were basically three chords, so I could improvise over them."

A song so simple, a child could play it, the garage-band standard "Gloria" was a staple of these rehearsals. Though the band knew the original by Van Morrison (with his early band Them), they modeled theirs after the crunchy recent hit cover by Chicago garage-rockers Shadows of Knight. "It had a real sense of teen angst that Van's didn't," Kaye says. "It had a real sense of gathering. As you peaked into the chorus, the celebratory nature of the song was inescapable. Plus it was just the one that was on the radio more then!"

## A song so simple, a child could play it . . .

Before long they were auditioning second guitarists by playing "Gloria" for forty minutes or more to see who dropped out first. "We had a lot of kids who played blues licks over it, we had a lot of traditional Chuck Berry licks," Kaye remembers of those marathon tests. "Most of them were mystified and soon left. But Ivan Kral just kept on chugging with us and was able to open our sound without changing it. By then, we were starting to see that we were becoming ourselves, which is of course the great journey of forming a rock-and-roll band."

**RIGHT:** The Patti Smith Group performing on the April 17, 1976, episode of *Saturday Night Live*. They performed "Gloria" and "My Generation."

Smith's poem "Oath" and Morrison's garage-band staple "Gloria" merged in a spontaneous moment one day in 1974. Playing regular concerts at Max's Kansas City and other small clubs, Smith's band practiced what they called "fieldwork"—what a different sort of band might call jamming. One day in their rehearsal room near Times Square, something magical happened.

"We had just bought a bass from Richard Hell, the copper bass he played in early Television," Kaye says. "Patti took it up, and she hit the big E string—*boonnnng boonnnggg*—so she could play it

Them's single of "Gloria" barely cracked the Top 100 in the U.S.

simplistically during one of the poems. She hit it and she sang 'Jesus died for somebody's sins but not mine.' *Boonnnng.*"

Smith recited more lines from "Oath" as she hit that E string over and over. As she neared the end, the band segued into another song that started on a similar big E chord: "Gloria." "With its repetitious chords and ease of playing, it seemed like a natural field to explore once we made the transition from 'Oath' into 'Gloria,'" Kaye says. "And of course it has a chorus that is about as rousing and as inspirational as can be."

From the moment Smith hit that big E note, "Gloria" ceased being a cover by the strictest standards. Over half the words in the final version are completely her own, and even the lines she takes from Van Morrison are often radically rewritten. Just as she had done with "Hey Joe," Smith took the bare bones of a well-known rock song and wildly rebuilt it.

"These songs were the fields of exploration that we gave ourselves each night for Patti to tell her cinematic tale," Kaye says, "for her to pull images from the air and create each night these different scenarios. We didn't know where these songs would lead."

From the original seed, "Gloria" grew. Smith continued writing lyrics until only the first six lines of "Oath" remained. The band began playing it live in late 1974, where it opened with a bass guitar playing the familiar piano riff, reminiscent of that first bass-note inspiration.

For a live radio concert in 1975, Smith even used the occasion to put the call out for a drummer, the last missing ingredient in the transition from poetry to rock-and-roll band. After a little self-mythologizing about how the band got together, she reaches the next stage while the band vamps behind her: "So they got together and they looked for a drummer. And I know you're out there! And I'm waiting for you!" and right back into the song. After the show ended, Clive Davis went backstage with the contract for a seven-album deal on his new label Arista. And before long, they added Jay Dee Daugherty on drums.

With a record deal in place and a real rock-and-roll drummer behind her, the band set out to record their first album. Going into the studio in August 1975, Smith wanted to keep covers to a bare minimum. "On my record, I'm trying to reveal as much about myself as I can," she told music magazine *Crawdaddy* around that time.

Some have written that Kaye talked Smith into including "Gloria" on the album, a story he disputes. "Nobody needed convincing, because we were all on the same page," he told *Rock Town Hall*. However, there was little question that this song was closer to his heart than hers.

Kaye had been performing the song in its more traditional form since before he met Smith and has often called it "the national anthem of garage rock" (he was the undisputed authority on the subject, having released the lauded *Nuggets* compilation a few years earlier). "It's a song that's been very important to me over the years," he

> ## "I'm trying to reveal as much about myself as I can."

says. "I still remember playing it at the Middlesex County Fair in 1967 and singing it to a girl who I recognized from the back of the school bus, who I always had a crush on and never really knew. I'm singing it, and from all the way in the back I can see her beautiful brown eyes looking at me. That to me is my most beautiful version of 'Gloria.'"

Smith didn't seem to feel as strongly about the song. In her earliest interviews, she constantly mentions a trinity of musical heroes: Jimi Hendrix, Brian Jones, and Jim Morrison. Yet that other Morrison—Van—never comes up. Like Jim Morrison, Van had proven himself able to bridge the worlds of rock-and-roll raunch and highbrow poeticisms, a model Smith herself would draw upon. Nevertheless, Kaye—or good sense—prevailed, and the recording of "Gloria" got under way at Hendrix's Electric Lady studios.

The sessions for the *Horses* album were contentious. Before they even started, Smith's first choice of producer got vetoed. "I had lined up another producer first," she told the *Independent* in 1995. "I didn't know anything about producers and just picked Tom Dowd because I admired him. But he was on Atlantic, and Ahmet Ertegun [former head of Atlantic Records] was really against me."

Smith's second choice to produce was the Velvet Underground's John Cale, but once he agreed and the sessions began, she began thinking she'd made a mistake. "My picking John was about as arbitrary as picking Rimbaud [as my favorite poet]," she told *Rolling Stone* in 1976. "I saw the cover of *Illuminations* with Rimbaud's face—y'know, he looked so cool, just like Bob Dylan. So Rimbaud became my favorite poet. I looked at the cover of *Fear* [Cale's 1974 solo record] and I said 'Now there's a set of cheekbones.' The thing is I picked John . . . in my mind I picked him because his records sounded good. But I hired the wrong guy. All I was really looking for was a technical person." When she told him she'd chosen him because his albums were well recorded, he reportedly responded "You bloody fool, you should have picked my engineer!"

Over the month-long recording sessions, Smith and Cale fought over everything from the band's cheap instruments (Cale made them buy new ones) to the amount of improvisation—Cale pushed for more, eventually nudging the formerly four-minute track "Birdland" past the nine-minute mark.

Despite Smith's reluctance about recording a cover—even one with as many original lyrics as "Gloria"—it soon became clear that the song not only belonged on her debut album, but that it needed to be the *first* track. "We went in there without a sense of programming," Kaye says, "but its opening declaration ['Jesus died . . .'], Patti's affirmation that she's taking responsibility for her life and not leaving it toward someone-Else-with-a-capital-E, is really one of the declarative statements of her art. It was something we believed in as a band, that one's personal responsibility to one's art is paramount and that you have to seize that moment and make it yours. As the album progressed, I believe that became more apparent to us. It was a way in which to claim and affirm our territory."

The band—Smith, Kaye, Kral, Daugherty, and Sohl playing the studio's massive grand piano—recorded the track totally live, according to engineer Bernie Kirsch in *Mix* in 2009. "The band was a live group; they were playing in the clubs and they had the songs down, so when they went in the studio it was mostly a matter of picking which performance was best," he said. "There were not a lot of fixes [that] I can recall."

By the time it came to mix the record, Cale was gone. "I'm not sure what occurred, but he didn't complete the project," Kirsch said. "If I recall, he wasn't there for most of the mixing. I don't know what the politics were—it wasn't in my domain. So I basically took over and did the mix with Patti."

The fighting between the band and Cale didn't appear to damage "Gloria," though. The song emerged relatively unchanged from the recent live versions that the band had been playing around town.

**Was this a call to arms for atheism?**

*Horses* was released on December 13, 1975, with "Gloria" leading it off. The critical reaction was immediate, with plenty of praise (the *New York Times* called it "extraordinary") and a few detractors (*Village Voice* derisively labeled it "an 'art' statement"). But whatever the reaction to the album, many reviewers homed in on "Gloria" in particular.

Perhaps not surprisingly, many focused on the first line of the album, that opening declaration so powerful that it doubled as a band mission statement. "Jesus died for somebody's sins but not mine." Was this a call to arms for atheism? A reflection of Nietzsche's "God is dead"? Just your everyday punk-rock provocation?

For anyone following Smith's career, an irreligious attitude wouldn't have been a surprise. She speaks about rebelling against her strict Jehovah's Witness upbringing in many early interviews. "My father taught us not to be a pawn in God's game," she told Andy Warhol's *Interview* in 1973. "He used to blaspheme and swear against God, putting him down. I got that side of me from him. The religious part I guess is from my mother, who is a complete religious fanatic."

Yet anyone outraged perhaps missed the sense of humor, the tongue just a little in cheek. In her first-ever interview in 1972, when she was already regularly performing "Oath" live, Smith told Victor Bockris, "When I say that bad stuff about God or Christ, I don't mean that stuff. I don't know what I mean; it's just it gives somebody a new view, a new way to look at something. I like to look at things from ten or fifteen different angles, you know. So it gives people a chance to be blasphemous through me."

Smith's definitive statement on the matter may have come twenty years later, when she reflected on "Gloria" to Terry Gross. "People constantly came up to me and said, 'You're an atheist, you don't believe in Jesus,' and I said, 'Obviously I believe in him' . . . I'm saying that, y'know, that the concept of Jesus, I believe in. I just wanted the freedom. I wanted to be free of him. I was twenty years old when I wrote that, and it was sort of my youthful manifesto. In other words, I didn't want to be good, y'know, but I didn't want him to have to worry about me, or I didn't want him taking responsibility for my wrongdoings, or my youthful explorations. I wanted to be free."

Many critics shared their opinions. The obvious question remained: What did Van Morrison think? If he ever said anything to her privately, Smith hasn't said. Kaye says he never heard anything from Morrison, or his people, either. Morrison's sole public statement on the matter, in a *Rolling Stone* profile two years later, does not prove particularly revealing.

"Yeah, I've heard that," he said when asked about Smith's cover. "I could even dig that for what it is. It doesn't floor me like some things. I'm the type of cat that would listen to black soul music or black gospel music . . . that's what I would listen to. But if something comes along like what Patti Smith is doing, I have a tendency now to accept it as what it is and get off."

Since then, other artists have been more forthcoming. "The opening to 'Gloria' might be one of the greatest moments in American music," Rage Against the Machine's Zack de la Rocha said when inducting her into the Rock and Roll Hall of Fame. The Smiths' Johnny Marr called her song "a massive influence on me" and said that "she gave new energy to American garage rock." Even Madonna named the song as an inspiration in an HMV ad campaign a few years back.

With *Horses* having raised her profile outside of New York, Smith continued to tour and perform "Gloria" as her regular set closer. She performed the song on the first season of *Saturday Night Live*, coincidentally singing the "Jesus died" line right as the stroke of midnight signaled Easter Sunday's arrival. CBGB tuned all their TVs in the bar to Channel 4 so everyone could watch—and earned themselves a shout-out at the performance's end. Show comedian Gilda Radner later got a lot of mileage out of a Patti Smith parody named Candy Slice.

In January 1977, Smith's relationship with the song changed forever. Six songs into a show in Tampa, opening for Bob Seger, she fell fifteen feet off the stage and broke several vertebrae in her neck. After an experience that could have killed her, she began reevaluating the irreligious message of "Gloria." In fact, she blamed her attitude toward the divine for her injury.

"I fell during [the song] 'Ain't It Strange,'" she told *Melody Maker* not long after the accident. "Just like the guy at Altamont got shot during 'Under My Thumb,' I fell just as I was saying 'hand of God, I feel the finger.' And I did feel the finger push me right over. It was like, I spend so much time challenging God when I perform and in everything I do . . . that I feel it was his way of saying, 'You keep battering against my door and I'm gonna open that door and you'll fall in.'

"I did say, 'Jesus died for somebody's sins but not mine,' and I still believe that," she continued. "I wasn't saying that I didn't like Christ or didn't believe in him, just that I wanted to take the responsibility for the things I do. . . . I'm a one-to-one girl and I have always sought to communicate with God through myself. And I feel that was one of the reasons I fell offstage."

"I think Patti changed [after the fall] and came to grips with her own spirituality and some sort of a spiritual system," her drummer Jay Dee Daugherty said in the punk oral history *Please Kill Me*. "I think she didn't feel that way anymore. This is something I've not talked to her about, this is my own observation. She was working out some theme of resurrection and coming to a different place."

> **She blamed her attitude toward the divine for her injury.**

When Smith returned to performing, the song stopped getting played quite as often. Then on September 10, 1979, in Florence, she played her biggest concert ever, her last before a sixteen-year retirement. For the first time ever, she opened with her usual show-closer: "Gloria." And she made one dramatic change to reflect her new beliefs. "Jesus died for somebody's sins," she sang. "*Why not mine?*"

The one-word change from "but" to "why" was "a long time coming," she said about that moment in the *Philadelphia City Paper* in 1995. "I was very involved with Christianity in my youth and had grown skeptical of church dogma. . . . As I got older, I did more New Testament studying, especially through Pasolini. His words were enlightening, portraying Christ as a revolutionary. I reassessed [Jesus Christ] and realized that he gave us the simplest and greatest ideas: to love one another, making God accessible to all men, and giving people a sense of community, that they would never be alone. It's not reconciliation as much as it is a tip of the hat."

She didn't perform it on her comeback tour with Bob Dylan in 1995, but by the following year it was back in the setlist—original line intact.

Smith continues to perform "Gloria" regularly at her concerts, with the opening line in its original form. All the years later, Kaye says that that first sentence on that first album remains one of the most important things the band has done.

"I'm glad that the message of 'Gloria'—that one takes responsibility for one's art as their

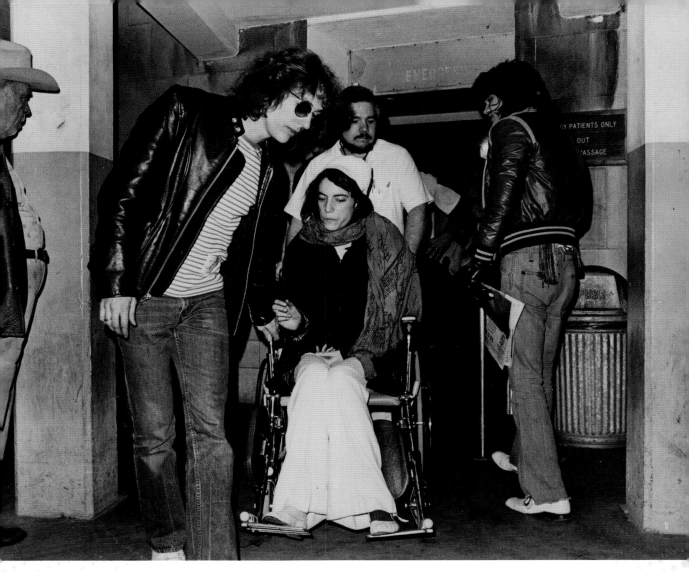

Patti Smith being wheeled out of a hospital after her fall from the stage during a Tampa concert, 1971.

mission in life—has inspired so many people over the years," Kaye says. "Many artists and groups have come up to me over the years, ranging from the most famous to the most infamous, to talk about it. Many of them don't even sound like us. But they took the core of what Patti was saying and converted it into their art. That to me is the greatest compliment of all." ◉

# TALKING HEADS
## "TAKE ME TO THE RIVER"

⚡ **AL GREEN COVER** ⚡

SONG
**"TAKE ME TO THE RIVER"**
[B/W "THANK YOU FOR SENDING ME AN ANGEL"] (1978)

WRITTEN BY
**AL GREEN, MABON "TEENIE" HODGES**

FIRST RECORDED BY
**AL GREEN (1974)**

David Byrne is sweating.

He's only been in the suit for a single song, but rivulets are already pouring down his face. It is a big suit—*the* big suit, as it was in fact known. This suit was not just a couple of sizes too large; it was a specially made costume, twice the width of Byrne's narrow shoulder blades. What stilts are to height, the suit was to width. It made his head appear to have been shrunk by a

voodoo priestess. It was also a lot of fabric to wear under heavy stage lights.

Byrne and the band kick into "Take Me to the River," the second song in the big suit. Within a couple of minutes, Byrne loses the jacket. This ruins the effect—the whole reason he's wearing this silly contraption—but this is not a song to be overdressed for. The way the Talking Heads performed "Take Me to the River" would make someone wearing shorts and a T-shirt sweat.

By the time of this iconic performance, captured in Jonathan Demme's 1984 concert movie *Stop Making Sense,* Byrne and the Talking Heads had scored a number of hits—"Once in a Lifetime," "Burning Down the House," "This Must Be the Place (Naive Melody)." But those had all been played earlier in the evening. The concert's big climax, as it was every time the band performed, was the lesser-known "Take Me to the River."

It wasn't their biggest radio hit, by far. But "Take Me to the River" was still the Talking Heads' showstopper, the roof-shaker, the number they could count on to push a crowd into a frenzy. And it wasn't even their own song.

As students at the Rhode Island School of Design in the mid-'70s, Byrne and Talking Heads drummer Chris Frantz were huge Al Green fans. Frantz says he even used to play Green records to woo his classmate Tina Weymouth. Byrne and Frantz formed a college band called the Artistics. In addition to a handful of early Byrne compositions, they began including an Al Green cover in their sets: "Love and Happiness."

Unfortunately, no recording exists of this proto-Talking Heads group covering "Love and Happiness." But both Byrne and Frantz say it presaged "Take Me to the River" by differing quite a bit from Green's original. "There's no way I was going to be able to sing it like Al Green," Byrne says, "so it ended up as something else."

When Frantz graduated from college in 1974, he and Byrne (who quit school) moved to New York City and formed a new band, adding Frantz's then-girlfriend, soon-wife Weymouth on bass (the Al Green records had worked!). They continued covering Green, but to celebrate the formation of the band they dubbed Talking Heads, they learned a new song of his: "Take Me to the River."

Although Al Green's *Explores Your Mind* was released in 1974, one year after his religious conversion, it was still plenty romantic.

Green and his guitarist Mabon "Teenie" Hodges had written "Take Me to the River" only a couple years earlier, in 1973. Though Green's version was never a single, it had been a hit for his labelmate Syl Johnson in 1975. Byrne says the song's lyrics first drew him in. "There's a mixture of the secular and the sacred, the sacred and the profane. It's sex and gospel and God and Jesus, all mixed together. That to me was fascinating. On the face of it, it seems like an unexpected mixture."

Like "Love and Happiness" before it, the Talking Heads' cover of "Take Me to the River" dramatically diverged from Green's original. Green's was yearning and emotional, every note dripping with sex. The Talking Heads' arrangement sounded less like seduction and more like an academic giving a talk about seduction. It sounded, in other words, like the Talking Heads: tender in the band's own dispassionate way, but a step or two removed from any raw expression of sensuality.

This difference was not entirely intentional. These art-school kids played their best approximation of Southern soul . . . but their best approximation simply wasn't very accurate. "As much as we hoped it would sound like Al Green, it never did," says Frantz. "I'm sure at the time I felt like, 'Oh, wow, this is really funky,' but it still sounded like a bunch of white kids from the suburbs."

Pretty soon the trio of Byrne, Frantz, and Weymouth added Modern Lovers guitarist Jerry Harrison to complete the band lineup. They had to teach him "Take Me to the River" from scratch, since he'd never heard the original. As far

as Harrison was concerned, it was just another Talking Heads song. "When I finally listened to Al Green's version years later, I was like wow, this is *different!*" he says. "The Talking Heads version is a more strident, driving song, whereas the original versions—both Syl Johnson's and Al Green's—are more delicate."

Even in those early days, Talking Heads was performing several songs that would become among their most famous. But as they gigged around New York City, they quickly realized that nothing connected with crowds like "Take Me to the River." This wasn't because their crowds at punk-rock clubs like CBGB knew the song—just the opposite, in fact. "The normal influences for bands in that place and at that time would have been pre-punk bands like the Stooges, Velvet Underground, or David Bowie," Byrne says. "We had those influences as much as any of the other bands did, but we wanted to also point out that we listened to a lot of R&B music and disco. That would have been anathema to some of that crowd."

Frantz takes this a step further. "A lot of the people down at CBGB were, when it came to music, pretty racist," he says. "If it was any black musician other than Jimi Hendrix, they weren't really very cool about it. You didn't hear anybody talking about how James Brown or Otis Redding are really great. All the talk was about David Bowie or Iggy Pop or Lou Reed. Performing a song written and recorded by a black artist is something none of the other bands were doing."

OPPOSITE: Al Green in concert, 1973. RIGHT: With "Take Me to the River," the Talking Heads introduced the downtown art-rock crowd to real R&B.

Even if the CBGB crowds didn't know any Al Green, they loved "Take Me to the River" when Talking Heads performed it. It had a groove and danceability absent from much of the music performed on those punk stages. It became the band's surefire showstopper, even once they'd released their first album and had their own songs to draw from. "Psycho Killer" was a great song; but live, it proved no match for "Take Me to the River."

Though their first album *Talking Heads: 77* had not been a massive success (even the now-classic "Psycho Killer" reached no higher than #92 on the charts), their label Sire pulled out all the stops for album number two. They flew the band down to the Bahamas to record it and sent producer Brian Eno to record it with them. Though within a few years Eno would be the iconic producer of U2—

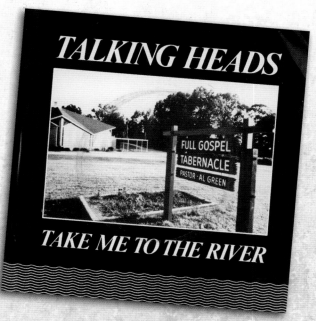

David Byrne and Brian Eno in the recording studio.

and, as we'll see shortly, Devo—at the time he was a relative novice whose only notable production was of the Velvet Underground's John Cale around the same time Cale was producing Patti Smith's *Horses*.

Remote as they sound, the Bahamas at the time actually weren't far from one of the era's major music scenes. Chris Blackwell of Island Records had recently found a niche recording Jamaican reggae artists like Bob Marley and Toots and the Maytals and had decided to set up a studio closer to where the action was. He opened Compass Point Studios in 1977 in the small island city of Nassau. Jerry Harrison remembers how hard it was to even find the place:

"I fly down at 8:00 p.m. one night and I tell the cab driver that I want to go to Compass Point. The cab driver goes 'What's Compass Point?' I tell him it's a recording studio and he goes 'Oh, yeah, I think I know where it is.' Eventually we get to the right village, which was like chickens walking around a single streetlight. There's just a bunch of dark buildings around us now. And he goes 'This is it, get out.' I'm thinking oh my god, what am I going to do? So I get out and a door opens and Robert Palmer walks out. He says 'I believe you must be in need of a cocktail!'"

If the studio's outside appearance was rugged, the inside was not much better. When the Talking Heads showed up a year after Compass Point opened, construction still wasn't complete. "We felt like pioneers," Harrison says. "There were times where a storm would knock out the power and the generator would come on. The salt air would cause corrosion in some of the equipment, so you started having breakdowns. Replacement equipment would have to get through customs through Miami, so then you'd get a couple of days off. You had to have a tolerant attitude."

As they set to recording their second album, "Take Me to the River" became a point of contention. Having seen how much crowds loved their cover, Eno was pushing them to include it. Byrne resisted. The band hadn't had a real hit yet, and he didn't want a cover song to be their first, not when he was writing so many originals that he was proud of.

"There's always a little bit of resistance to recording a cover like that because it's kind of a crowd pleaser," Byrne says. "I'd seen it happen before, where radio DJs who pick what they're going to play will often pick a cover song. Something that's already familiar to their audience is less risky. So then a band gets known for covering somebody else's song as opposed to writing their own material. They have to go through a struggle for years to get identified with their own songs."

Eventually Eno and Byrne's bandmates (who wanted a hit and were less invested in whether Byrne himself had written it) prevailed. "Take Me to the River" was one of the final songs the band recorded for the album, which was then operating under the working title *Tina and the Typing Pool*. And though Brian Eno would later earn a reputation as a hands-on, assertive producer, in those early days he sat back and let them play. He only had one major suggestion for the song: slow down.

"The Al Green version is actually a pretty up-tempo song, and we had been playing it at a fairly fast tempo," Frantz says. "Brian suggested, 'Why don't you play it as slow as you can?' We tried it, and it really worked. The version that ended up being on the record is way slower than how we were playing it live."

Having honed the track over so many shows, the foursome recorded it live in the studio. Eno wanted everything simple and basic. "He gets bored very quickly," Harrison says. Eno even tried recording the whole band—vocals, guitar, bass, drums, keyboard—using only two microphones planted in the middle of the studio (this sounded terrible and he reverted to a more traditional setup). "Brian saw that we were a good live band and felt like 'My main job at this point is just to capture what's already there,'" Byrne recalls.

Eno forbade the band members from tinkering too much with his live recordings. He even imposed a rule that overdubs had to be no more than one note every few bars. And the band obliged, to a fault. Frantz remembers overdubbing a percussion part on a little wooden box, hitting it only once every ten or fifteen seconds. When he finished, Eno said, "Maybe that was a little *too* sparse."

Eno did not, however, follow his own rules. The band might have been forbidden from tinkering, but he wasn't. Though the facilities at Compass Point were limited, Eno had brought his own gear. Frantz remembers Eno running the drums through a briefcase-size synthesizer, plugging pins into holes, just like at an old telephone switchboard, to get certain effects. Eno added what he called "epi-events"—little blips and bloops that gave the track a little weirdness. He then ran the whole recording through a limiter

**The Talking Heads never released another cover.**

that distorted the audio as the track progressed, creating the effect of it gradually getting louder without actually changing the volume. He called this a "psychological trick," telling the BBC it "makes your ears think they're hearing something that is getting louder all the time."

Harrison says that with all the delays and effects Eno was using, the sounds he and the band produced on their instruments were not always what they anticipated. "It was a very interesting experience making that album, because what you played would not necessarily be what ended up on the tape."

The band eventually left the Bahamas, and Eno put the final touches on the song and the album, rechristened with a new name. Supposedly, while they were casting around for a title to replace the unpopular *Tina and the Typing Pool,* Weymouth asked, "What can we call an album that is just more songs about buildings and food?" Harrison responded "We can call it exactly that."

*More Songs About Buildings and Food* came out in July 1978. "Take Me to the River" was the first single, and it soon became the band's first real hit, reaching #26 on the charts. It offered an entry point into the Talking Heads world, something just familiar enough that people could latch on.

"I think that after our first album," Harrison says, "everyone was like 'What is this music? What is it even influenced by?' And then we put out 'Take Me to the River' and people were like

**RIGHT:** The Talking Heads, seen here in 1977, were one of many not-exactly-punk bands that played at New York punk-rock landmark CBGB.

'Oh, it's R&B!' It sort of solved the puzzle for people."

It certainly solved the puzzle for radio DJs. Many DJs still avoided anything that sounded like punk music, but an Al Green song held no risk of backlash from listeners with more conservative tastes. Byrne's predictions proved exactly right. "Radio programmers played it safe," he says. "They thought 'This is an Al Green song. We're not going totally with an unknown here.' It's like people doing movie sequels or Broadway adaptations. Something's already been a success."

Having a genuine hit was an unmitigated joy for the others, but Byrne had mixed feelings about

It should be noted that the cover art for *More Songs About Buildings and Food* features neither.

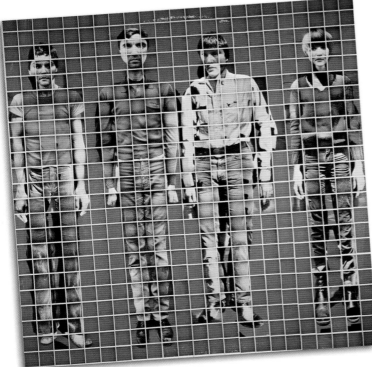

being best known for a song he hadn't written. He'd worried about becoming famous for a cover song, and that's exactly what happened. The Talking Heads never released another cover, and Byrne confirms that the success of "Take Me to the River" was the major reason why. He says, "You want to make sure you don't fall into that trap" of being known as a cover artist.

Even once the band had original hits, "Take Me to the River" remained their biggest concert crowd-pleaser. Byrne wrote many beloved songs but never one that electrified crowds like the Al Green cover. Frantz thinks he knows why. "Most of our other songs you wouldn't call sexy," he says. "Not that they weren't interesting and really good, but they didn't have that." Harrison attributes that to the song's structure: "It has a drama and it reaches an impassioned peak, so it's a great song for the end of the evening."

As the band's live performances grew, the song grew with them. Within a couple of years, Byrne began writing bigger song arrangements that required more musicians. By the time they filmed *Stop Making Sense,* the foursome was augmented by backing singers, another keyboardist, and a second drummer (not to mention a big suit). "After [our album] *Remain in Light,* David said, 'Oh, we can't possibly play this music live,'" Frantz says. "The recording of *Remain in Light* was done with a lot of overdubs and different parts, more than he believed we could play. He didn't think it would sound like the record and didn't want to tour anymore. I believe it was Jerry who came up with the idea of what if we toured with extra music playing the other parts to fill out the sound? David liked that idea."

"Take Me to the River" proved perfectly suited for this growing concert setup. It had begun life as a soul song, and adding backing singers nudged the Talking Heads' version back in that direction. "It was still our groove as opposed to Al Green's groove," Byrne says, "but the bigger band brought a lot of the gospel stuff back into it."

The Talking Heads themselves never met Al Green, but in later years the various members met musicians connected to the earlier "Take Me to the River" recordings. They all have stories.

Chris Frantz once met Syl Johnson, Green's labelmate who'd recorded the first hit version, in a Japanese hotel. "The jet lag is something serious when you get to Japan, so I woke up in the middle of the night," Frantz remembers. "I couldn't wait to get some breakfast, so I got down to the restaurant before it even opened. I was waiting outside and there was this really nice-looking black guy waiting there, too. We started talking, and he introduced himself. It was Syl Johnson." Johnson said he loved the Talking Heads' version of the song he'd made a hit.

When working on a Memphis-music documentary titled *Take Me to the River,* Harrison had the opportunity to play the title song with iconic soul musicians like William Bell and co-writer Teenie Hodges's brother Leroy Hodges, who played bass on both Green and Johnson's recordings. Harrison of course tried to play it in the original arrangement, but the muscle memory of so many years playing the Talking Heads' version proved hard to shake. "It worked best if I could sit next to Leroy and be watching his hands," he says. "I could see that he was about to move and the chord change was going to come there."

Byrne ran into Teenie Hodges himself a few times, even once inviting him onstage to join in on the song. But he made Hodges do the Talking Heads' version. "He was incredibly happy that we covered his song and, I think, probably also happy that we realized that he had a part in it," Byrne says. "He wasn't just some faceless songwriter. That acknowledgment, I think, meant something."

As for Al Green himself, on the few occasions when he's been asked about it, he had nothing but good (if somewhat generic) things to say. "I think Talking Heads are a super little group," he said. "I thought they were great. I guess the public thought so, too. . . . The record sold quite a bit. It's just fantastic."

If he doesn't go into more detail, perhaps it's because the song the Talking Heads recorded sounds little like the song Green wrote. "Our version, it does seem very much like it's ours," Byrne says. "That what makes a successful cover, I guess. You own it, as opposed to copying somebody else's version. You make it yours." ◉

**DEVO**
PRODUCED BY BRIAN ENO

WBS 8675
(WAA 8152)S
2:38

ABKCO
Music Inc.
BMI

From the
Warner Bros.
Album
BSK-3239
Q: ARE WE
NOT MEN?
A: WE ARE
DEVO!

**(I CAN'T GET NO)
SATISFACTION**
(Mick Jagger/Keith Richard)
℗1978 Warner Bros. Records Inc.
a Warner Communications Company

# DEVO
# "SATISFACTION"

⚡ **THE ROLLING STONES COVER** ⚡

SONG
**"(I CAN'T GET NO) SATISFACTION"**
**[B/W "SLOPPY (I SAW MY BABY GETTIN')"] (1977)**

WRITTEN BY
**MICK JAGGER, KEITH RICHARDS**

FIRST RECORDED BY
**THE ROLLING STONES (1965)**

Everything was riding on Mick Jagger's reaction.

Mark Mothersbaugh and Gerald Casale—the two prime architects of Devo—were fidgeting in a New York conference room one afternoon in 1978. The meeting with Jagger had been arranged by their label. Devo had recorded an odd cover of the Rolling Stones hit "(I Can't Get No) Satisfaction"—so odd that their label said they needed Mick's blessing to release it. Mothersbaugh put the tape in a boom box and pressed play.

As the strange sounds of the cover filled the room, Jagger sat stone-faced. He may not have known what to think. What he was hearing sure didn't sound much like the "Satisfaction" he'd written. Keith Richards's iconic riff was gone, and the original melody was nowhere to be found. Instead of Jagger's lusty swagger, Devo's version sounded like sexless robots lurching about. Was this an homage, Mick must have wondered, or were they mocking him?

"He was just looking down at the floor swirling his glass of red wine," Casale remembers today of that tense moment. "He didn't even have shoes on, just socks and some velour pants. I don't know what his habits were then, but this was early afternoon and it looked like he had just gotten up."

For thirty seconds or so, Jagger, Mothersbaugh, and Casale sat in silence, listening to the weird robo-funk coming out of the boom box. Then something changed.

"He suddenly stood up and started dancing around on this afghan rug in front of the fireplace," Casale says, "the sort of rooster-man dance he used to do and saying [in Jagger voice], 'I like it, I

**Was this an homage, Mick must have wondered, or were they mocking him?**

like it.' Mark and I lit up, big smiles on our faces, like in *Wayne's World*: 'We're not worthy!' To see your icon that you grew up admiring, that you had seen in concert, dancing around like *Mick Jagger being Mick Jagger*. It was unbelievable."

"We were less than nothing," Mothersbaugh adds. "We were just these artists that nobody had ever heard of from Akron, Ohio. It was a dream to actually meet him and to see him dance to a song that we had recorded. It was his song, but for us it was the most amazing thing that had ever happened in our lives."

Mick's rooster dance was all the approval they needed. Devo's wild reimagining of "Satisfaction" was ready to be released.

If Mothersbaugh calling Devo "artists that nobody had ever heard of" is an exaggeration, it's a small one. After forming in 1972, Devo had spent the subsequent half-decade building up a huge fan base in the Midwest but had not made a dent beyond. To get gigs, they would lie to clubs and say they were a Top-40 covers band (once promoters figured out they weren't, they were rarely invited back).

One impediment to the band's wider success was that, as far as they were concerned, Devo wasn't a band at all. Devo was an art project created to advance Casale's theory of "de-evolution." The concept was that instead of evolving, society was in fact regressing ("de-volving") as humans embraced

**PREVIOUS**: Devo (musically) bringing their theory of devolution to New York's Bottom Line, 1978. **OPPOSITE**: Mick Jagger shows off that signature strut at a Rolling Stones show in Atlanta, 1978.

their baser instincts. Music was only one facet of Devo's larger identity and not necessarily the main one. They were also creating satirical visual art, writing treatises, and filming short videos. The first of those videos included the band's first-ever cover, of Johnny Rivers's spy-show hit "Secret Agent Man."

"Secret Agent Man" could be seen as a template for "Satisfaction": a pop hit everyone knew radically deconstructed into an industrial lurch by a bunch of art-school weirdos. Devo's secret agent was "more like a janitor than a gigolo," Mothersbaugh says. They released their cover on a nine-minute film called *The Truth About De-Evolution* that they would screen before their concerts.

A band that doesn't call itself a band and subjects its audience to lengthy diatribes on obscure quasi-scientific theories does not seem poised for mainstream fame. But, for all their quirks, Devo craved success. And to get there, they needed a way to package their oddball identity for mass consumption.

No one in the band ever set out to cover "Satisfaction." They were attempting to write an original song at the time. But, to quote another Stones lyric, you can't always get what you want.

Devo used to rehearse in their practice space outside of Akron, in the very Devo-esque location of an abandoned garage behind a car wash. They had no heat and would rehearse wearing winter coats and gloves with the fingers cut off to play their guitar strings.

One January afternoon in 1977, as the band practiced—the phrase "jamming" seems wrong to apply to a band so removed from the hippie scene, but jamming is what they were doing—Casale's brother Bob (who passed away in 2014) came up with a guitar line, the robotic seven-note opening that would replace the original "Satisfaction" riff. Drummer Alan Myers joined in with a typically bizarre Devo beat. "It sounded like some kind of mutated devolved reggae," Casale says of the rhythm. "I started laughing, and I came up with a bass part that I thought was a conceptual reggae part. We just kept playing it, and Mark just started singing."

The song Mothersbaugh sang was a Rolling Stones song, but it wasn't "Satisfaction." Mothersbaugh first tried to sing "Paint It Black."

That he would pick a Rolling Stones song wouldn't surprise anyone who knew him. Though his own band's sound was very different, Mothersbaugh was a huge Stones fan. "Satisfaction" was one of the first singles he ever bought, and it opened his eyes to the subversive possibilities of pop music. "I just loved it because they smashed together two different rhythms on the guitar and the bass that didn't really fit, and it was the punkiest thing," he says.

One day as young Mark sat on his living room floor listening to it, his mom's church friend overheard and was appalled. "This woman says to my mom, 'Mary, why are you letting that boy listen to that song? It's dirty.' I went 'Wow.' Then I took it to the basement and I listened to it a million times. I kept trying to figure out what was dirty. I couldn't figure it out, but it made it all the more

> For all their quirks, Devo craved success.

interesting." Likewise, Casale had first picked up a guitar (before later switching to bass) after hearing the Rolling Stones. Though some would later wonder whether Devo's "Satisfaction" was mocking the Stones, these two were diehard fans.

As the band futzed around in their practice garage that day, they couldn't get the "Paint It Black" lyrics to match their jerky rhythm. "It was my brother, I think, who said try 'Satisfaction,'" Casale says. "Mark started singing 'I can't get no satisfaction' to our jam, and that did it. We stopped and figured out the two chord changes that would make it 'Satisfaction'—or at least a facsimile of it. Then we rebooted it and started up again."

Several hours later, the band emerged with the rough skeleton of their next single, a cover of "Satisfaction" mutated almost beyond recognition.

Though Devo's "Satisfaction" had come about by chance, the band soon realized that it offered an ideal vehicle to bring their de-evolution philosophy to the masses. "This was so whacked out that it was an example of what de-evolution meant musically," Casale says. "We had taken a massive worldwide hit that everybody knew and showed them, graphically, what you can do if you rethink it. It was a way into Devo for a lot of people. It made the Devo manifesto more understandable."

They weren't covering the song, Devo would say, they were "correcting" it. "I think those are some of the most amazing lyrics that were ever written in rock and roll," Mothersbaugh says,

"dealing with conspicuous consumption and the stupidity of capitalism and sexual frustration all in one song. It pretty much encapsulated what was going on with kids at that time, much more than any of the hippie songs as far as I was concerned."

The band began playing it live, and "Satisfaction" quickly became a showstopper. "We started playing it at our local little club gigs, and we got an amazing reaction," says Casale. "People would start going nuts."

The more they played it, though, the more the song evolved (or, rather, devolved). Early videos show a version much slower than it would become, a midtempo rumble that wore out its welcome by the end. Interesting conceptually and no doubt a fun surprise for concertgoers but not necessarily something you'd want to listen to repeatedly. "The versions that we were doing of all our songs in the early days were very slow and more bluesy, like Captain Beefheart material," Mothersbaugh says.

The Rolling Stones do look distinctly unsatisfied on their 1965 single cover.

"Comparatively speaking, [the first arrangement] plods along—but everything did in those days." They even recorded a "Satisfaction" demo in that slower tempo, though it has never seen the light of day.

As the band got bigger gigs, they realized that they needed to raise the shows'—and the song's—energy level. "We started off at Akron speed," Casale jokes. "But then once we went to New York and saw the amazing energy of the Ramones and the Damned, it just put a fire under us."

Partly because of their live cover of "Satisfaction," the quintet started getting some music-industry interest. David Bowie even introduced the group onstage at one of their 1977 New York shows, calling them "the band of the future." Their gigs were getting them the buzz that their first single "Mongoloid," released earlier that same year, had not. The band decided to capitalize on their momentum by going off to L.A. to record a second single: "Satisfaction."

Despite having no plans to sign with them, Devo took advantage of one small label's interest to use their studio to record. Unlike Elvis's "Hound Dog" or Hendrix's "Watchtower," this cover was pretty polished and ready to go when Devo arrived in the studio. They recorded the version as a single without much headache and released it on their own label.

This first single of "Satisfaction" helped grow their cult following—Mothersbaugh remembers eleven separate Devo bootlegs being traded among fans before they even had an album out—but didn't lead to any radio play or chart success. But it did help them get their foot in the door with major labels, who started a bidding war over the Ohio oddballs.

Amid the label drama, the band decamped to Germany to record their debut album with producer Brian Eno and their fan David Bowie, who wanted to assist. Though at the time they still had not signed a record deal, Eno believed they would get one, and they recorded the album on spec (he was right: Warner Bros. signed the band soon after).

From the start, there was tension. Eno was regarded as a sonic architect—but in Devo's mind, their sound was pretty much built already. They found themselves unable and unwilling to collaborate with Eno as the Talking Heads would in the Bahamas only a few months later (Eno recorded "Satisfaction" before he did "Take Me to the River," but the latter was released first).

"They were a terrifying group of people to work with because they were so unable to experiment," Eno later said. "When they turned up to do this record in Germany, they brought a big chest of recordings they'd already done of these same songs. We'd be sitting there working, and suddenly Mark Mothersbaugh would be in the chest to retrieve some three-year-old tape, put it on and say, 'Right, we want the snare drum to sound like that.' I hate that kind of work."

The reason they were so rigid, Mothersbaugh says, is that they had been burned by music industry types so many times already. At one point, Mothersbaugh says the (in)famous producer Kim Fowley called him and said, point-blank, "I heard your band the other day and I want to know, how can I make money off of you?" Another time, Virgin label head Richard Branson flew them down to Jamaica and, after getting them thoroughly stoned, tried to browbeat them into appointing the Sex Pistols' Johnny Rotten their new lead singer (he was supposedly waiting in the next room).

Having already gone through the ringer of music-biz shenanigans, they were unwilling to compromise, even with geniuses like Eno and Bowie. "By the time we finally got to Germany, we just thought 'we just want to do what our vision is,'" Mothersbaugh says. "Our goal was to just try and make it as faithful to what we were doing as we could. But Brian and David added on extra harmony vocals, and they put in synth parts. When we weren't in the studio, Eno would go in on his own and record extra parts over top of our songs. Most always we took all the stuff out that they did."

No one can quite remember how much this happened with "Satisfaction" specifically, but if there was a dispute, Devo appears to have won. In the end, the song basically emerged unchanged from their prior recording. The difference between the early single version and the eventual album cut that most people know is mostly a manner of polish and production values.

Once their label learned that Devo wanted to put "Satisfaction" on their debut album, they demanded that Devo get it approved by Jagger's people. From a legal standpoint, it's a little unclear why. Cover songs don't need anyone's approval; you can cover anything you want as long as you pay the original copyright holder and don't change the words.

Casale thinks Warner may have been worried that their cover was so different, it might have been considered satire—a separate legal entity for which one needs permission (Devo had run into a similar issue covering Johnny Rivers's "Secret Agent Man" and ended up using a sneaky runaround to get

> **They were unwilling to compromise, even with geniuses like Eno and Bowie.**

permission from his Japanese publisher since Rivers himself refused).

Cover-song legal expert Jon Garon thinks the most likely reason was that the label simply wanted to avoid any issues down the line. Devo could not afford a lawsuit, even one they likely would have won. Even if someone in the Stones made a stink in the press, that could sink a baby band's career before it started. Better to get the Stones' permission, just to be safe.

That's what put Devo in that conference room with Mick Jagger. That's what let them see their childhood hero dancing around. *I*'s were dotted, *t*'s were crossed, and they had Jagger's official blessing. (They later learned that their manager had strong-armed Jagger's manager to make sure Jagger signed off, but the band still believes his enthusiasm was genuine. There was no reason to put on the rooster-dance routine if all he was doing was an obligatory paperwork-signing.)

When the album was ready to be released, Warner mentioned in a meeting with Devo that they had a $5,000 promotional budget. When the band asked what that would go toward, Warner made some noises about cardboard cutouts of the band for record stores. Mothersbaugh and Casale had a counteroffer: give us the money to make a music video.

From today's perspective, this seems a logical suggestion, but a label executive in 1978 must have had a different reaction: What's a music video?

MTV was still three years away. Every now and then, a label would make a TV commercial—

usually just spliced-together clips of the artist performing the song (when you find a YouTube "music video" from a song released before the 1980s, this is usually what you're watching). But the idea of using video as its own creative medium to promote music was novel, or maybe just boneheaded. "They thought we were crazy," Mothersbaugh remembered. Where would they play such a thing?

The band prevailed, and their impulse to make music videos was prescient. Their reason *why* they made the videos was not. They made videos not because they foresaw MTV but because they foresaw another wave of the future: laser discs. These large discs—like a metallic vinyl record—had just hit the market, and industry buzz indicated that they were going to replace VHS cassette tapes. Devo wanted to make music videos to take advantage of the sure-to-be-huge laser disc market. "We believed all this stuff we were reading in *Popular Science* and *Popular Mechanics*," Casale says. "We thought the laser disc wave was just around the corner and that this was going to revolutionize everything. And when it did, we would be right there and be the only people doing it."

The fact that I just had to explain what a laser disc looked like tells you how that revolution worked out. But though Devo's predictions about laser discs were dead wrong, they still benefited from creating this backlog of unreleased music videos. When MTV launched in 1981, very few bands had videos ready for them to play. So the one band that earned endless rotations and became a household name as a result: Devo. And one of those videos on endless MTV rotation was their clip from three years earlier for "Satisfaction."

Casale came up with the "Satisfaction" video concept: finding outrageous examples of the lyrics. "We were trying to think of graphic examples of being denied satisfaction," Casale says, "like where desire causes pain, or being rebuffed romantically. Classic, universal, easily understood."

The video's vignettes ranged from a son being denied satisfaction when his dad yells at him for kissing a girl (Mothersbaugh's actual dad played his father) to their Booji Boy baby character sticking a fork in a toaster with predictable results. "I had read something about a kid getting electrocuted when he stuck his spoon in the toaster," Casale says. "But we made it a fork because it was funnier." They

Devo's 1978 album *Are We Not Men*? failed to make much of a dent on the charts but was hugely influential artistically.

even included a freak they'd seen in L.A. named Spazz Attack who could do a full forward flip onto his back without hurting himself.

The first thing Devo did with that $5,000 was get a wardrobe. Image was always important to the band, but they didn't want to look like rock stars—they wanted to look like anything but. "We didn't want to be lumped in with rock and roll, and we thought the way people dressed in rock and roll was stupid," Mothersbaugh says. "We were looking for something more interesting and more theatrical and more dramatic. What can we do to let people know we're not the same?"

Casale still had a day job at a janitorial supply company, so he would bring home the sales catalogs for inspiration, searching for the ugliest janitorial outfits they could find. That was where they found their famous yellow waste suits. "The yellow suits were great, because they had this look that was totally the opposite of something that hugged your balls or your butt, or showed off your physique in any way," Mothersbaugh says. "It was kind of the opposite; they hid us. We ended up looking like five cheeseburgers onstage."

The famous yellow suits—which they still wear in concert today—made their debut in the "Satisfaction" video (though they had not yet discovered their equally iconic red helmets). Mothersbaugh also built a guitar to look like Devo sounded, a metallic Frankenstein's monster covered in duct tape with electrical wires shooting out and a big metal modulator stuck to the front. "Every now and then you got a little shock from it," he laughs. "Either sweat or beer or spit or rain or something would inject its own permutation into the song."

They rented out an Akron theater to perform in, filmed the video on the cheap, and got it ready for its big laser disc debut. Though laser discs went nowhere, the "Satisfaction" video helped make the band unlikely MTV stars just a few years later.

The video was done, the album was out . . . and the public was not interested. Devo had started seeing flickers of success in the UK, but in America the buzz in the cool downtown New York crowd was not translating to the rest of the country. They were hip, but had no hit.

Their big break finally came when they performed "Satisfaction" on *Saturday Night Live* (coincidentally the week after the Rolling Stones themselves appeared). While ordinarily a little-known band like Devo wouldn't even merit consideration by *SNL*, they now shared a manager with Neil Young. Their manager dangled the possibility of a Young performance over the producers' heads to persuade them to book Devo (a sneaky trick, since he didn't bring Young on the show for another decade).

Rather than tone down their shtick for mass appeal, Devo performed at their most Devo-esque. They wore the yellow waste suits and pitch-black sunglasses, did the same jerky robo-motions as in the video, and Mark had a guitar even more Frankensteinian than the last. The one concession to mass appeal: you can briefly hear Mothersbaugh play Keith Richards's original "Satisfaction" riff before segueing into his own.

Instead of turning people off, though, their performance mesmerized a large portion of *SNL*'s audience. People home watching weird comedy on a Saturday night were, as it turned out, exactly Devo's target demographic. "Overnight, we went from being this little club band to having to rebook our upcoming tour to larger venues," Casale says. Without that "Satisfaction" performance on *SNL*, Devo might not have had a career.

Even four decades and many hits later, the band still thinks Devo owes a lot to "Satisfaction." Mothersbaugh calls it "the quintessential Devo tune," despite its not even being one he wrote. Casale says when they're long gone, "Satisfaction" and "Whip It" are the two things they'll be remembered for.

And none of that success would have happened without that conference-room afternoon with Mick Jagger. Forty years later, Mothersbaugh still can't quite believe it happened: "When I walk out in front of a car later today, not paying attention to traffic, and get squashed like a bug, and I'm looking up through one eye and there's a gardener with a blower that he hasn't turned off yet, standing over top of me with a cigarette, ashes floating down, and he's talking to somebody in some language I don't understand, and I'm watching all the good moments of my life zip by real fast . . . I know that one will go by a couple times." ◉

**RIGHT:** Devo's set at New York's Bottom Line in October 1978 showed a predilection for protective gear and alarmingly short shorts.

# "WEIRD AL" YANKOVIC
## "POLKAS ON 45"

⚡ **VARIOUS ARTISTS COVER** ⚡

SONG
**"POLKAS ON 45" (1984)**

WRITTEN BY
**VARIOUS**

FIRST RECORDED BY
**VARIOUS**

No name is more associated with parody songs than "Weird Al" Yankovic. Since he first turned a Queen hit into an ode to mass-transit hassles on "Another One Rides the Bus" back in 1981, Weird Al has elevated the parody song to an art form. Kurt Cobain famously said he wasn't sure he'd made it until Al parodied Nirvana. His parodies are sometimes as successful as the hit songs he's satirizing. Al's most recent album, in a career now in its fourth decade, became his first #1 album.

One could view a parody song as the cover song's opposite. In a parody, you keep the music but change the words. In a cover, it's the reverse.

> **Weird Al still isn't sure why his parents first bought him an accordion.**

If a parody is the opposite of a cover, then why are we talking about Weird Al in a cover-songs book? Because Weird Al *does* do some covers, and they pioneered one of the biggest cover-song trends in the age of YouTube: the novelty cross-genre cover.

Weird Al still isn't sure why his parents first bought him an accordion. "I can only conjecture, but I guess they thought that if you played the accordion, you're a one-man band, the life of any party," he says, laughing (many of his sentences end with a laugh). "They were just looking out for my social life."

As part of his early accordion lessons, Al listened to a lot of polka music. People often assumed he was related to accordionist Frankie Yankovic, who in the 1940s earned the nickname

"America's Polka King" (he's not, though the two Yankovics did collaborate on a special polka for the 1986 Grammy Awards). Even when Al wasn't trying to play polka music, whatever he *was* trying to play still sounded like polka. "Everything I play on the accordion—anything from rock to reggae— winds up sounding sort of like a polka to many people," he jokes. "I learned early on that there was humor to be gleaned from the juxtaposition of rock and roll and polka music."

He first explored that juxtaposition in college in the late 1970s, as an architecture student performing at California Polytechnic's campus coffee shop. "Mostly it was guys coming in with their acoustic guitar playing Dan Fogelberg covers, very mellow and laid-back," he remembers. "I used to go up with my accordion and my friend Joel who played the bongos, and we'd do what we called 'A Medley of Every Song Ever Written in the History of the World.' It was just random songs—everything from the theme to [soundtrack album *2001: A Space Odyssey*] to 'Hava Nagila.' The more random, the better. We went for ten minutes stringing these little snippets of songs together, and the crowd went nuts. That's when I first thought 'People like this.'"

Unlike the parodies Al later became famous for, these polka-fied medleys of popular songs were honest-to-goodness covers. He sang the words straight, not adding any of his own lyrical jokes. The humor came in the music, recontextualizing well-known songs into ridiculous accordion-and-bongo arrangements. "You're hearing something that's familiar in a very different way, which is also part of the reason parodies are funny," he says.

"As has been said many times, a lot of comedy is the element of surprise. It's taking you down a road and then making a sharp left turn. The polka medleys are similar, I think. It's something that's familiar, but it's tweaked a little bit. It's not how you're used to hearing it."

He was particularly inspired by comedy music predecessors, like 1940s bandleader satirist Spike Jones, who occasionally performed a zany polka cover of some serious composer like Tchaikovsky. "I listened to a lot of polka music because I want to make sure it passes muster with a hard-core polka enthusiast," Al says. "But it's comedy, so my medleys owe as much to Spike Jones as they do to traditional polka music."

As he continued his open-mic performances, Al began recording early song parodies on his tape player and gained some local notoriety on Dr. Demento's comedy-music radio show. Even once Al got a real band and regional fame in southern California (among a small group of comedy nerds), he kept the polka covers in his setlists. Soon, bongo-playing Joel was no more, replaced by Al's longtime drummer Jon "Bermuda" Schwartz.

"We weren't playing for a thousand people or anything like that," Schwartz remembers, "but our

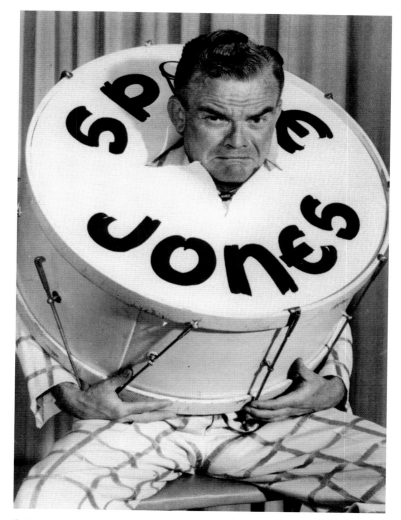

Spike Jones's penchant for the unusual piqued the interest of gag-rockers like "Weird Al" Yankovic.

crowds back then really liked the polkas. He'd sing them sort of sweet; that was half the gag. We were usually playing for the Dr. Demento audience, and they were into anything wacky."

In those early days, Al would throw random songs into his polka medleys, "local-interest kind of stuff, things that maybe people outside of L.A. wouldn't know," as Schwartz puts it. One early

Dr. Demento, the novelty radio DJ who helped popularize Yankovic's early work.

polka medley included tracks by Bad Brains, Suburban Lawns, and the Normal—not exactly "mass appeal" choices (also a Plasmatics song called "Sex Junkie," a rare bit of early vulgarity before Al committed to an all-ages career).

The polka medleys remained a concert-only gag, though. When Al recorded his debut album in 1982, it blended original comedy songs with parodies of current artists like Joan Jett ("I Love Rocky Road" for "I Love Rock 'n' Roll") and the Knack ("My Bologna" for "My Sharona"). There were no polkas to be seen—though, as he points out today, the accordion was so prominent that *every* song sounded kind of like a polka.

The polka covers transitioned from a live novelty to one of the most enduring components of his career when Al realized one thing: the medleys were funnier if you knew the original songs. The local-interest choices had to go. From now on, he would only polka-fy huge hits.

Al first recorded one of his polka cover medleys on his second album, 1984's *In 3-D*. Gone were the obscure oddities from the live shows, the Plasmatics and Bad Brains, replaced by Clash and Talking Heads hits. "I rejiggered it to make it more mainstream and classic rock, to make it more palatable to the average music listener," he says.

The resulting song "Polkas on 45" kicks off with Devo's "Jocko Homo" and rockets from there into Deep Purple, Berlin, and the Beatles. In the polka context, these disparate bands blend together into a zany accordion-fueled sprint. The more somber the original, the funnier to hear it goofed up (a chipper "In-a-Gadda-Da-Vida" is particularly inspired).

"I like to think that my parodies are funny even if you're not familiar with the original song material," he says. "But I think in a polka medley, the humor is a bit more reliant on being familiar with the songs. It doesn't hold as much punch if you're not familiar with the angsty or hard-rocking original."

Angsty or hard-rocking is right; Al tries to pick hits that sound as far away as possible from the jaunty polka beat. The more mopey or edgy the original song, the better. "Comedically, I like something that just seems *wrong* done polka-style," he says. "If it's a song that's already upbeat and happy and bouncy, it's not nearly as funny. It's funnier to do Nine Inch Nails as a polka."

Since that first album, he's recorded a polka cover medley on nearly every album, polka-fying the era's biggest hits in every one. If the early coffee-shop polkas were "A Medley of Every Song Ever Written in the History of the World," these became more like "A Medley of Every Song Ever Written in the Past Twelve Months."

The song choices often end up being hits he tried—and failed—to parody. On 2014's *Mandatory Fun,* Daft Punk's massive hit "Get Lucky" would have been one of the most obvious songs to parody. But all Al's attempts failed, simply because the song has so few words. ("You need enough syllables to be able

Sure, *"Weird Al" Yankovic in 3-D* had the Michael Jackson spoof-hit "Eat It," but the underrated classic "Theme from Rocky XIII" should not be ignored.

to actually make jokes," he says.) So it ended up in the polka medley. As did Miley Cyrus, One Direction, and Macklemore, and seven other recent pop hits.

"A lot of those songs would be great as parodies if I could think up a clever enough idea," he says. "But try as hard as I might, I couldn't come up with an idea I was happy with. So I thought, okay, well, it will work in the polka medley, at least."

Combining a dozen of the day's biggest hits into a four-minute polka has, he admits, "gotten a little formulaic" by now. But the formula works for a reason, and his past attempts to change things have met with mixed results. In 1989, for the soundtrack of his movie *UHF,* Al did a Rolling Stones–only polka medley. And in 1994, after *Wayne's World* made Queen's "Bohemian Rhapsody" a hit again, he recorded a full-length polka of the entire song. But then on the next album, he went right back to the hodgepodge-of-hits approach he'd started with "Polkas on 45."

"As much as I like going with the tried-and-true, after a while you want to see if something else is going to work," he says. "Both those polkas were sort of experiments. And both worked okay. But in general, I found that people tended to like the full-on random medleys better. Like, the Stones thing was a nice tribute, but there wasn't as much of a surprise going from song to song. It was like 'Oh, and here's another Stones song.' And I think a big part of the humor in the medleys is the random, jarring juxtaposition of one song to the next, done polka-style. I thought 'Well, I tried that, now let's go back to what works.'"

**The formula works for a reason.**

OPPOSITE: Yankovic shows off his Michael Jackson jacket at an awards show, circa 1984 (sadly, no glove).

Since Weird Al's now done a dozen polkas using more or less the same formula as the original "Polkas on 45," recording them these days should be easy. It isn't. Al is a perfectionist in the studio, taking these silly songs very, very seriously. As Schwartz says, "He's extremely . . . I won't say anal, but I will say *meticulous.*"

For example, Al always wants his song parodies to perfectly mimic the original music. The easy way to achieve this would be to just sing his new lyrics over the original backing track. But he doesn't; the band members have to deconstruct how each instrument on the song was played and recorded and then re-create it exactly. And this same studio perfectionism comes out on the polka covers. He could just sing over a basic polka beat—he could even use the same one for every polka—but he doesn't.

In the thirty-plus years since "Polkas on 45," his polka recording process hasn't changed much. Al combines all the song snippets together and records a demo at home, then brings it into the studio with his band—the same band that's been with him since the very first polka. They record the main band (drums, bass, banjo—as always, from scratch), the accordion, and Al's vocals. But where most people would call that polka done, for Al that's where the real work begins.

Schwartz says a good example of Al's meticulousness comes when it is time to record the horns. Horns propel much traditional polka music, but it's a safe bet that few Weird Al listeners pay a whole lot of attention to the horn section on a comedy song. The live circus tuba used when he sings the Police's "Every Breath You Take" (accompanied by theatrical gasping for air) is a nice touch, but inessential to the joke. Al doesn't care.

"Where a lot of guys would just do the horn parts on a synth and nobody would know the difference, Al knows the difference," Schwartz says. "We bring in the same live horn section almost every time: tuba, trumpet, clarinet, maybe trombone. It's important to him to have those things sound live, just the little inflections that make a live tuba sound different than a synth tuba are important to him."

The silly sound effects and funny noises that make the polka covers more *The Simpsons* than the symphony are also done live. "The quacks, the wacky horns, the fart cushion—they're live every time," Schwartz says. "I keep telling him, I've got samples from the last one, we could just assemble them. He'll say, 'No, I want to do them live.' We've done like five or six takes on a toy siren whistle until he gets it exactly right. You wouldn't believe it, to see him standing there conducting this thing. It has to be exactly the right 'quack' on the duck call—and if it's not exactly right, you're going to do it again."

When pressed, Al explains why he puts so much effort into the polkas' goofy sound effects—again, it's not clear anyone would notice if he just played computer files:

*Honestly, it's just more fun that way. One of my favorite parts of recording in the studio is being with my whole band, sitting in a circle around a microphone and doing claps. We certainly have so many clapping samples at this point that we could just use those, but that's not fun! For example, on [nonpolka original song] "Weasel Stomping Day," we went through a lot of iterations of trying to come up with sound effects for weasels being stomped and crushed and bones breaking and weasels squealing. We literally had a microphone over a trash bucket, and we would try every single fruit—biting into an apple, crunching celery— until the waste barrel filled up with food items and various other things we broke and mangled and bit into to try to get the proper sounds. I like doing it the organic, hands-on way. It's just one of the simple pleasures in life.*

Once recorded, there is one more hurdle to clear before a polka cover's release, and it shows another way in which a parody and a cover song differ: legality. Artists don't need anyone's permission to cover a song, but they do need to buy a mechanical license. With a parody, though, one needs neither permission nor any sort of license. A parody is considered satire and falls under a totally different law. Yankovic does get permission from the artists he parodies, but only because he wants to, not because he has to (most of his parody peers don't bother).

When he is recording the polka covers, though, he, like anyone else, needs to get a license. In fact, he needs a *bunch* of licenses: one for each song he's covering. "Polkas on 45" contained thirteen songs, so he needed thirteen licenses: from the Beatles, the Police, Devo, etc. Which brings up a particular quirk of cover-song copyright law.

When you cover a song, you need to pay a set royalty rate—but the same rate applies even if you only cover *part* of that song. In Yankovic's polka medleys, he is sometimes covering only five or ten seconds of a song, but the law doesn't make that distinction. A cover is a cover, and the royalty rate does not change no matter how little of the song he uses.

Which presented him and his label with a problem. Thirteen licenses is a lot to buy. Especially in the early days, the license fees would add up to more than his budget for the entire album. So he and his longtime manager Jay Levey worked out a system that they still use to this day. When Yankovic finishes recording a polka medley, they figure out exactly what percentage each song takes up, and negotiate with that song's publisher to pay that percentage of the regular royalty.

For instance, on that first polka, The Clash's "Should I Stay or Should I Go" takes up roughly 7 percent of the song. But the five seconds he sings of Talking Heads' "Burning Down the House" takes up only 2 percent. The Clash's publisher would have to agree to take 7 percent of their usual fee, and Talking Heads' publisher 2 percent. Instead of paying thirteen royalties, Al would pay one royalty, split thirteen ways.

"It's daunting from a legal standpoint," Yankovic says. "My manager has to go to every one of those publishers that owns the song rights and get their permission to use it in a medley. If we had to pay full royalties on every single song, I would lose money and the record company would lose money. For every polka medley, my manager has a thick file of paperwork to deal with regarding just the legalities."

With this system, though, he loses one of the main protections copyright law offers cover songs. If you're asking for something other than the standard mechanical license—like a discount—the publisher *can* say no. And occasionally they do. Yankovic once tried an all-U2 covers medley that died when the publisher wouldn't agree to his royalty system.

> "We've done like five or six takes on a toy siren whistle until he gets it exactly right."

Weezer's "Buddy Holly" had to be struck from a medley when the publisher demanded the full rate (they relented a decade later, letting Al polka the band's "Beverly Hills").

"At this point, thankfully, I've got a track record so we get very few turn-downs from publishers," Yankovic says. "The artists themselves generally have a good sense of humor about it. A lot of times if a publisher is giving us a hard time—and sometimes they do because they'd only make a fraction of what they'd normally make and don't think it's worth their time—I have to go to their artist and say, 'Hey, your publisher's not playing nice with us. Can you please get on that?' Some of these artists have grown up on my music at this point, which is of course very flattering, but it's also helpful when I'm trying to get permission for things."

Not all artists are flattered, though. Mick Jagger had loved Devo's cover, but his bandmate proved less enthusiastic towards Al's. "In the late '80s, I had just done the Rolling Stones polka medley," Al says. "I was in New York in an elevator, and I realized the only other person in the elevator was Charlie Watts, the Stones' drummer. I just started saying, 'Oh, Charlie Watts, hey! I just did a Rolling Stones polka medley and blah blah blah.' I was just rambling on, and I kind of got the feeling he had no idea who I was. I think he probably pushed a button to get off on a different floor than he wanted to 'cause he just wanted to get away from me so quickly."

Weird Al's latest album, *Mandatory Fun,* was the biggest hit of his thirty-plus-year career—his first-ever

#1 album. It was also the last album on his longtime contract with RCA Records. During interviews, he repeatedly claimed it might be his last album, *period*.

He's long complained that the traditional album cycle is ill-suited for parody songs; due to needing to produce a dozen tracks and then deal with labels and press CDs and records, the parodies risk coming out after people have forgotten the originals. He may switch to just releasing singles in the future, putting out a new parody song as soon as he's done with it.

But without an album—and without a record company's budget to license all these cover songs—is there a future for the polka medleys? Al doesn't know.

"That's a very good question. It is a lot of work, particularly for my manager, but I know that fans like them a lot. One option is maybe I won't record them anymore, maybe it will just be something I do live in concert. Maybe when I go back on the road, maybe there will be a new polka medley that is just concert-only. Or maybe I will release a new polka as a single. Now that I'm in the free-form stage of my career and not beholden to releasing albums, I can do anything I want to. I guess I just don't know what I want yet."

He's tried to retire the polka covers before, though, to no avail. For his fifth album *Even Worse* (with his hit Michael Jackson parody "Fat"), he didn't bother doing a new medley. "I thought, well, I've done three polkas now, I think people have gotten the joke," he says. "But there was a huge public outcry. Fans were running wild in the streets, crying and gnashing their teeth and throwing bombs and holding picket signs. I thought 'I can't be responsible for that public unrest!'" More

seriously, he adds: "Fans made it pretty clear that, for a lot of them, the polka medleys are their favorite part of the albums. So I decided 'well, I'm going to make this just a part of the album formula—half parodies, half originals, then we'll throw in a polka medley.'"

He hasn't released an album without a polka-covers medley since.

Even on the off chance that Weird Al never records another polka cover, they will live on in another way: their many imitators. Though Al is quick to admit that he did not invent the cross-genre novelty cover, he certainly popularized it, and many others have followed in his wake. He and Schwartz both cite Mark Jonathan Davis, who under the name "Richard Cheese" has been performing lounge-style covers of big pop hits for going on twenty years. Then there's Hayseed Dixie, who have been performing bluegrass AC/DC cover songs nearly as long. And there are now hundreds of albums in the "The [Genre] Tribute to [Artist]" mold: *The String Quartet Tribute to Nirvana*, *The Lullaby Tribute to Michael Jackson*, etc.

**In the YouTube era, genre mixup covers have become a cottage industry.**

In the YouTube era, genre mixup covers have become a cottage industry. Over the ten years since the *Cover Me* blog was started, cross-genre tributes have become a huge percentage of the songs we get emailed. A cappella covers are popular, as are ironically mellow covers of aggressive rap songs. Someone has even made their own polka medley—of all Weird Al's own songs!

Yankovic celebrates his Best Comedy Album Grammy for *Mandatory Fun*, 2015.

Ever humble, Al refuses to take too much credit for his cross-genre-cover followers. "I'd like to think that—just from the sheer fact that I've been around as long as I have—I've been an inspiration to some people making their living in music and comedy," he says. "I'm not going to claim total responsibility for all those other genre-crossing covers, but if people want to claim me as an inspiration I'd be very flattered."

One unexpected person does claim Weird Al's polka covers as an inspiration: Lin-Manuel Miranda. Miranda told the *Washington* Post in 2017 that he and fellow Weird Al superfan Jimmy Fallon once sang along to Al's 1986 medley "Polka Party!" in Fallon's basement and that they both knew every word. In 2016 he told Marc Maron that he might never have written the record-breaking Broadway rap-musical *Hamilton* without Weird Al as inspiration. When Maron asked him how he got first the idea to blend musical theater and hip-hop, Miranda responded:

*I always loved music that told stories, so genre becomes fluid. A huge help in that was fucking Weird Al Yankovic. When you listen to Weird Al, you realize genre is just the clothes the artist puts on. Like, he'll do a polka version of [the Rolling Stones], and you're like, 'It's the same chord progressions, the same melody, it's just played on an accordion.' And suddenly, it's a polka.* ◉

# PET SHOP BOYS
# "ALWAYS ON MY MIND"

⚡ ELVIS PRESLEY/BRENDA LEE COVER ⚡

SONG
"ALWAYS ON MY MIND"
[B/W "DO I HAVE TO?"] (1987)

WRITTEN BY
MARK JAMES, JOHNNY CHRISTOPHER,
WAYNE CARSON THOMPSON

FIRST RECORDED BY
GWEN McCRAE
[AS "YOU WERE ALWAYS ON MY MIND"] (1972)

The lineup of artists for the 1987 UK-televised Elvis tribute *Love Me Tender* could not have been more stereotypically 1980s. A bedazzled Boy George crooned "Are You Lonesome Tonight." Kim Wilde sashayed her white trench coat through "Treat Me Nice." Meat Loaf strutted and sweated through "American Trilogy" (if you squinted, he actually kind of looked like late-'70s Elvis).

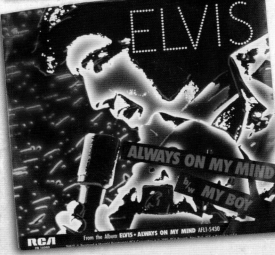

But this was 1987 masquerading as 1957. The acts played sound-alike Elvis covers in front of a cheesy *Happy Days*–esque diner set. All the performances were instantly forgotten. All except one.

From the opening seconds of the Pet Shop Boys' number, it was clear that they had very different ambitions. Gone is the neon-lit diner. Instead, they sit on an industrial platform billowing with smoke. The stage contains few instruments Elvis would have recognized. Instead, a man whose leather outfit screams "motorcycle dictator" plays a towering stack of synthesizers.

Anyone watching this performance after the preceding parade of King karaoke would have had many questions. The first almost certainly would have been:

"Wait . . . isn't this a Willie Nelson song?"

"Always on My Mind" wasn't a Willie Nelson song, nor was it an Elvis song. At least, not originally. The song started life in 1972 as a schmaltzy ballad dashed off in ten minutes by songwriter Wayne Carson, then best known for the Box Tops' 1967 hit "The Letter," and his partners Johnny Christopher and Mark James (they added the "Tell me that your sweet love hasn't died" bridge). A soulful version by Gwen McCrae and a country-pop take by Brenda Lee, both released in the first half of 1972, failed to chart.

**PREVIOUS:** The Pet Shop Boys' Neil Tennant in concert. **LEFT, ABOVE:** The Pet Shop Boys' "West End Girls" hit #1 on the charts in 1986. **LEFT, BELOW:** The 1985 rerelease of "Always on My Mind." **OPPOSITE:** Willie Nelson playing on the Pet Shop Boys' home turf in London, 1982.

Later that year, Elvis Presley heard the song. He was enjoying one of his periodic late-career comebacks, having just hit #1 with "Burning Love." Life on the home front was not going well, though: his wife Priscilla had recently left him after having had an affair with her karate instructor. When Elvis read the heartbroken lyrics to "Always on My Mind" for the first time, he reportedly asked his producer, "What are you trying to do to me?"

Elvis's "Always on My Mind" cover was a modest success, reaching the Top 20 on the country charts. But it wasn't enough to make the song a classic. In fact, it remained obscure enough

**Neither . . . Neil Tennant nor Chris Lowe even particularly liked Elvis.**

that when the song's cowriter Johnny Christopher offered Willie Nelson the song to record a decade later, Nelson thought it was a new composition. Christopher, not wanting to jeopardize his chances at a Willie cover, didn't correct him.

Actually, it wasn't just a Willie cover Christopher was angling for. At the time, Nelson was in the studio with Merle Haggard, where in 1981 they were in the early stages of recording what would become their blockbuster duets album *Pancho and Lefty.* "I wanted Merle to hear it to see if maybe he and I would do it together," Nelson wrote about the song in his autobiography. "Merle didn't particularly like the song. He didn't hear it well enough, I think. As soon as Merle and I finished our album . . . I stayed in the studio with the band to do a few more tunes. I wanted to see how 'Always on My Mind' would sound with just me singing it. . . . We'll never know what would have happened if Merle had really heard the song right."

Willie definitely heard the song right. He recorded a solo version that topped the country charts in 1982, immediately eclipsing Presley's and Lee's. Given a third life by Nelson, "Always on My Mind" quickly became a standard of country crooners and lounge singers across the nation. Nelson had set the template that the rash of covers that came after followed: sentimental crooning and string orchestras, the stuff American-songbook standards are made of.

Earlier in 1972, Brenda Lee failed to make a dent with her cover of "Always on My Mind."

Nelson's template held firm until the Pet Shop Boys needed an Elvis song to play on a tribute show.

In 1987, the Pet Shop Boys were recently minted stars. The electronic-pop duo's debut album the previous year had spawned huge hits in "West End Girls," "Suburbia," and "Opportunities (Let's Make Lots of Money)." But they were still only one album into their career, and a big national television appearance in the company of other young celebrities must have seemed worth taking some time away from the recording studio.

So often, artists cover their heroes and inspirations to pay heartfelt tribute. This was not one of those times. Neither Pet Shop Boy Neil Tennant nor Chris Lowe even particularly liked Elvis. Lowe put it bluntly, saying, "I'm not a fan of Elvis Presley," though he acknowledged a slight fondness for the "bloated Vegas period" (perhaps he'd seen the King's cover of "Unchained Melody").

"We were approached by Central TV to be on a program called *Love Me Tender,* commemorating the tenth anniversary of the death of Elvis Presley, and for some reason, we agreed to do it," Tennant said later. "Rob Holden, who worked with our manager, Tony Watkins, got us a load of Elvis cassettes and the first track on the first one Chris picked up, *Magic Moments with Elvis,* was 'Always on My Mind.'" They picked that track so they wouldn't have to listen to any more.

Elvis's take on "Always on My Mind" was the B-side to his 1972 single "Separate Ways."

"We knew everyone else was going to do their songs very much in the style of Elvis Presley, so we wanted to make sure ours was very different," Tennant continued. "It was around the time that acid house [a minimalist dance-music genre] was starting, and everyone had their own idea of what it might sound like, so we wanted this to be ours."

Whereas most performers on the show only needed to spend a few minutes learning the words to "Jailhouse Rock" or "Don't Be Cruel," building a new cover from the ground up required a lot more prep work. Lowe and Tennant holed up in the studio for two days, tinkering with the song.

Despite a penchant for cowboy hats, Pet Shop Boys' cover was inspired not by Willie Nelson but by Elvis.

They changed the chord structure to make it closer to disco and came up with the synthesized-brass riff that repeats throughout the song. By the time they were done, the song was barely recognizable as the standard popularized by Elvis and Willie.

As can happen with a great cover, Lowe and Tennant's new music changed the tone of the lyrics. To the band's ears, the narrator no longer sounded remotely sympathetic, but cold and unfeeling. Despite not changing a single word, their cover gave the romantic ballad a dark new interpretation. Read this way, the song's lyrics might not have unnerved Elvis so.

"The song is sung from the point of view of a selfish and self-obsessed man, who is possibly incapable of love, and who is now drinking whiskey and feeling sorry for himself," Tennant said. "It's a completely tactless song. 'And I *guess* I never told you,' or, you know, 'I *guess* I could have held you.' So, actually, 'maybe I didn't love you' is a completely logical conclusion."

They brought their new recording to the TV taping and lip-synced along in their industrial-smoke setting. It couldn't have stood out more from the other covers that night. But they considered that to be the end of the line for their new cover. It was a lark for a TV opportunity, nothing more. They had their own album to record.

But when *Love Me Tender* aired, Tennant and Lowe began hearing from viewers and friends: You have to release "Always on My Mind" as a single! They eventually caved. Releasing the track was easy enough—all they needed to do was go into a studio to flesh out the tribute-show demo they'd already recorded.

"I'd heard they would record their cover only a few days before the session," says their producer Julian Mendelsohn. "They'd done a fair bit at home by the time they came into the studio, maybe 75 percent. The main thing it really needed were new vocals."

The still-young Tennant was not a confident singer. "Tuning was always a problem for him in the early days," says Mendelsohn diplomatically. "I saw him perform recently and actually said to him 'Boy, you've really improved your vocals,' and he said 'Yes, I have, haven't I?'"

Tennant's trouble belting a tune had an unexpected upside. That understated singing over the huge synthesizer chords emphasized the narrator's dead-eyed attitude—though Tennant says that was not intentional. "I thought I sounded very sincere and my voice was dripping with emotion,

until people started congratulating me on being so deadpan. That was when I realized that there was a big difference between how I thought my voice sounded, and how everyone else did."

## The cover quickly went to #1 in Britain.

The duo also added little production touches, most notably sending producer Mendelsohn out one night to record fireworks exploding at a friend's party. "There were sometimes occasions where we went out into the field to get certain effects," Mendelsohn says. "For the song 'It's a Sin' we went to London Oratory and did recording there. In this case I went to someone's house where he was having a big fireworks party. I think I had to videotape it and then record the audio off the video soundtrack. It was quite crude in those days, not a matter of just plugging it into your iPhone."

The cover quickly went to #1 in Britain—which, after the response to the TV performance, was not a shock. More surprising was the reaction from the original songwriter, who had written what he thought was a straightforward country ballad fifteen years earlier.

"Everybody had told me 'You're not going to like [their cover]. They changed some of the melody, they changed a couple of words, and they added all these synthesizers and things,'" Wayne Carson said shortly before his death. "But I just kept an open mind, and when I finally heard it, I thought 'Hell, that's a great record.'"

# WHITNEY HOUSTON
# "I WILL ALWAYS LOVE YOU"

## ⚡ DOLLY PARTON COVER ⚡

### SONG
### "I WILL ALWAYS LOVE YOU"
[B/W "JESUS LOVES ME," "DO YOU HEAR WHAT I HEAR?"] (1992)

### WRITTEN BY
### DOLLY PARTON

### FIRST RECORDED BY
### DOLLY PARTON (1974)

In 1974, Dolly Parton got the sort of break that young songwriters dream of: Elvis Presley wanted to cover one of her songs. "I Will Always Love You" had recently become a #1 country hit, and Elvis and his manager loved it.

"I got the word that he was going to record it, and I was so excited," Parton told *CMT* in 2006. "I

**PREVIOUS**: Whitney Houston performing in 1993 during her *The Bodyguard* world tour. **BELOW**: Dolly Parton rerecorded a new version of "I Will Always Love You" for the 1982 movie *The Best Little Whorehouse in Texas*.

told everybody I knew 'You're not going to believe who's recording my song!' . . . Then Colonel Tom [Parker, Presley's manager] gets on the phone and said 'You know, I really love this song,' and I said 'You cannot imagine how excited I am about this. This is the greatest thing that's ever happened to me as a songwriter.'"

But Parker had called with more than pleasantries. He informed her of an arrangement he had made a regular practice for Elvis by this point: younger songwriters had to sign over half of their publishing rights to any song the King was going to record. That meant Elvis would be credited in perpetuity as a song's cowriter, though he never wrote a word. In addition to his standard performing royalties, Elvis would earn half of Parton's songwriting royalties—and not just from his version but from that of anyone else who covered it as well. Back in the early days of "Hound Dog," he and Parker would have been laughed out of the business for trying a stunt like this. But after nineteen #1 singles, they could often get away with it. Parker had strong-armed many desperate young songwriters into agreeing to this predatory arrangement. But Parton was no pushover.

Parton said she told Parker "'Well, now, it's already been a hit. I wrote it, and I've already published it. And this is the stuff I'm leaving for my family when I'm dead and gone.' And he said, 'Well then, we can't record it.' I guess they thought since they already had it prepared and already had it ready, that I would do it. I said 'I'm really sorry,' and I cried all night."

Parton never got to hear Elvis cover "I Will Always Love You." But standing her ground paid off two decades down the line.

For a time, Parton was almost as well-known for her roles in movies as for her singing. Whitney Houston, on the other hand, worked only briefly as an actress.

Though some later called "I Will Always Love You" the best love song of the 1990s, it wasn't written in the '90s, nor was it exactly a love song. Parton wrote it in 1973 about a business partnership ending.

For the first decade of her career from the mid-1960s on, she had worked regularly with her mentor, country music icon Porter Wagoner. She'd recorded albums with him, toured with him, and appeared often on his popular television show. Their work together had done well enough, but her more recent solo work had done even better. She decided that she needed to sever their professional ties for good.

**Parton was no pushover.**

"I was trying to get away on my own because I had promised to stay with Porter's show for five years. I had been there for seven," Parton explained to *CMT*. "And we fought a lot. We were very much alike. We were both stubborn. We both believed that we knew what was best for us. Well, he believed he knew what was best for me too, and I believed that I knew more what was best for me at that time. So, needless to say, there was a lot of grief and heartache there, and he just wasn't listening to my reasoning for my going."

She wrote her feelings into the lyrics of "I Will Always Love You." Lines that would later sound heartbreakingly romantic really described two business partners going their separate ways.

"I took it in the next morning. I said, 'Sit down, Porter. I've written this song, and I want you to hear it.' So I did sing it. And he was crying. He said 'That's the prettiest song I ever heard. And you can go, providing I get to produce that record.' And he did, and the rest is history."

Parton's recording became her third #1 hit on the country charts in 1974, and the song became a country staple. In 1982, Parton rerecorded it for the soundtrack to *The Best Little Whorehouse in Texas* and had *another* #1 hit with it, making her the first artist to top any chart twice with the same song. Eventually, though, the song began to fade from popular culture. For a decade after Parton's second recording, no one of note recorded any covers.

But while the song faded from country radio rotation, over on the R&B side of the charts, one name was starting to appear more and more often.

While Parton's rise to the top of the charts took her ten years and thirteen albums, Whitney Houston started out on top. Her debut album in 1985 spawned three #1 singles. Her next album had four #1 singles (and not #1 on a genre-specific chart like Parton's country hits, but #1 *overall*). By the time Houston began filming her first movie, *The Bodyguard,* she had the third-most #1 hits of any woman ever—and she wasn't even thirty years old.

For her first acting role, she played a famous singer—not exactly a stretch—while Kevin Costner played her titular bodyguard. By this point in his

career, Costner was more than an actor, having won Academy Awards the year before for directing and producing *Dances with Wolves.* No longer content to wait for his cues and say his lines, as the star and producer he was involved in every aspect of *The Bodyguard*—and that included curating the soundtrack.

For Houston's big musical number, Costner had chosen Jimmy Ruffin's Motown hit "What Becomes of the Brokenhearted." No one other than Costner was particularly enthusiastic about the choice, but they tried to faithfully execute his vision. Houston's producer David Foster spent two days with a studio band recording a workable demo track to play for Houston.

"She was shooting a performance scene at the Mayan Club, in downtown L.A., and when they wrapped we met in her trailer," Foster wrote in his autobiography *Hitman.* "I played her the demo, and she looked at me blankly. I knew what she was saying: she didn't like it. At all. 'I'm sorry,' I said. 'I can't get my head around it. And to be completely honest, I don't think it's a good choice.' 'You're probably right,' she said. 'But please go back and try it one more time.'"

As they continued wrestling with how to make "What Becomes of the Brokenhearted" work for the film, they had a stroke of luck. Singer Paul Young had covered the song for the recent movie *Fried Green Tomatoes,* and his version was moving up the charts. They'd been beaten to the punch. If Houston sang this song now, she would appear to be riding Young's coattails. The producers had all the excuse they needed to scrap it. Foster broke the news to Costner, and asked if he had any other ideas for the film's big number. A day later, Costner did: "I Will Always Love You."

"Dolly's song was a song that I just always really, really loved," Costner told *ABC News* in 2009. "And truth be told, the musical side of [Houston's] camp was very unsure about this little country song."

Foster didn't know the track, but went out and bought the only version he could find, a Linda Ronstadt cover from 1975. As he wrote in his book, "the heavens split open the moment I played it. I could literally hear the finished Whitney recording in my head—the key change, the rousing strings, the big finish—and I knew *exactly* what I had to do to make it soar."

However, not everyone shared Foster's vision. Costner hadn't just chosen the song; he had his own ideas about the arrangement. He wanted Whitney to sing the intro *a cappella,* and once again he butted heads with her team. The idea of starting a major single with forty-five seconds of slow, unaccompanied vocals was anathema to music-industry veterans. They didn't just want to make a great record; they wanted another #1 hit. Radio wouldn't play a song like that, and MTV viewers would change the channel. But Costner didn't care, so to placate the star they agreed to try it. Foster and a few studio musicians recorded a demo in the new arrangement and flew down to Miami to meet Houston (with Foster quietly planning on adding instruments under the intro later).

Houston was in Miami, filming *The Bodyguard*'s final scenes. The movie would end with a tearful airport farewell between her character

and Costner's, intercut with footage of Houston performing "I Will Always Love You" onstage. The film's producers assumed she would record the song in a studio and then just lip-sync to give them the performance footage they needed.

> **Houston had the third-most #1 hits of any woman ever— and she wasn't even thirty years old.**

"She said, 'I don't do that,'" remembers recording engineer Peter Yianilos, who ran the mobile recording studio they used. "Lip-syncing is not something Whitney Houston thinks is very funny. She'd spent her whole life honing her voice and insisted she was going to sing it live, period. I'd recorded her doing her famous National Anthem at the Super Bowl, too, and the producers there suggested the same thing, because it is almost

Houston's "I Will Always Love You" cover was so connected to her legacy that it was played at her funeral in New Jersey in 2012.

Kevin Costner whisks Houston away from danger in a scene from *The Bodyguard*.

impossible to hear yourself sing in a stadium. She insisted on doing it live."

It wasn't just Houston singing live. Against the producers' strenuous objections, she flew her entire band down to Miami to play live as well. "This was a big deal," recalls her longtime saxophone player Kirk Whalum (whom she'd nicknamed "Bishop" for the backstage Bible studies he led). "She wanted us because she was familiar with us. It was a known fact that she depended on us for more than just backing her up musically. We *prayed* with her, not just played with her. When she asked for us to be flown down to play with her, they said, 'We can't do that.' Apparently she told them something like 'Go ahead and do it whatever way you want to do it, then—but

you're going to have to find a singer.' Eventually she won out."

Houston and her band learned the arrangement and prepared to tape it live. But the night they were set to record, Foster got an unexpected phone call.

On the line was Dolly Parton. She had heard that Houston was recording her song and had one note. "Don't forget," she told Foster, "there's a third verse that Linda Ronstadt never did on her version." "What are you taking about? *What* third verse?" Foster asked. She read it to him over the phone. He ran into rehearsal and taught Houston the extra lyrics.

The night of the recording, everyone arrived at Miami's Fontainebleau Hotel to find a grand ballroom arranged with a huge gold lamé curtain behind the stage. It looked great on film, but setting up a live taping that would sound decent in the cavernous space proved difficult. The film crew arranged the band offstage and then wrapped a heavy curtain around them to muffle their sound. Whitney would not be able to see her band, nor could they see her.

Because the ballroom did not have the requisite recording equipment, Foster and the engineers were all parked in Yianilos's recording truck out in the hotel's alley. It was pouring rain, and the raindrops hit the truck's roof so loudly that it was hard to hear what they were recording.

Kevin Costner was in the truck as well. He had nothing to offer in terms of technical ability, and he wasn't acting in this scene, but he showed up for moral support. "He was really Whitney's cheerleader," Yianilos says. "He encouraged her and gave her a lot of confidence, I think more than anyone else on the session."

Despite having so many #1 hits, Houston needed all the support she could get that evening. Yianilos has never forgotten one particular moment he shared with her. "I was asked at one point to go up to her and switch to a slightly different type of microphone," he says. "And I wanted to make sure she understood that this was not a flaw with her performance, so I just gave her a smile and an encouraging nod, like things are going great. I recall that she looked terrified. Just frozen, like a deer in the headlights. I'll never forget that. I expected a bold, brash hit-maker persona and encountered what seemed like a scared girl."

**Whitney needed all the support she could get that evening.**

Whalum, who played with her for eight years, says this was not unusual. "She was always a nervous, jittery person. Her hands would always be shaking—I don't want to say trembling, exactly, but just *nervous*, moving fast. In retrospect, I'm sure some of that was drugs, but I think she was just a nervous, wiry person anyway."

When the tape started rolling, however, the star shone through. "We would see her with all that nervous energy, and then she'd open her mouth and blow us away, like she didn't have a care in the world," Whalum says. "This lady was born to sing. It was inspiring to see her settle into her zone."

They did five takes of "I Will Always Love You" that night, Whitney singing live with the band she couldn't see. Everyone knew the moment they got the one.

"As a music person, you just can detect when you get that magic," says Yianilos. "You can feel it, where you're poised on the edge of your seat at every beat, at every measure, just waiting for that thing you know makes a record perfect. That final take was just a really heartfelt performance from her. There were big smiles all around."

"When she opened her mouth," Foster wrote in *Hitman,* "I realized that Kevin Costner had come up with one of the greatest ideas in the history of movie music."

The tapes flew back to Los Angeles with mixing engineer Dave Reitzas, David Foster's right-hand man. "David came to L.A. to listen to some Michael Bolton mixes I was doing, and he came in with the multi-track of 'I Will Always Love You,'" Reitzas says. "He said, 'Dave, can you do a quick mix that I can send to Clive Davis so he can hear the new arrangement? Just make sure there's a lot of vocal, but do it really quick. You don't have to spend a lot of time on it.' So I spent about an hour doing a quick mix—all from the heart, no brain—just thinking we have to let Clive know where we're at."

The mix was very rough. The strings weren't loud enough, Houston's vocal needed technical polish to sound more like a studio recording, and Whalum's climactic high note in his sax solo was sharp. They didn't hear anything back from Davis, so they set about polishing the track. Foster and Reitzas spent two months adding synths, bringing in guitarists to record new parts, reducing the background noise of the hotel, and running Houston's vocal through various effects. "Just the typical things you would do to take it from a Miami ballroom recording into a professional studio-type sound," Reitzas says. They sent the final track off to Davis to approve.

This time he responded immediately—and angrily. "What did you do to it?" Davis reportedly told Foster. "I *hate* it. Why did you make all those changes?" Davis wanted to release that first mix, the rough one Reitzas had made in an hour.

Reitzas tried to compromise, to remove some of the new instruments they'd added but keep the polish and fix the most overt mistakes. "I went up to Clive's office and played him all our mixes," Reitzas recalls. "He kept saying, 'The mix that you guys sent me first is the one I want to use.' It got

> **"When you think about how many rules that song broke for radio—it was a ballad, it was an R&B singer doing a country song, it's got that a cappella part. . . . It was a perfect storm."**

so heated that at one point Clive said to David, 'We better hang up the phone now before we never talk again—but I'm using that rough mix.' David had to tell him we didn't even have it anymore. But Clive responded, 'I have it right in my pocket. I've been holding on to it since you sent it.'"

Reitzas still hears all the technical imperfections, and Kirk Whalum says he still cringes any time he hears his off-pitch sax solo, but Houston agreed with Clive. She was never shy about correcting mixes—Reitzas once had to drive all night to Whitney's house to fix another song's mix she didn't like—but, he says, "She really trusted Clive Davis's judgment. If he felt something needed to be a certain way, she always deferred to that."

That mix also included Whitney's long a cappella intro, the one Kevin Costner had demanded. "When we decided it would be a cappella for the movie," Costner said in 2009, "They said it would never play on the radio with this a cappella thing in front. I said, 'I don't really care. But I wouldn't be too sure about that.'"

The single was released on November 3, 1992, two weeks before *The Bodyguard* hit theaters. Rough mix or not, everyone involved knew the recording was great. But they didn't know if it would be a hit. "When you think about how many rules that song broke for radio—it was a ballad, it was an R&B singer doing a country song, it's got that a

A scene from *The Bodyguard*, in which Costner scans the crowd for threats.

cappella part, it's long," Foster told *Entertainment Weekly.* "It was a perfect storm."

They needn't have worried. "I Will Always Love You" went to #1 and stayed there for fourteen weeks—the longest run atop the charts *ever* at the time (though it wouldn't last long; three years later, Mariah Carey and Boyz II Men took the crown with their sixteen-week #1 "One Sweet Day"). Radio programmers adored the unconventional song, a cappella intro and all, and played it constantly. Reitzas remembers once hearing it playing on one radio station, changing the station when it finished to find another station playing it, then changing the station a third time to hear—what else?—Houston's recording yet again. It was inescapable.

The first time that the song's original writer heard it was on the radio. "One day, I was riding along in the car and had just turned the radio on, and I heard her start that a cappella, like 'If I should stay . . .'" Dolly Parton said. "And it took me, like, a few seconds, and I thought, what is that? That's so familiar. And then when she went into the 'I will always love you,' I just about had a heart attack and died. I just about wrecked. It was a great feeling, though."

Parton had been crushed when Elvis wouldn't cover her song; but two decades later, her foresight in hanging on to her songwriting credit had paid off. "When Whitney [Houston's version] came out," she said, "I made enough money to buy Graceland!" ⦿

# FUGEES
# "KILLING ME SOFTLY"

⚡ ROBERTA FLACK/LORI LIEBERMAN COVER ⚡

SONG
"KILLING ME SOFTLY" (1996)

WRITTEN BY
CHARLES FOX, NORMAN GIMBEL

FIRST RECORDED BY
LORI LIEBERMAN
[AS "KILLING ME SOFTLY WITH HIS SONG"] (1972)

In 1971, an obscure singer named Don McLean found himself with the #1 song in America, "American Pie." Touring to support his sudden success, he played a show in southern California. An even more obscure singer named Lori Lieberman, just nineteen at the time, was invited to attend.

"When my girlfriend asked if I wanted to go to a concert to see Don, I was lukewarm about it," Lieberman remembers today. "I knew the hit, but I wasn't really expecting much else. Sitting there, though, I listened to him for the first time; and when he sang 'Empty Chairs,' it just blew me away. I really felt like he was singing right to me."

When the concert ended, instead of leaving with the rest of the crowd, she stayed at her table scribbling on a napkin. She wrote a poem about how much McLean's song moved her. The poem described how the singer seemed to be singing her life with his words, as if he was reading her letters.

The next day, Lieberman called up her producer (and boyfriend at the time), the iconic songwriter Norman Gimbel. Twice Lieberman's age and with far more music experience, Gimbel had written hits like "The Girl from Ipanema" and "I Will Follow Him." Gimbel and his songwriting partner Charles Fox had discovered Lieberman after auditioning dozens of singers at clubs in search of one to sing their material. They were looking for, as Fox puts it, "the Diane Warren to our Burt Bacharach and Hal David."

The three were working on her debut album at the time, and her label said they still needed one more song. When Lieberman called Gimbel and

read her poem to him, she asked whether it could be turned into a song. He thought it could and took out his notebook. In it, he'd written down hundreds of unclaimed song-title ideas he'd had over the years. He flipped through until he found a title that seemed to fit her experience: "Killing Me Softly with His Blues."

Gimbel changed "Blues" to "Song," since neither Don nor Lori sang the blues, and polished Lieberman's poem into lyrics. Fox put the words to music. Lieberman recorded the finished song in the soft folk-pop style popular in the early 1970s, and they brought it to their label. "They said, 'This is it, this is the single,'" Fox recalls. "We all knew we had something special." They promptly released the first, now little-remembered version of "Killing Me Softly with His Song."

Anyone who bought the single would have only seen two songwriters in the credits: Fox and Gimbel. Despite having written the poem that inspired the lyrics, Lieberman was not credited as a songwriter on her recording or any thereafter. But she didn't think anything of it. She was certain that she would earn her royalties as the song's performer—as long as *she* had a hit with it, and not someone else. . . .

"I was really naive," Lieberman says now. "I had just come to L.A. from Switzerland, where I grew up. I was shy and in this very dramatic relationship with Gimbel. I was so thrilled to have my first record deal that I gave [the songwriting credit] away unknowingly. I didn't fight for anything. I didn't even know that was an option."

When the single was released, the label pushed it halfheartedly. Very few radio DJs played it, so almost nobody heard it. One of the few people

**Very few radio DJs played it, so almost nobody heard it.**

PREVIOUS: The Fugees (L-R): Wyclef Jean, Lauryn Hill, and Pras.

who *did* hear it, though, was sitting on a TWA airplane bound for New York City.

Roberta Flack's career was in a very different place than Lori Lieberman's in the early 1970s. Though also new on the scene, Flack's debut album had shot to #1 on the strength of her 1972 hit single "The First Time Ever I Saw Your Face" (her version of the much-covered Ewan MacColl song). Proud of her sudden success, she would page through entertainment magazines to see if she was mentioned. Which is what she was doing to kill time that day, flipping through TWA's in-flight magazine. Her name wasn't in it. But someone else's was.

"I'm [usually] more interested in seeing who's the featured artist than hearing the music—just to see if I'm on there," Flack recounted a few years later. "But I'd never heard of Lori Lieberman, so I thought I'd see what she'd got going for her that I didn't have."

Flack plugged her headphones into the in-flight radio to hear the Lieberman song with the unusual title. By the time the plane landed, she knew she had to record it. "For me, that song wasn't finished," she said. "Sometimes a song will be done by a Streisand or someone like that, and I simply feel there's no need for me to do it. But this song was not finished. . . . I knew I'd be able to add something to it."

When she landed, she called songwriter Charles Fox. He answered the phone and heard a voice say, "Hi, this is Roberta Flack. We haven't met, but I'm going to sing your songs."

Lori Lieberman's original "Killing Me Softly With His Song" shared very little with later iterations.

She began singing "Killing Me Softly" in concert, and it got a great reaction. *Too* great a reaction, in fact. After one show, the crowd erupted so much that her producer Quincy Jones told her not to sing the song again until she'd recorded it. He didn't want another artist to beat her to the market.

The recording process took three long months. Perfectionist Flack tinkered endlessly with layered vocal parts and a soulful arrangement that was far from Lieberman's poppy folk. When Flack finally released her cover in 1973, though, all that tinkering paid off: it was an immediate smash.

The song was every bit as big as the songwriters had thought it would be—just not under their singer. It gave Flack a second #1 single and both Record and Song of the Year Grammys.

The latter, a songwriters' award, was accepted on the Grammy stage by the two credited songwriters: Charles Fox and Norman Gimbel. Lieberman was not standing with them on that stage. She says today that she had not even been invited.

Today, though, she's not bitter. "When I first heard Roberta Flack's version, I thought 'Well, that will never go,'" Lieberman says. "It just didn't make sense to me. I came from a real folk era—James Taylor and suspenders and no makeup. My song was a very simple folk song. It just didn't have any of the flash and flair and choral effects that she had. She made it something I never would have thought of, though, and I applaud her. Without her, it would have just been another folk song."

And without the Fugees, "Killing Me Softly" would have just been another soul song. Twenty years after Flack's hit, the hip-hop trio was deep into work on their second album and feeling pressure to make it a hit. Their much-hyped 1994 debut album *Blunted on Reality* had disappointed commercially and artistically, and there were rumblings that their label might drop the once-promising rappers if the follow-up flopped as well.

Sweating through long days in their hundred-degree New Jersey basement studio, they searched for a way to make this album stand above the hip-hop competition. They worried that producers had pushed them too far in the direction of conventional rap on *Blunted on Reality,* since they considered themselves more than just rappers. Fugees member Lauryn Hill said at the time that they wanted to make "a hip-hop version of [the Who's] *Tommy*"—a sprawling magnum opus that paid little heed to genre lines. And one of the ways to do that was through Hill herself, who, in addition to being a capable rapper, was also a brilliant singer, a highlight of their live show not reflected on the first record.

One evening, Hill and her Fugees bandmate Pras were driving her mom's car to the studio. "There was this radio station called KISS FM that used to play a show called *Love After Dark,*" Pras remembers today. "After, like, ten [o'clock], they just played love songs or ballads or whatever. As I was getting dropped off, we were just talking, and then [Roberta Flack's] 'Killing Me Softly' came on. We sat there and listened to the whole entirety of the song. I looked at her and said, 'Yo, this is the record you have to do.' She was like 'Really? You think so? I don't know. . . .'"

Pras eventually overcame Hill's resistance. Sure, a 1970s soul song didn't exactly scream "hip-hop." But he promised they could find a way to connect it with their audience. They commissioned music from Kool and the Gang founder Ronald Bell for Lauryn to sing over. But what Bell sent back didn't work at all.

**When Flack finally released her cover in 1973, though, all that tinkering paid off: it was an immediate smash.**

**OPPOSITE:** Roberta Flack, performing in 1973.

"It sounded like Roberta Flack, part two," Pras says. "It was very musical, and he had all the strings, the horns. I was just like 'Oh, no. The hip-hop generation is never going to relate to that.'"

This dilemma continued to bother them. How do you take a vintage soul song with no rapping and make it something that might fit on a hip-hop radio station? They wanted to build a bridge to a wider audience, but not by abandoning the rap fans who were filling up the clubs for them. The solution came suddenly, at a concert far from the studio.

Fugees shows always began the same way. Wyclef Jean, the trio's third member, would enter first. He would introduce the other two like pro wrestlers, each with their own entrance song culled from hip-hop history. Hill would come onstage to Mary J. Blige's "What's the 411." Then Pras would enter to A Tribe Called Quest's "Bonita Applebum."

But at this particular concert, Pras missed his cue. "We were performing at a high school football field," Pras remembers. "I was in the locker room and when 'Clef was calling my name from the stage, I didn't hear him at first. When I finally realized 'Clef had started the show, I started running. It was probably three or four hundred feet to the stage, and all I could hear was 'Clef repeating my intro. 'Praswell . . . ['Bonita Applebum' beat] . . . Praswell . . . ['Bonita Applebum' beat]. . . .' I'm running and listening to this beat over and over, and I don't know why, but while hearing the beat in my head, I was [singing the lyrics to] 'Killing Me Softly.' When I finally jumped onto the stage they were pissed off at me, but I had this big smile on my face, like 'Yo, I think I got it!'"

Pras's inspiration was to have Hill sing the Roberta Flack song over the Tribe Called Quest background music, just as he had sprinting that day to the stage. That way, they could showcase Hill's amazing singing but add enough hip-hop flavor to make it fit into the Fugees sound.

They tried to sample the original "Bonita Applebum" as they had sampled many other songs, but the beat didn't line up precisely enough with the "Killing Me Softly" melody. So they had to rerecord the music from scratch, trying to get the same sound as Tribe had five years earlier.

Since they were changing the instrumentation so aggressively from the famous Roberta Flack version, they wanted to keep Hill's vocal parts as similar as possible. Flack had obsessively blended her many vocal tracks into a seamless whole, and now they had to try to pull those parts apart again so Hill could re-create them.

"We wanted to keep the essence of what Flack had, so we had to dissect her," Pras says. "We took turns listening to it. 'Yo, there's this one harmony here.' 'Here's this other harmony here.' 'Did you hear this harmony here? Oh, my God, this harmony is crazy.'"

Their recording engineer Warren Riker (who earns Hill's shout-out "Warren up in here!" in the outro) estimates there may be thirty separate tracks of Hill singing background harmonies on the song. "I said let's create a massive, really dense vocal track that would put a whole new dimension on the simplicity of the track," he says. "I spent a day or two with Lauryn just singing those background parts."

Once they had layered all thirty background tracks together, Hill recorded her lead vocal. Unlike reassembling the intricate background arrangement, this was easy. She stepped up and did it in one or two takes. They thought the track was done.

However, in the chorus, Hill did not sing "killing me softly." She sang "killing the sound boy." This caused a major problem.

"Sound boy" was a Jamaican term Pras and Wyclef Jean knew from their Haitian roots, a derogatory term for a rival musician (a rough analog would be calling someone a wannabe or a poser). For the same reason that they used the Tribe Called Quest beat, they thought this tweaked chorus would appeal more to the hip-hop community.

"Killing the sound boy" might seem a small change—they kept every other lyric the same. But legally, it mattered a lot. Though anyone can record a cover without the original songwriter's permission, if an artist revises even a word of the lyrics, the situation changes. In that case, the new cover is considered a "derivative work" and requires the original songwriter's blessing before it can be recorded and released. Which the Fugees asked for. And were denied.

"We just felt that it's our song," songwriter Fox explains about his and Gimbel's decision. "We don't ever give permission for anyone to change the words of our songs. We get all kinds of requests, too. A company once sent me a record that they wanted to release called 'Killing Me Softly with Kung Fu.' Everyone is free to write their own songs, but no one is free to change my songs."

Pras says they never considered scrapping the track—they were already too far in—but it was a crushing disappointment nonetheless. "Killing the Sound Boy" sounded like a hip-hop song title. "Killing Me Softly" did not.

The songwriters' denial also presented a serious logistical problem, because Hill hadn't just sung "killing the sound boy" once on the lead vocal: she had repeated it thirty times in all those background tracks. She and Riker had to sit down and painstakingly rerecord each one to the original lyric.

"It was a pretty big nightmare for us," Riker says. "We had to go in and replace certain words. It was a downer 'cause we were all so happy with how it came out originally. To have to tear that painting apart to touch a color up was a drag. But we did."

The graphic design of *The Score* intentionally evoked a 1970s movie poster and played off the dramatic structure of the songs themselves.

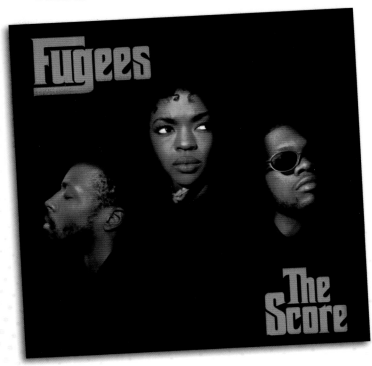

> A 1970s soul song didn't exactly scream "hip-hop."

Pras feels that it was worth it. He says that though "Killing the Sound Boy" might have connected to hip-hop listeners who knew the reference, it risked alienating everyone else. "In the end I was glad they rejected that, because it wouldn't have worked," he says. "It wouldn't have been iconic the way it is now if you made something that only worked for that moment. This version right here is everlasting."

The Fugees' second album *The Score* was released in January 1996, with "Killing Me Softly" as the eighth track. The first single, though, was the more traditional rap song "Fu-Gee-La." The band knew "Killing Me Softly" was good, but still worried about it not being hip-hop enough. "Fu-Gee-La" did well, but as soon as radio DJs heard the full album, they began spinning "Killing Me Softly" instead.

The record label—no longer harboring any desire to drop the band—began pushing to scrap the planned follow-up single and switch to "Killing Me Softly." The band was still worried. "The label was like 'We're probably going to have to pull [the other single] back. We're going to have to go with "Killing Me Softly,"' Pras says. "We're like '"Killing Me Softly"? No, we need hip-hop for the streets.' They said 'Forget the streets! We have to get off the streets and start selling records.'"

The label prevailed, and the "Killing Me Softly" single exploded. The band discovered that Roberta Flack herself loved their version, even performing it with them on that year's MTV Movie Awards. "I'm not going to hold on to that song with my heart and bleed to death while someone else covers it," Flack said. "I'm a music lover who has enough experience and common sense to know that it's good they recorded it and had a hit. I had a hit with it too, but I wasn't the first person who recorded it." Today she says in concerts that the Fugees "kicked [the song] into the twenty-first century."

But the song's success came at an unexpected cost. The three Fugees had always considered themselves equals in the band, but to the casual listener "Killing Me Softly" might as well have been a Lauryn Hill solo track. Pras and Wyclef Jean's vocal contributions were limited to background ad-libs. Only a dedicated listener poring through the CD booklet would realize how much work Pras, in particular, did on the instrumentation. The narrative surrounding the Fugees became that it was only a matter of time before Hill left the other two behind—which she did, not long after. Thanks to "Killing Me Softly," *The Score* became the Fugees' breakthrough album. It also became their last.

For his part, Pras doesn't resent how much credit outsiders gave Hill for "Killing Me Softly." "It was a team effort," he says. "It doesn't matter: the guy who makes the last shot to win the championship, the whole team has to win. 'Killing Me Softly' was equivalent to our Super Bowl Championship, our NBA Championship, our Olympic Gold Medal. We won big." ◉

# THE GOURDS
# "GIN AND JUICE"

⚡ SNOOP DOGGY DOGG COVER ⚡

SONG
"GIN AND JUICE" (1998)

WRITTEN BY
CALVIN BROADUS, HARRY WAYNE,
"K. C." CASEY, RICHARD FINCH,
ANDRE YOUNG

FIRST RECORDED BY
SNOOP DOGGY DOGG (1993)

Music fans who used Napster in the late 1990s and early 2000s might remember a cover of "Gin and Juice" by Phish that circulated widely in the early days of file sharing. Or maybe they remember a "Gin and Juice" cover by Blues Traveler; Widespread Panic; Ween; or even the country music supergroup of Garth Brooks, Kenny Chesney, and Tim McGraw.

The thing is, none of those bands ever covered Snoop Doggy Dogg's "Gin and Juice." That country supergroup never even existed. The song that circulated under their names—and many others—was by an Austin band whose name the millions of people who downloaded it probably never learned: the Gourds.

With their "Gin and Juice" cover, the Gourds recorded the first song to go viral, before that word meant anything besides an infection. But their story also exposed an unforeseen peril of sharing music on the Internet. Despite reaching millions

online with a hugely popular cover, they found the recognition of that success stolen in an odd case of musical identity theft.

They would have been a one-hit wonder, except no one knew they had a hit.

In 1998, the Gourds were four years into their career and doing okay. They didn't play outside of Texas that much, but their shows in the region were packed. They had one album under their belt, a new contract with a respected local indie label, and a promising future on the Texas alternative-country circuit.

That spring, singer Kevin Russell went to visit his sister down in Denton. She was a hip-hop aficionado and would often play him her favorite new songs. "I wasn't really into rap music much," he says today. "The extent of my rap music knowledge had been Run-D.M.C. But my sister was heavy into NWA and the whole West Coast scene that was happening." On that visit, she played him a song he'd never heard, though it had been a hit a few years earlier: "Gin and Juice," by a Dr. Dre affiliate then going by Snoop Doggy Dogg.

Russell loved the song and, as a musician, his first impulse was to figure out how it was constructed. He started playing around with the rhythm on the guitar and soon had a pretty decent

> **They would have been a one-hit wonder, except no one knew they had a hit.**

**PREVIOUS:** Lead singer Kevin Russell at a Gourds show in Falls Church, Virginia, in September 2010. **LEFT:** Snoop Dogg's 1998 debut solo album *Doggystyle* established him as a bona fide solo artist and not just comic relief in the Death Row stable. **OPPOSITE:** Once Snoop Dogg bestowed his approval upon the Gourds cover, no further proof was needed of their hip-hop credibility.

approximation—it was only two chords, after all. "I wrote the words down as best I could understand them, but some of it was probably wrong," he says. "I didn't know what 'macking' meant at the time."

Playing a gangster-rap song on acoustic guitar didn't strike him as odd. He often quoted Johnny Cash's mantra "a good song is a good song," regardless of genre, and he'd toyed around with other songs like that before. This one, though, seemed to have a little more potential, maybe even something he could play in public.

He knew the crowds he played to might be skeptical, if not worse. "The Americana [music] world, I wouldn't call them racist, but they're certainly paranoid people, and they don't really trust black people or brown people very much. And at the time, people in Texas were terrified of rap music."

Russell, though, considered rap to be very much in the folk tradition of the poor and downtrodden expressing hardships through song. To his way of thinking, all the people railing about the dangers of rap music just didn't realize that the more outrageous lyrics were a joke, an act in the same way that Americana singers sometimes took on an artificial suspenders-and-straw-hat persona. He respected rap, and wanted Americana fans to as well.

"I hoped people weren't going to see me as Pat Boone doing 'Tutti Frutti,'" he says of his worries about sharing his cover with others. "I was like, I'm going to have to pull it off in a way that's not aping it or making fun of it."

> **Pretty soon, "Gin and Juice" was the band's surefire showstopper.**

Russell soon had a chance to try. He and Gourds bandmate Jimmy Smith were both scheduled to play solo sets at a friend's birthday party and made a bet. "We were having a fun little contest to see who could do the better cover," Smith says. "I played 'Let's Spend the Night Together' or some shit like that, and then he busted out with the 'Gin and Juice' thing."

"I didn't know how strong the reaction would be, but I felt people would think 'Oh, that's pretty clever,'" Russell says. "So I played it at this party, and people just were rolling around. It was great. I thought wow, that was quite a reaction."

Gourds multi-instrumentalist Claude Bernard was there, too, and remembers the moment: "People were going crazy! I remember I was getting a drink and this guy was like 'Man, is this the craziest thing you ever heard?' I was like 'Yeah it's cute.' I didn't get it at all, honestly."

But other people did, and the song soon made its way to the full band. "We were playing at the Electric Lounge one night, and we had a great crowd," Russell says. "We had really just started taking off in Austin and we had an encore situation. I was like 'Hey, you guys remember that song I did at the party, right? Look, it's just A and D chords. Just play that over and over and follow me. We'll see what happens.' We never rehearsed it. We never discussed doing it or anything. We just did it as an encore for this night. The rest is history, as they say."

None of the band had even heard the original, but it didn't matter. True to the Gourds' loose spirit, they made up their parts as they played. The crowd loved it, and pretty soon, "Gin and Juice" was the band's surefire showstopper. "It would decimate whatever band was playing before or after," says drummer Keith Langford, who saw an early live incarnation of the song shortly before he joined the band.

Before long, the band's manager and label were pressuring them to record the cover. "For months, I was saying, 'We should record that thing,' and they didn't want to do it," says Mike Stewart, their manager at the time. "Jimmy, in particular, was afraid that it would pigeonhole them in some way."

"We didn't really want to," Russell agrees. "We just felt like it was a fun cover. We're like, you got to be careful with things like this. Our fear was that it would be really successful and we would be stuck with it."

The business interests eventually prevailed, but the band demanded that it not be put on a proper Gourds album. Instead they cut a quick version in Austin's Arlyn Studios for an odds-and-sods EP with some live stuff, an outtake, and another cover recorded the same day (David Bowie's "Ziggy Stardust"). On "Gin and Juice," Russell played mandolin and sang, Smith played bass and tambourine, Bernard played acoustic guitar, and Langford, a recent addition to the band, played a simple drum pattern.

The band doesn't remember much about the session itself. At the time, it didn't seem particularly notable. They slammed the song out in a few hours, the basic rhythm track plus a few instrumental overdubs. They tried to keep the live feel—Stewart says he has never seen a band so good at bringing that packed-show energy to a sterile studio environment—and Smith says they'd played it enough at that point to be comfortable "bringing it to the studio without losing the wildness of it."

The label wanted them to record a separate, censored version to pursue radio play—as Snoop himself had done—but the band put their foot down. It was one thing putting the song out for the fans, but they'd be damned if they were going to mount a full-scale campaign promoting this thing. They didn't want to be pigeonholed on the off chance it became popular.

Named for a line in the movie *Goodfellas,* the *Gogitchyershinebox* EP came out in September 1998. It was a hit with the local fans, with the *Austin Chronicle* singling out the band's Snoop Dogg cover as "a must for homeboys as well as hicks." But it didn't make much of a ripple outside of Austin.

Then the following June, a new service called Napster went online. Pretty soon someone shared the Gourds' cover of "Gin and Juice" on the service. But that someone, it seemed, had mislabeled the MP3 file. The MP3 credited the song to the jam band Phish.

The "Gin and Juice" cover went viral, the first song to do so (the term "viral" wouldn't even start being used for another year). The other top downloads were all songs that were popular elsewhere: radio, TV, etc. This song was only popular in one place—online—but it spread wildly.

**The "Gin and Juice" cover went viral, the first song to do so.**

Which should have been a windfall for the Gourds, except no one other than hard-core fans knew it was by them. "People started emailing me saying, 'Hey, your song is labeled as Phish on this thing called Napster. I keep telling people that's the Gourds, but nobody believes me,'" Russell says. "After I got these for a month or two, I thought, well, I'll look into it."

No one in the band had yet heard of Napster. The song went viral early enough in the service's run that one would have had to be pretty plugged-in to know about it, and these four decidedly were not. "I didn't even have a computer," Smith says. "All I had was a tape deck and all I was interested in was writing and recording. This was all going on around me and I was oblivious."

The song was Russell's, though, so he took it upon himself to try to sort out the credit confusion. He went as far as calling Napster headquarters, but he said they told him there was nothing they could do. "I said, 'If I understand you right, I could upload Lynyrd Skynyrd's whole catalog under the name of my band?'" he says. "They're like, 'Yeah.' I was like 'Okay, but I think this is a really bad idea that you guys have come up with.'"

Though Phish was the most-seen name attached to the Gourds' Snoop Dogg cover, many other bands were credited with it, too, from Blues Traveler to Garth Brooks. The fact that the song didn't sound like any of those bands—no one in Phish even *played* a mandolin—didn't slow the misinformation's spread.

The Gourds, 2011 (L–R): Max Johnston, Kevin Russell, Claude Bernard, Keith Langford, Jimmy Smith.

Adding to the confusion was that three months after the EP had come out, the band's label Watermelon Records declared bankruptcy. A prominent local Austin label cofounded by songwriting giant Robert Earl Keen, Watermelon had earned a reputation in the early 1990s as an artist-friendly destination, but things quickly soured. By the time the Gourds signed with them, the writing was on the wall to anyone in the know—which the Gourds weren't.

As a result, the band's EP was no longer in stores when the Napster thing took off. That, coupled with their decision to forgo a radio single, meant there were no official channels where one *could* hear their cover. The song was effectively a Napster exclusive, and the Gourds had no way to get the word out that this huge Internet hit was actually by them, not Phish or anyone else. "If we had been smart, we would have rerecorded it and sold it ourselves instead of just waiting for this bankruptcy thing," Russell says. "We knew it had potential, but then we did things to sabotage it. I don't know why. That's just the culture that the Gourds was."

"So many people were online at that time and it's such a thing in their minds that no amount of PR would ever overcome the volumes of people that understood that to be Phish," says Langford. Smith adds: "We couldn't control Napster. We couldn't control the fact that people thought it was another band. We couldn't do anything about it. It probably did more good for Phish and all those other bands than us."

Even the members of Phish felt bad about the confusion. When the Gourds played Burlington, Vermont, Phish's home base, Phish bassist Mike Gordon came backstage. He introduced himself to Russell, and said he and his bandmates were all sorry for inadvertently hijacking the band's one hit. "I was like, 'Why are you apologizing? It's not your fault,'" Russell remembers. "He goes 'We feel bad about that.' I never understood why he apologized. He had nothing to apologize for."

Eventually, though, some small percentage of the downloaders figured out that the Gourds were behind the hit. The band finally did rerelease it in 2001 when they found a new label, which helped. It also helped when the cover reached the song's originator.

When a *SPIN* reporter sat down for a videotaped interview with Snoop Dogg (who had by this point dropped the "Doggy"), he asked Snoop if he had heard the cover. The reporter played it for him, and Snoop started nodding along. "I like that shit!" he exclaimed.

The band promptly put the blurry video footage on its website. "The audio is garbled but it was just amazing," says Bernard. "He's rocking it out and sort of trying to sing along with it but not being able to figure out what the cadence of the new version is. Man, if that's not street cred, what do you need to do?"

At one point Snoop's people even reached out to the Gourds about a possible collaboration. He was cohosting the first week of Jimmy Kimmel's new late-night show in 2003, and Russell got a call at home to see if the band could perform on the show with Snoop. "I don't know how they got my number but some producer called me and said, 'We want you to be on the show tonight,'" Russell says. "I said, 'I live in Austin, but I can come tomorrow.' They're like, 'You live in Austin? We'll get back to you.' They never did."

No collaboration ever took place; but in an interview with Canadian radio personality Nardwuar years later, Snoop remembered the cover. "I know the Gourds!" he said. "They redid my shit with a twist on it. They on some country shit, and they hard as a motherfucker. I fucks with them. I like them."

As downloaders—at least a small percentage of them—learned the cover's true origins, the venues the band played grew, and the crowds came to fill them. "You're talking about us going from playing to a handful of folks and only being able to go to a handful of states, to nationwide and European tours," Smith says. "That song was a really big deal for us."

Many in the crowds were only there to hear "Gin and Juice," though, and were not shy about requesting it. The band grew frustrated; this was exactly what they'd feared when they recorded it. Not only were they now expected to play their one big song ad nauseam, but it wasn't even a song they wrote (and they couldn't help wondering how much bigger the venues would be had it gone viral under their own name). "It sucked when people don't do anything for the entire show, [but] they get out there" when "Gin and Juice" began, Bernard says. "It's basically a big fuck-you to everything you just did when they're finally dancing for the last song."

The band tried to retire it a few times over the next decade, but that never lasted. "It is not so much that we hate playing it as much as we HAVE been playing it for so long," Russell wrote in response to a fan's online question in 2009. "We cannot play it every night. That is what some folks don't understand. Of course it might be their only show of the year and they want to hear that song. Or they brought their friends and told them about the song."

On the other side, the Gourds had a solid group of hard-core Texas fans who couldn't stand to hear the "Gin and Juice" cover live and resented that it was the thing for which the band was best known (even if under another name). "There were people who would tell us 'I would rather hear three original Gourd tunes in that span of time than hear that stupid shit,'" says Smith. "It would swing back and forth like that. Sometimes

> **Many in the crowds were only there to hear "Gin and Juice."**

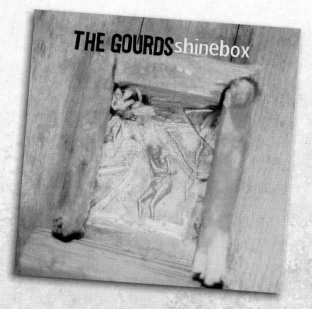

After the Gourds' "Gin and Juice" went viral on Napster without a purchase option for fans, they rereleased it on their 2001 LP, *Shinebox*.

THE GOURDS ON "GIN AND JUICE"

at the end of the night Kevin would bust into it and people [start] to go crazy, but then you've got three or four people who are booing."

The band members themselves all admit to fluctuating feelings over the years. In a comment on the Gourds' Yahoo! fan page, Russell wrote they couldn't play it "without throwing up in our mouths a little bit." Many other times, though, he was the one leading the charge.

"I definitely had moments where I felt like that, like, 'Goddammit, maybe we shouldn't be doing this, or maybe we should've stopped playing this,'" Langford says. "Then at some point I just decided to quit overthinking it. If anybody really felt like it was cheapening our band, they weren't listening to the other ninety minutes of music. I ended up just liking the people that liked it more than I liked the people that hated it."

To keep themselves interested, the band gradually began turning "Gin and Juice" into a medley with other covers, often improvised on the spot. Innumerable songs found their way into those medleys. In one performance alone, the Gourds might mix in songs by Stevie Ray Vaughan, Sam Cooke, the Temptations, Al Green, Cheap Trick, Michael Jackson, and the Sex Pistols, plus the *Dukes of Hazzard* theme. They sometimes incorporated songs from the towns they played in. In New York, they might throw in some Lou Reed. In San Antonio, they sang some of the old Charley Pride hit "Is Anybody Goin' to San Antone."

As the band's two main songwriters and strongest personalities, Russell and Smith often butted heads. Over the years, "Gin and Juice" became a particular sticking point. The band would often agree not to play it some night, but then Russell would independently break into it at the end of the show. At that point, as Smith says, "You don't have a fucking choice. You can't say 'No, I'm not doing it.' Because he's already hit the first three chords of it and people are starting to go crazy. Kevin didn't care if we had a say in it or not. I think it was Kevin's way of passive-aggressively trying to control a band that was primarily a democracy. We were at his mercy."

"Near the end of the Gourds' career, it was definitely an issue that came up in bitter conversations between us, which I had to bear the brunt of," Russell says about the albatross of the song's success. "It's my fault. How was I supposed to know?"

The rest of the band also had no say in the songs in the medleys. Langford and Bernard were generally game for whatever, but Smith and Max Johnson, a fiddle player who had joined not long after "Gin and Juice" was released, resented being thrown into songs they might not even know. "It just got really annoying because Kevin would start playing stuff and we would have to find a way to get into a Michael Jackson song that didn't really fit," Smith says. "Again, you don't have a choice. You have to play it. It turns into this big freaking cover mash-up thing. I felt like, 'Okay, this is stupid. Let's end the song and get on to something that we wrote.'"

"Gin and Juice" had become a symptom of much deeper personal problems within the band, and eventually things boiled over. In 2013, nineteen years after they began, the Gourds announced they were breaking up. Officially it was an "indefinite

> Over the years, "Gin and Juice" became a sticking point.

hiatus," but everyone in the band knew better. "The only reason we said 'hiatus' was that we didn't want to say it was done," Russell told Tennessee's *Daily Times* a year later, "because that would be final."

These days, though, the band members mostly look back fondly on "Gin and Juice." "You have to give the devil its due," Smith says. "It did everything it was supposed to do. It was almost a rock-and-roll cliché that just fell into our laps, and it was great."

"I don't know how long the Gourds would have been together, period, without that song," Bernard adds.

At the same time, they can't help wondering what could have been without the Napster naming issue. "[At the time] I was already seeing success, at least in my eyes, so I didn't have this overwhelming sense of being ripped off at all by Phish or by the Internet," says Langford. "But now in hindsight, I realize that there was a whole other level of success and, perhaps, money that we could have had that we didn't."

Smith calls this "the big question mark, the big unknown." "I think that plagues all of us,"

> "You have to give the devil its due."

he says. "Had that one mistake not happened, had that [song] not been attributed to Phish, and had we gotten the credit for doing it from the get-go, would it be the difference between us being a bottom-feeder, or would we be actually in Widespread Panic or Wilco world where you're headlining huge venues?"

Because Napster came along when it did, they'll never know. Without the advent of file sharing, maybe no one outside their small Texas circles would have ever heard the cover in the first place. Or maybe they would have, *and* they would have known it was by a band called the Gourds. "Everything about it was just—I don't know if 'cursed' is the wrong word, because it was a helpful tool for our band—but like all of it was just shrouded in ambiguity," says Langford.

On the whole, they all now see it as a net positive, even Smith. "'Gin and Juice' was a big deal," he says. "It was a huge game changer and helped us accomplish the next twelve years of our existence, and it took us everywhere. We had the greatest times, and some of the worst. It will be the headstone song for the band. No one's going to remember anything else, and that's fine." ●

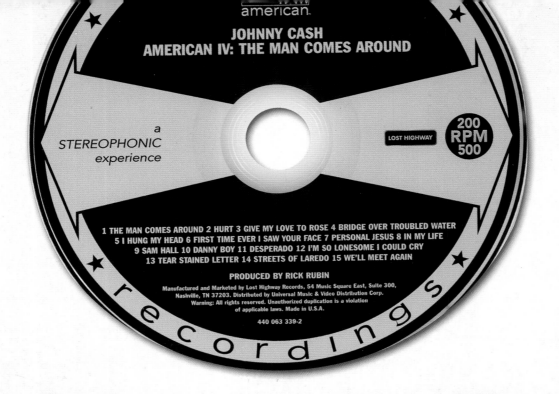

# JOHNNY CASH
## "HURT"

⚡ NINE INCH NAILS COVER ⚡

SONG
"HURT"
[B/W "PERSONAL JESUS," "WICHITA LINEMAN"] (2002)

WRITTEN BY
TRENT REZNOR

FIRST RECORDED BY
NINE INCH NAILS (1994)

> **"Nobody's song is safe out there from me. I go through 'em all, picking and gleaning, picking and gleaning."**
>
> —*Johnny Cash,* Unearthed *liner notes, 2003*

When Trent Reznor of Nine Inch Nails first heard Johnny Cash's cover of his song "Hurt," he was not impressed. He'd thought the idea sounded "a bit gimmicky" when his friend Rick Rubin, who was also Cash's producer, suggested it. When Reznor got the CD in the mail, hearing the song sung by someone else felt "invasive." "It sounded weird to me," he told *Alternative Press* in 2004. "That song in particular was straight from my soul, and it felt very strange hearing the highly identifiable voice

**PREVIOUS:** Johnny Cash, the Man in Black, in 2002. **BELOW:** Nine Inch Nails' *The Downward Spiral* created a singularly dark landscape—exactly the kind of world that Cash liked to explore. **OPPOSITE:** Nine Inch Nails' Trent Reznor—who also wore little besides black—performing in 1994.

of Johnny Cash singing it. It was a good version, and I certainly wasn't cringing or anything, but it felt like I was watching my girlfriend fuck somebody else."

When Rubin asked what he thought, Reznor didn't mention this metaphor. He said something noncommittal and put it out of his head.

Then he saw the video.

When Johnny Cash stepped into the studio a few months earlier, he was riding a comeback three albums deep. After a fallow 1980s, his partnership with Rubin had catapulted him back to the cool kids' table. "Before Rick Rubin came along ten years ago, I had declined to the bottom of the ladder," he wrote in the liner notes for the outtakes collection *Unearthed.* But Rubin pulled Cash back to his roots with a simple pitch: play whatever songs you want. "I said, 'What're you gonna do with me that nobody else has done to sell records for me?'" Cash remembered in a 1997 interview with Terry Gross. "He said, 'Well, I don't know that we *will* sell records. I would like you to go with me and sit in my living room with a guitar and two microphones and just sing to your heart's content, everything you ever wanted to record.' I said, 'That sounds good to me.'"

The albums made by the country legend and the hip-hop hippie—"the bard and the beard," some called the pairing—came to be known as the *American* series. By the early 2000s, the albums had won three Grammys, incorporated high-profile collaborators from Tom Petty to Sheryl Crow, and even in one case earned a rare five-star review from

A publicity still of Cash in his earlier years, suggesting he might just hop that train to who-knows-where.

*Rolling Stone.* Cash's daughter Rosanne called Rubin her dad's guardian angel for reviving his career.

The *American* albums were so successful that they began a music-industry trend of revitalizing flagging careers through cover albums. Cash singing covers was hardly novel—many of his early hits were covers, and he'd also been singing covers on his little-noticed albums released right before Rick came along. But the *American* series was specifically pitched to audiences as "Cash sings covers," and labels took note of their success. Soon everyone from Ray Charles to Herbie Hancock was finding new life with cover albums, no one more so than Rod Stewart with his endless *Great American Songbook* series. And if the song choice

was unexpected, all the better. We might never have heard Jerry Lee Lewis singing Led Zeppelin or Aretha Franklin singing Adele without Cash's late-career success with covers.

What the *American* albums hadn't done was generate a hit song. Rubin's line that they might not sell much proved prescient. Critics loved them, but critics don't buy records. Album sales typically stalled around 65,000—certainly not bombs, but far from runaway successes. (In comparison, Cash's seemingly unending stream of greatest-hits CDs continued to outsell his new material.)

One reason for the tepid sales is that the country-music industry never supported the albums the way the critics did, and country radio—still the major gatekeeper to break a hit song—wouldn't touch them. This was the heyday of polished pop stars like Garth Brooks, and this raw new Cash just did not fit that mold. "They ignored the albums," says his longtime manager Lou Robin. "Johnny Cash wasn't on their radar by that point."

After the second album won the Grammy for Best Country Album, Cash and Rubin ran a full-page ad in *Billboard*. The text sarcastically read, "American Recordings and Johnny Cash would like to acknowledge the Nashville music establishment and country radio for your support." The accompanying image was the famous 1969 photograph of Cash shooting the middle finger at the camera, which graces countless T-shirts and dorm-room posters today.

When a third album generated more of the same—critical praise and commercial stagnation—Cash wondered if enough was enough. "I'm getting good write-ups and I'm proud of the albums, but they're not really selling all that much compared to the other acts Rick works with," he said later about that period. "So I felt I was overstaying my welcome with Rick."

Rubin disagreed, though, and they began working on album number four.

Over the course of their work together, Cash and Rubin developed a system to exchange song ideas. Rubin would send Cash a mix CD with twenty or so songs and see which ones Cash responded to. "I would always suggest songs for him based on lyrics," Rubin said. "Everything else could change, but the lyrics were always what made a song suitable."

The lyrics drew Rubin to the dark and desolate Nine Inch Nails song "Hurt." Rubin and the band's leader Trent Reznor had worked together several years earlier on a remix of the Nails song "Piggy" and struck up a friendship. "'Hurt' stood above everything," Rubin said in Robert Hilburn's biography *Johnny Cash: The Life* about his pick for Cash. "To me, it was a song about an older person reflecting on their life with remorse. It was so heartbreaking."

He put the song as track one on the next mix CD and waited to hear what Cash thought. When Cash responded, though, he liked a couple other songs but made no mention of "Hurt."

Undeterred, Rubin led the next CD with "Hurt," too. Maybe Cash had overlooked it, Rubin thought, or needed a second listen. Once again, though, Cash ignored the song.

Ordinarily Rubin would have just dropped it. He was constantly sending suggestions that Cash ignored (R.E.M. was a perpetual white whale). That was the whole point of the process: give Cash a bunch of songs and let him pick one or two to try. Everything else would be discarded. But Rubin felt so strongly about "Hurt" that he made an exception to the rule. He tried again on a third CD, and this time he appended a personal note, asking Cash to give it extra attention. "I think this particular song is a really special one," he wrote. "I feel like the words have a lot of power, and with you singing them it's really going to take on a whole new light."

Cash trusted Rubin's judgment, and as he read the lyrics he started seeing what Rubin saw in it. He related to the pain and regret, but still thought it too much of a stretch. Though tame compared to many other Nine Inch Nails songs, "Hurt" still contained blasts of feedback and screaming. It didn't sound like a Johnny Cash song. "I [told Rick] 'I think it's probably the best anti-drug song I ever heard, but I don't think it's for me,'" he recalled in his final interview, with *Time*. "And he said, 'Why?' I said, 'Because it's not my style, it's not the way I do it.' And he said, 'What if it were?'"

Rubin got a few musicians together and recorded a new version that sounded more like a Johnny Cash song. He had done the same with Soundgarden's "Rusty Cage"—an obvious precursor to a Nine Inch Nails cover—and it had worked. He wanted Cash to see how "Hurt" *could* be his style.

"I don't think anybody but Rick knew how big that song was going to be," Cash's engineer David Ferguson says. "He had a vision. That's absolutely his brainchild. It wasn't treated just like any old song."

Rubin's persistence paid off. Cash finally agreed to give "Hurt" a try. He told the idea to his son John Carter. Cash occasionally turned to his son for advice on Rubin's more out-there suggestions. The younger Cash had grown up listening to this sort of hard rock, even dragging his dad to Metallica and Iron Maiden shows. John Carter dutifully gave his take: don't do it.

"I was hesitant because it was such a dark song," he says today. "I said, 'Dad, do you really want to go there?' My father said, 'This is as true a statement as I can make about my life. I have to sing it.'"

Johnny Cash's *American IV: The Man Comes Around* was released in November 2002 and included a diverse range of material written by Cash, Paul Simon, Sting, and Hank Williams.

Due to his failing health, a lot of Cash's recordings by this point were done from his home in Tennessee, but Rubin wanted to wait until Cash came to Rubin's studio in Los Angeles to do "Hurt," to make sure they did it right.

When Cash flew in, Rubin convened three musicians to form the backing band: guitarist Mike Campbell and keyboardist Benmont Tench from Tom Petty's band the Heartbreakers—who had been working with Cash and Rubin since the beginning of their partnership—and guitarist Smokey Hormel, who had just finished touring with Tom Waits. Cash would just sing; arthritis had robbed him of the ability to play guitar a few years before.

"Rick's studio was in this old Hollywood mansion that had belonged to Peter Lorre," Hormel says. "It was

In the studio, (L-R): Cash, Tom Petty, Rick Rubin, and Marty Stuart.

a very goth setting. The room we were recording in was full of weird keyboards, pump organs, and toy pianos—half of them broken. Then here's Mr. Cash all dressed in black, but it's faded, so it's sort of gray. You couldn't have made it more perfect."

Rubin played the Nine Inch Nails version for the assembled musicians (at deafening volume, the way he listens to everything). Then Hormel sat with Cash to work out a vocal arrangement. Cash's range had grown limited with age, so they had to find notes he could still hit. The plan was for Cash to return to record his part the next day.

The following day, the band arrived before Cash to record the backing parts. They met with

Rubin and Ferguson upstairs above the studio. Rubin laid out his vision for a somber acoustic number, then they went down to the studio to hammer it out. The key thing was finding the right rhythm.

"I spent a lot of years listening to Mr. Cash's early Sun records, and the thing I realized about him is that he always had to have a really solid beat behind him, even when there's no drummer," Hormel says. "I knew going in that my job was to give him that support. Even on a song like 'Hurt.' It's a slow song, but he still really needs to know where the beat is."

So they developed a simple arrangement that emphasized rhythm. Having played with Cash many times before, Campbell took the lead guitar parts, and Hormel took rhythm. He tried to guess what Cash would have played if he could still play guitar, careful not to do anything that would overpower him. "You had to remember he's a sick old man who doesn't have a lot of power," Hormel says. "You have to provide support but leave him a lot of space. That was the challenge."

Tench added keyboard parts. "There's several different pianos on there," Ferguson remembers. "There's a grand piano, there's a tack piano, there's the mellotron, and then there's a little bitty kid's toy piano hitting those eighth notes when the track gets at its biggest point. He knew where to make it big and small and explosive toward the end." The low cello-like drone was actually Tench manipulating an organ's bass pedals.

When Cash showed up, the track was ready for his vocals, but he struggled from the start. "The song threw him for a loop" is how the Heartbreakers' Mike Campbell put it. Ferguson agrees: "He didn't really understand it. He'd tap his foot and come in where it felt natural, but songs like that, you'd wait forever before you come in." The song's sudden dynamic shifts were an issue, too. Ferguson remembers telling him, "It's going to get really big, but then it's going to get small where you don't think it's going to get small, Johnny. It ain't going to start off small and just keep getting bigger."

Cash soon tired. Eventually, they gave up for the day. To prep him to try again the next day, someone in the room recorded a guide vocal to demonstrate what he should sing—memories differ as to who

> **"He made it a Johnny Cash song."**

among them did it—and Cash returned to his hotel room with a burned CD to study. "I probably sang the song a hundred times before I went [back] in," Cash said later, determined to find his way in.

The following day, he came back in, sat down in front of the microphone, and nailed it immediately. "We were all just blown away by how much he had transformed that song," Hormel says. "He made it a Johnny Cash song." John Carter, who was in the studio that day, adds, "Suddenly, the song became his own." They just did two or three takes, and it was done.

"We all knew it was special," Hormel says. "When we heard the first playback with the good vocal on it, you just knew this is really something else. Then you hope, 'Okay, well, the people at the label, are they going to want to put it out? When Johnny hears it in three weeks, is he still going to like it?' You never know what's going to get in there."

When you talk to Cash's collaborators, the word they use most often to describe his performance on "Hurt" is "honesty." The song's power comes from his ability to project both vulnerability and resilience without trying to hide his age or ill health. "It's enduring honesty that made that recording possible," says John Carter. "Even through the weakness that he was having, through the sadness he was enduring, through the physical struggles, there was a sense of persistence and tenacity that was far greater than those things. Even though his body was failing in many different ways, in other ways he was strengthening creatively."

Cash had been in poor health since the 1980s, diabetic and prone to pneumonia (not to mention the damage done by years of alcohol and pills). But his deterioration had accelerated in the mid-1990s, around the time he recorded the second album with Rubin. He developed symptoms that looked for a time like Parkinson's disease—trembling, dizziness, weakness—and began losing hair rapidly. He grew almost blind, had to retire from touring, and began spending more and more time confined to a wheelchair.

The eventual diagnosis was diabetic autonomic neuropathy—a collection of symptoms related to bad nerve damage. Though it had forced him off the road for good, Cash continued to fight. "I've made it a point to forget the name of the disease and not to give it any space in my life," he told *USA Today* in 1999. "I just can't do it. I can't think that negatively. I can't believe I'm going to be incapacitated. I won't believe that."

Despite the constant pain, Cash made it a point to keep recording. Many collaborators noted that he never seemed more energized than when he was in the studio. "When he started singing, all his illness just seemed to fall away," said Nick Cave, who had duetted with him on his third album. "He became energized by that. There was just this real strength—this force of nature that came out of him."

"I found strength to work just to spite this disease," Cash said. "Sometimes I came to the studio and I couldn't sing—I came in with no voice when I could have stayed at home and pouted in my room and cried in my beer or my milk, but I didn't let that happen. I came in and opened up my mouth and tried to let something come out. There are tracks I recorded when that was the last thing in the world I thought I could do, and those are the ones that have the feeling and the fire and

the fervor and the passion. A great deal of strength came out of that weakness."

"Hurt" embodied the culmination of that strength out of weakness. Cash didn't hide his pain, his ravaged voice, his failing physical state. Cash related the song's lyrics specifically to his past drug problems, but paired with his voice the song sounded like a man nearing the end, looking back on a long life. "When Johnny sings it, all of a sudden it becomes a different song," Rubin said. "It has a different weight to it when he sings the lyrics. He has a way of personalizing the music and communicating the emotion of the lyrics that very few people have."

"That fearlessness at looking at your own mortality is the sign of a great artist," his daughter Rosanne Cash said. "It sent waves through the entire culture."

Not immediately, though. On November 5, 2002, "Hurt" was released as the second track on the album *American IV: The Man Comes Around*. Compared to the previous three albums, reviews were more mixed. *Rolling Stone*, which had given the first installment a perfect five stars, gave this one only three. They wrote "cover versions that once seemed inspired now feel somewhat obligatory." They did not highlight "Hurt," nor did many other critics. Cash himself didn't seem to be emphasizing "Hurt," either—in the liner notes he wrote for the album, he doesn't even mention the song, focusing exclusively on his own composition, the title track "The Man Comes Around."

Sales were, as usual, soft. Like the previous *American* albums, big Cash fans purchased it, but copies weren't exactly flying off the shelves.

Visionary music video director Mark Romanek's revelatory take on Cash's "Hurt" turned the song into a hit.

Christmas came and went without a noticeable sales bump, and as the new year dawned, it seemed this album was being forgotten. Perhaps Cash had been right. Maybe he had overstayed his welcome with Rubin.

Director Mark Romanek had wanted to work with Cash for years. He had come close once when he was slated to direct the "Delia's Gone" music video for the first *American* album, but Anton Corbijn took over instead. As a friend of Rubin's, Romanek had been bugging the producer to let him make a Cash video, but two more albums went by without his involvement. Finally, soon after *American IV* came out, Rubin agreed to give him a shot.

> **If [Romanek] wanted to make any video at all, he needed to get to Cash's home in Nashville quickly.**

"I had pestered [Rick] for eight years to allow me to make a video for John," Romanek said. "He played me the rough mixes of 'Hurt' and a few other tracks and I said, 'I'm doing a video for that song. Period.' Without Rick's entrée, I could never have made such an intimate piece. Rick very graciously said to John 'Just trust this guy. He's a true fan.'"

Romanek was given three song choices (the other two were "The Man Comes Around" and "Danny Boy"), and "Hurt" jumped out at him. An acclaimed video director, he had worked with Trent Reznor himself twice before, most notably on Nine Inch Nails' breakthrough video for "Closer" in 1994. "The truth is, I would have done a video of Johnny singing 'Happy Birthday,'" Romanek said. "I wanted to work with him so much. But 'Hurt' was something more. It was so powerful. I definitely had chills listening to the song."

The concept he developed for the video was this: Cash would appear alone on a soundstage in Los Angeles, surrounded by junk. It was "a rip-off of a Samuel Beckett play called *Krapp's Last Tape,* where a person was dwarfed by this pile of crap they had accumulated during their life," Romanek said. As he sang the song, workmen would come and start taking away the things, one by one. There would be a few celebrity cameos among the workmen—Johnny Depp and Beck were discussed. At the end, Cash would be sitting alone on the stage, nothing left but the music.

As they were preparing for Cash's arrival, though, his health took a sudden turn. Instead of coming to L.A. to film, he and June booked a flight to Jamaica, where he often went to rest. Romanek, an obsessive who prepared for weeks for a shoot, was given four days' notice that if he wanted to make any video at all, he needed to get to Cash's home in Nashville quickly. He had to discard the elaborate plan for the stage, the pile of junk, the celebrity cameos.

"I'm someone who usually takes a minimum of two weeks to prep a video, but this was Johnny Cash," he said. "So I jumped on a redeye to Nashville with my producer and a cameraman and

**"This is the time. Let's be bold."**

arrived on Friday [the day before Cash was leaving] with no idea of what I was going to make. I looked around the house and made a few suggestions of where we might film Johnny performing. I was making it up off the top of my head."

Then he went to Cash's museum, located in his old home, known as the House of Cash. Due to flooding, it had been closed for years, a formerly glorious monument now broken with age and neglect. Romanek immediately saw a metaphor reflecting Cash's own situation. "When I saw the state it was in, I went, 'Wow, this is great, this is really interesting,'" he said. "And the idea of showing the museum without prettifying it or fixing it back up kind of led me to the idea that, well, you know, let's just show Johnny in the state that he's in."

Not everyone wanted to give the crew access to the run-down museum, though. Several years earlier, the label had tried to shoot an album cover there, perhaps having a similar idea, but Cash's manager Lou Robin forbade it. Robin tried to put his foot down again this time, for fear of giving a misleading impression that Cash was living in squalor.

"I had told the people at the office not to let the film crew in, because the place was a mess, but I wasn't in town, and they did," Robin says now. "His museum had been closed earlier due to flooding, and the sprinkler system broke loose twice, so it just destroyed almost everything. I didn't care much for the portrayal of him being penniless. It gave the impression that that's how he was living."

By filming in the wrecked museum—rather than in the Cash family's current, very nice home not far away—the video might give the impression that Cash was destitute. But the point, Romanek said, was to mirror the song's lyrics—the theme he drew on was "impermanence."

To fit that, he emphasized Cash's weakness. Though undeniably sick, Cash wasn't "quite as frail as he appears in the video," Romanek said. "The song is slow and somber, and it required a subdued and serious performance. In between takes, he was a lot more spirited and frisky (making jokes, etc.) than he appears on camera. So the video is, in some ways, by necessity, not really a fully accurate account of his actual state of health at the time. He was a bit infirm, but not that infirm."

Though Cash struggled during filming—due to his limited eyesight, he occasionally had trouble locating the camera lens—he improvised one of the video's most memorable scenes himself. When the shoot was nearing its end, Cash was sitting at a banquet table piled with food. Romanek told him "'This is the last thing we are going to shoot, so if you want to do something crazy, go for it—if you want to sweep the food off the table, this is the time. Let's be bold.' He said, 'I think I've got something, Mark.' And that's when he poured the wine onto the table. It was totally him, and that turned out to be one of my favorite moments in the video."

The other big spur-of-the-moment addition is the shot of June looking on with loving concern from the stairwell. Romanek caught her doing that as they were filming and asked if he could put it on camera. She acquiesced (but only after running upstairs to put on makeup). The worried look she gave, and that millions saw later, seemed to be one of a wife watching her husband as he approached death's door.

But what Romanek didn't know, as the cameras caught that moment, was that the sickest person in the room that day was not Johnny: it was June. The day before the shoot, she had been diagnosed with a serious heart-valve leak, one that she knew would be fatal at her age. As writer Robert Hilburn puts it in his Cash biography, "As she stood on the stairs in such despair, she was likely thinking not so much about what she would do without John as what John would do without her."

"All of our anxiety had been focused on Dad for ten years, and the whole time she was slipping away," Rosanne Cash said a few years later. John Carter agreed: "I think my mother knew very well that she was a lot sicker than everybody else thought she was. I think she knew." (June Carter Cash passed away on May 15, 2003, four months before her husband. In his final interview, Johnny said he was glad she had lived long enough to see the attention "Hurt" got.)

The filmmakers returned to L.A. and began editing. They cut a version from the footage they had gotten in Tennessee; but when they watched the results, it seemed like something was missing. The images were striking, but they worried that an unbroken montage of Cash looking frail would lose its power by the time the four minutes were over. It felt incomplete.

When they had visited the museum, they had been escorted to Cash's film archives, a room which included video of every movie and TV appearance Cash had made. To be polite, they had taken the boxes they were given, but they weren't planning on using any of the material. When they realized that they didn't have quite enough new footage to sustain a compelling four-minute video, though, they decided to pop something in. They pulled, somewhat at random, a clip of a young Cash riding a locomotive and threw it in the middle of their new footage. When they watched it back, the pairing stunned them.

"It was that juxtaposition that gave the video its power," Romanek said. "It's the shocking contrast of a man in his prime smacked one frame right up against someone who is coming toward the end of his life."

Over the next three weeks, they dug deep into the boxes and inserted more old footage, much of it taken from the 1969 documentary *Johnny Cash: The Man, His World, His Music* and from Cash's 1973 religious film *The Gospel Road*. Then they presented the final video to Rick Rubin.

"It really upset me and it really affected me," Rubin said. "I thought it was beautiful, but it was so unlike any video I'd ever seen before, and so extreme, that it really took my breath away, and not in a good way. I didn't know how to handle it; it was overwhelming."

The Cash family wasn't sure how to handle it, either. Was it strong, or was it exploitative? Did the bleak imagery make Cash look like a survivor, or like an invalid? Cash told Rubin he needed a few days to talk with his wife and children about whether to release it. "I was devastated," Rosanne said when she watched it. "I was crying like a baby. He was sitting next to me, patting me on the shoulder. I told him it was the most powerful video I had ever seen. I said it wasn't even a video. It was a documentary."

His other daughter Kathy had the same reaction: "The first time he showed me 'Hurt' was in his office. I just started crying, and he asked, 'What's the matter, honey? And I said, 'It's so sad

**"I didn't know how to handle it; it was overwhelming."**

but it's beautiful!' He said, 'Aw, that's art! It's part of life.'"

In the end, Cash looked at it from an artistic standpoint. "It was obviously so sad," says John Carter. "It was so powerful, but it was so sad. But my Dad was like a kid. He was like, 'This is great! Everybody's going to love this!' I'm not kidding. He was just so excited because he saw that it was a masterpiece."

Meanwhile, Rubin and Romanek were anxiously awaiting his decision. It had taken some time for Cash to show everyone, so because it was taking so long, they assumed the worst. "I remember sitting in my car in Santa Monica, looking at the ocean while talking to Johnny, having a feeling that nobody's ever going to see this video," Rubin said. "I thought for sure he was going to say no. But he decided it should be seen."

The video was released in early 2003. It was included as a bonus track on the CD single and offered to the usual music video channels. At first, it made no impact.

MTV, then in its final years as the gatekeeper for music videos, was aimed toward teenagers; the videos in heavy rotation around that time were John Mayer and Maroon 5. The channel wanted nothing to do with the old man they saw on screen. "They thought ['Hurt'] was a little heavy," says manager Lou Robin. "They thought this was a downer."

In that era, with YouTube still a couple of years away, a video without MTV support was dead in the water, so Rubin put all his effort into pushing the song. He made a personal trip to tastemaker L.A. radio station KROQ to have them play the single on air. They did, and listeners responded. It entered heavy rotation there, and other radio stations began playing it too. Before long, the song became popular enough to force MTV's hand. They added the video. Once viewers finally saw it, it became a sensation almost immediately.

"If you watch what [else] is on MTV, you don't see anything like this," Rubin told the *Associated Press* once it took off. "You won't see anything from any artist in Johnny's age range, and you won't see anything with this kind of serious content. It really sticks out like a sore thumb."

It entered heavy rotation and became a water-cooler moment in a way few music videos do. "[Music] videos aren't really meant to have that kind of emotional engagement," Romanek said. "Most people don't have that set of aspirations; it's not the agenda to move people deeply. And it wasn't our intention. We didn't say, 'Wow, we're going to really move people.' But boy, were people moved."

The video's success led to a sales spike for the album. Before the video grew popular, *American IV* was down to selling 6,800 copies a week. The week after MTV started playing the video, album sales almost doubled, to 13,300. Then 18,100, then 21,000, then 26,500. The album went gold within a few months, and platinum not long after, making it the first Cash record to sell a million copies since *At San Quentin* in 1969. Critical acclaim was all well

and good, but now Johnny Cash had something he hadn't had in many years: a hit.

That summer, MTV nominated "Hurt" for six Video Music Awards, including Video of the Year. Such a pop spectacle might have seemed beneath Cash's stature, but for him it symbolized something meaningful: he was connecting with young people again, after so many years on the oldies circuit. "I have no illusions about who I am, how old I am, and what a stretch it might be to relate to these young people," he had written in his autobiography six years earlier.

Cash was seventy-one years old now; the average age of the other four Video of the Year nominees was twenty-eight. But early industry rumors said "Hurt" would win. Mostly housebound at this point, Cash began working with his doctors to ensure that he would be ready for a trip to the ceremony in New York.

It never came to pass. His manager learned from someone at MTV that the video would not, in fact, win. It would lose in five out of the six categories it had been nominated in, only taking Best Cinematography. Cash would have been making a difficult trip just to sit in the audience and clap politely for the people who beat him. The trip was canceled. When Justin Timberlake beat Cash for Best Male Video, he exclaimed in his acceptance speech, "This is a travesty! I demand a recount. My grandfather raised me on Johnny Cash, and I think he deserves this more than any of us in here tonight."

> **"I have no illusions about who I am, how old I am, and what a stretch it might be to relate to these young people."**

Cash didn't see Timberlake's speech. On August 26, two days before the ceremony, he was rushed to the hospital complaining of stomach pains. Just over two weeks later, in the early hours of September 12, 2003, he died.

Johnny Cash's passing led to a new wave of adulation for his final hit, adulation that has continued to this day.

*Rolling Stone,* which had damned the album with the faintest of praise upon its release, later named "Hurt" the fifteenth best song of the decade. Over in the UK, *NME* named it the greatest video of all time. BBC listeners voted it the best cover song ever.

Bono called it "perhaps the best video ever made" and added, "Trent Reznor was born to write that song, but Johnny Cash was born to sing it." Michael Stipe of R.E.M. (whose songs Cash had consistently declined to cover) said, "To be able to do a piece of work that is that powerful, that rises so far outside of the genre of what it is, I mean was phenomenal. The power of that video is something I can barely talk about. It really had a profound impact." And Joni Mitchell said, "It was almost too sad but beautifully done. I have mixed feelings about it. I'd have to see it again, but I don't really want to see it again."

**"I just lost my girlfriend, because that song isn't mine anymore."**

In the end, even Trent Reznor came around.

Even though he'd been underwhelmed by the song, when Rubin sent him the video during a recording session with Rage Against the Machine's Zack de la Rocha, Reznor dutifully put the tape in the studio's VCR. Once he saw the video, the song made sense.

"It's morning, I'm in the studio in New Orleans working on Zack de la Rocha's record with him," he said. "I pop the video in, and . . . wow. Tears welling, silence, goose bumps. I just lost my girlfriend, because that song isn't mine anymore." ◉

On the record label:

ADELE 19

SIDE B
C 730624
BL 886973062241
33⅓ RPM
STEREO

FIRST LOVE
(Adele Adkins) Universal - Songs of Polygram Int., Inc. (BMI)
RIGHT AS RAIN
(Adele Adkins and Leon Michels, Jeff Silverman, Nick Movshon & Clay Holley on behalf of
Truth & Soul) Universal - Songs of Polygram Int., Inc. (BMI) / Original Spin Music (BMI)
MAKE YOU FEEL MY LOVE
(Bob Dylan) Special Rider Music (SESAC)
MY SAME
(Adele Adkins) Universal - Songs of Polygram Int., Inc. (BMI)
TIRED
(Adele Adkins and Eg White) Universal - Songs of Polygram Int., Inc. (BMI)
HOMETOWN GLORY
(Adele Adkins) Universal - Songs of
Polygram Int., Inc. (BMI)

℗&© 2008 XL Recordings Limited / "Columbia" and ® Reg. U.S. Pat. & Tm. Off. Marca Registrada

# ADELE
# "MAKE YOU FEEL MY LOVE"

⚡ BOB DYLAN COVER ⚡

SONG
"MAKE YOU FEEL MY LOVE" (2008)

WRITTEN BY
BOB DYLAN

FIRST RECORDED BY
BOB DYLAN (1997)

One evening in 2006, producer Jim Abbiss was working with the promising young British singer-songwriter Jack Peñate. For one song they were recording, Peñate needed feminine backing vocals. He was trying to sing them himself, in falsetto. It didn't sound good, and Abbiss told him so. Abbiss asked if they could bring a singer in.

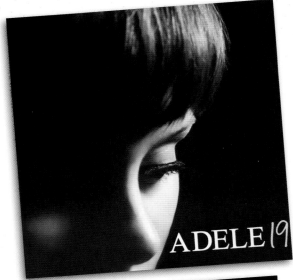

"There were plenty of singers that I knew who could come and do it," Abbiss remembers today, "but he said he wanted to ask his friend. I was little bit wary of somebody just bringing their friend in. It was already past 10:00 p.m., and I'm thinking I really don't want to be here all night waiting for someone I've never met to come and sing. He said, 'Trust me, she's really good.'"

The friend was eighteen-year-old Adele Adkins, who herself had just been signed to record her first album. As soon as she stepped up to the microphone, Adele put Abbiss's doubts to rest. "Within one take, I thought, 'My god, she has one hell of a voice,'" he says. "She did the whole backing vocal, double-tracked, harmonies in about twenty minutes."

Afterward, Abbiss and Adele chatted over tea on the recording studio sofa. She needed advice. As record labels sometimes do with new artists, her label XL Recordings was sending her to meet various producers to find a fit. Nothing was clicking. Abbiss, hot after producing Arctic Monkeys' record-selling debut album, was happy to offer his expert guidance.

"She was a little confused about the process and wasn't too sure about the people she'd met so far," he remembers. "I think she was a bit bombarded by people's expectations, all these producers telling her what they were going to do for her. We didn't have that kind of conversation because I wasn't pitching for a job. I just asked her, What sort of records do you like? She loved the Johnny Cash records that Rick Rubin had made.

**PREVIOUS:** Adele performing at a music festival in Brighton in May 2007. **LEFT:** Adele wrote or cowrote all the songs on her 2008 debut album except for "Make You Feel My Love."

She said it just sounded so natural and you can hear everything in his voice."

Adele went off and Abbiss went back to work with Jack Peñate. He didn't encounter her again for some weeks, until he got an unexpected call from her label. She still hadn't had much luck with producers and asked if he could produce some songs for her. "She just said, 'I felt so relaxed on your session, could we do some songs again?'" Abbiss says. "I said, 'Yeah, love to.'"

Though only eighteen when she joined Abbiss and Peñate in the studio that day, Adele had been singing since she was seven, most recently studying at the BRIT School, a performing-arts high school outside of London whose recent alumni included Amy Winehouse. XL Recordings' boss Richard Russell heard a demo Adele had posted on MySpace. He signed her but didn't anticipate that she would join the best-selling ranks of some of his other discoveries, such as the White Stripes and M.I.A.

"At the time we began to work with her, she was a fairly low-expectation artist," says Abbiss's studio engineer Richard Wilkinson. "I don't mean that nastily, but she'd signed for a relatively small amount of money, and I don't think [she] was signed with the expectation of being a million-seller. That's what was said away from Adele: We hoped people will like this record, but [we had] no expectation of fulfilling the numbers it ultimately did. More like, Let's try and do forty thousand records."

If Adele held any higher expectations for herself, she hid them well. Her public persona now is bold, chatty, and unfiltered—a big personality. But all three collaborators on this song say she was quieter (though still funny), humble, and down-to-earth.

"She's very natural and low-key when you meet her," piano player Neil Cowley says. "She doesn't run around and shout about what she's doing. If anything, the personality you see now is almost a caricature of herself. Like that Cockney voice she does. I'm from that part of the world, and you don't choose to talk like that! But she plays it up onstage now. At the time, she was perhaps a bit nervous but hiding it well."

During those early sessions, her self-deprecating humor helped keep the mood light and breezy. While recording her original song, "Hometown Glory," Wilkinson says she cracked everyone up, joking about how she wanted to license it for *Sex and the City*. The joke being that they all agreed the idea was absurd; there was no way she would become famous enough for something like that.

But disarming charm didn't hide Adele's musical self-assurance. "She was a completely confident singer even that early," Abbiss says. "She was slightly unsure about the industry, but she was completely confident in her ability to sing and how she wanted her songs to come across. She's very self-effacing and funny, but she knew when she hadn't done a great vocal and she was acutely aware of pitch and delivery. She was very mature for her years as a performer.

"She wasn't a dictator, though," Abbiss adds. "She wanted to collaborate and have a sounding board. But if we would try things she wasn't sure about, she would know it wasn't right."

She proved democratic, willing to entertain ideas from anyone in the room—even a low-ranking

**"Trust me, she's really good."**

engineer whose job was to roll tape and keep his opinions to himself. "I was quite close to her age, so we got along great," Wilkinson says. "Politically it was expected by Jim that I should keep my mouth shut and stay out of the way. But she would often look to me and say, 'Well, what do you think, Richard?'"

And nowhere did that collaborative spirit pay off more than on "Make You Feel My Love."

After five months in the studio, Adele's debut album was almost complete. She'd finished the few songs they planned to release as singles—for those, her label had paired her with more pop-oriented producers and cowriters—and recorded the other slower and more soulful album cuts with Jim Abbiss and his team. The record appeared to be a

BELOW: Dylan's widely praised, Grammy-winning 1997 comeback album of new material, *Time Out of Mind*. OPPOSITE: Bob Dylan performing in Birmingham on year eleven of his so-called "Never-Ending Tour," 1998; this show actually closed with a (sort-of) cover: Dylan and Van Morrison sang "Knockin' on Heaven's Door."

wrap, until one day her manager Jonathan Dickins rushed into the studio with one more suggestion. He sat Adele, Abbiss, and Cowley down and played them a Bob Dylan song he thought she could cover. It wasn't one of Dylan's big 1960s hits, the part of his songbook that singers usually delved into, but a newer ballad called "Make You Feel My Love."

None of the three knew the song, and they didn't learn until much later that during its brief existence it had already been covered by both Billy Joel and Garth Brooks. As far as they were concerned, it was some weird-sounding deep cut that didn't make any obvious sense for her. "Jim and I discussed it as, 'It's a weird choice, isn't it?'" Wilkinson says. "That was the word we used: weird. Dylan's version didn't really represent the record we had just made. There were more obvious tracks she could have covered. It felt like the label said, 'We've got the record done—oh, wait, here's one extra track.' And we thought 'Oh, really? This?'"

"When I first heard it, I wasn't quite sure about it," Abbiss agrees, "because it's a very traditional song, straight down the line with simple chords. That isn't to say Adele was making alternative, left-field, weird music, but there was always a little twist in her songs. The chord progressions or whatever were slightly unusual at times. 'Make You Feel My Love' was a very straight-ahead song. I wasn't sure how she would make it her own."

Dickins was more than a casual Dylan fan; his father is Dylan's longtime booking agent, Barry Dickins (himself the son of the founder of long-running British music magazine *NME*). The song came up in a chat the two had one day, and Jonathan thought it would be perfect for his new client. There had been talk of doing a cover on the album, and some song ideas had been batted around, but

nothing had even gotten to the recording stage. Too many of the song suggestions were iconic already; "hearing this new girl doing a famous Motown song or a standard was the last thing people wanted," Abbiss says. Jonathan thought this song could be different and pitched it to Adele.

She also didn't know "Make You Feel My Love," and she didn't even like it at first. But she trusted Dickins. "I don't like his voice—it really grates," she told the *Telegraph* when the album came out. "But I googled the lyrics. They are so stunning, and it kind of summed up what I'd been trying to say in all my songs. They are the most beautiful lyrics."

For not the first time in his career, Bob Dylan found a new fan who looked beyond his acquired-taste vocals to focus on the words themselves. Adele had spent the past several years writing the songs on *19,* only to discover that Dylan had already written the song she wanted to write—and done it better than she had.

"I wrote nine songs in a short space of time, all about this awful relationship I was in," she told the *Guardian.* "I never quite got down what I was really feeling in those songs, though. Although I was trying to. It wasn't that I was holding back or anything, but I just couldn't get it down. I was bitterly upset. And then my manager played me this Bob Dylan song, 'Make You Feel My Love.' The lyrics are just amazing and summed up exactly what I'd been trying to say in my songs. It's about regretting not being with someone, and it's beautiful. It's weird that my favorite song on my album is a cover, but I couldn't *not* put it on there."

OPPOSITE: A 2008 publicity still of Adele, which emphasizes the straightforward yet vulnerable quality that made her such a powerful soul singer at a young age.

The recording might not have worked but for one person: piano player Neil Cowley. He didn't know Adele or the producers, but had come in as a personal favor to his and Abbiss's shared manager. Adele's previous piano player had just bailed. He didn't think her career would go anywhere, so he didn't want to quit his job at the supermarket. This Dylan cover they were planning would only be vocals and a piano (some strings were added later), and they needed a ringer.

Cowley was a reluctant sideman at best—his main priority was his jazz project, the Neil Cowley Trio—but he agreed to lend a hand in a crisis. As it turned out, they made a perfect partnership. "I was ideally placed to accompany her, because I was coming from the same area of music," he says. "Some people say she's Etta James-esque, and that's precisely the sort of person I was designed to accompany. So she's manna from heaven, really. She's made this soulful pop balladry, and I was there at the same time. It was happy circumstance."

Cowley's piano influences are Carole King and Steely Dan's Donald Fagen—a less-is-more philosophy, nothing flashy or ostentatious. "When you book me, you book that," he says. "I think the art of a good session musician is just to know what's required and do no more. Leave as much space as you want."

That's what Adele and Abbiss wanted for "Make You Feel My Love": a very simple and stripped-down piano accompaniment to Adele's voice. "'She told me, 'These are the chords, play what you play, Neil,'" he says. "I was kind of left to my own devices."

To learn "Make You Feel My Love," Cowley just sat at the piano and played along with the Dylan recording. "I would immediately play that as if I was in the band with Bob Dylan and the rest of those guys," he says. "I would just play a piano accompaniment that would fit in with that band. The piano is such a wonderful, all-encompassing instrument, a whole orchestra under your fingers, so then you just go and strip the rest of the band away. My part would sound perfect in among the Bob Dylan band. I wouldn't sound out of place."

That approach—playing along with Dylan's band, then simply removing the band—led to a simple accompaniment that would give Adele all she needed to sing over without competing for attention in any way. Abbiss points to little jazzy touches Cowley came up with—"blue" notes that on paper don't fit the key, but give it texture—but nothing flashy or ostentatious. Cowley says that because he considers occasional session work just a side job, he has no ego about demonstrating his formidable piano skills. And that makes him more valuable to a singer like Adele.

"Adele wanted it to be a bare-bones version, very simple," Abbiss says. "She, Neil, and myself got together that first morning in the studio. He'd learned the song structure and chords, and she'd learned the words. Neil did what he does so well, which is to slightly bend chords, tweak the harmony slightly. We found a key within a couple of play-throughs. We lowered it so she could open the song in a lower register of her voice, so it was more intimate sounding, but still open up in the middle of the song."

Adele and Cowley recorded the song in the room together, facing each other across the studio. The recording process was as simple as the song itself, four takes at the most. "Most things I did with her were completely live," Abbiss says. "It was all about performance. She would be in the same room facing Neil for complete eye contact, only a few meters apart. She pretty quickly got inside the vocal and began phrasing it in slightly different ways. She varied some notes on the second verse, put some more blue notes in. It was becoming an Adele song. My initial concerns [about the song choice] were out the window."

The version you hear on the album was all done live with Cowley, in a single take. Or almost a single take. Cowley says they swapped out a line she had muffed when she went out to lunch one day. They never told her.

They brought in a small string quartet the next day to accent the song's second half but resisted temptation to add more instruments for a bigger pop production. "I've found as soon as you put a lot of instruments—especially rhythm seconds—on tunes, they become pigeonholed as part of a certain genre and compared to other artists," Abbiss says. "If it's kept bare, you just listen to the words and the voice because you're not distracted by anything else."

Adele and her studio collaborators all felt good about the song, but still considered it what it started as: just one more track to fill out the album, a deep cut for only superfans to find. For several years after the album 19's release, it remained just that.

19 and its first two singles, "Hometown Glory" and "Chasing Pavements," were unqualified successes, if nowhere near the level of her subsequent music. Eight months after 19 came out, her label released "Make You Feel My Love" as the album's fourth single—and as anyone in the industry will tell you,

an album's fourth single is rarely a track anyone is wildly confident about. The album was simply more successful than the label had hoped, and one last single might help boost sales for another month or two.

Sure enough, "Make You Feel My Love" went no higher than #26 in the UK—perfectly fine, but not as high as her previous three singles (and it didn't make the charts at all in the U.S.). It quickly fell back down and disappeared from the charts.

Then, a year later, something odd happened. The simplicity of Adele's "Make You Feel My Love" made it a perfect choice for the wildly popular new format of singing-competition shows: *American Idol, The X-Factor,* and their many competitors. A bunch of Adele wannabes began copying her cover whole cloth and, by doing so, pushed her single back onto the charts. It rose far higher than it had the first time, hitting #4 on the UK charts and cementing its place as one of her most popular songs.

"Make You Feel My Love" remains one of her most-performed songs today, the only cover she sings in every concert. A song she didn't even know before her manager suggested it has taken on such personal meaning that she sometimes can barely get through it. "I always envision someone that I love, or someone that's not here anymore, or someone that I'm not friends with anymore, and I always get a bit choked up [when I sing it]," Adele told the BBC. "I remember doing it in Birmingham, and I had to walk offstage. It was like full-on snot coming off my face!"

She thinks of Dylan's lyrics as bittersweet, and she regularly connects it to sad news events, dedicating it to Amy Winehouse after her death in 2011 and to victims of the Brussels bombings in 2016. But the song has taken on many meanings. There have been marriage proposals during that song in concert and first dances at weddings—including British royal couple Prince William and Kate Middleton. Even after she's had so many more famous singles, she says it remains one of the songs fans most connect with. "Sometimes I get letters from people asking me to sign wedding photos because their first dance was to 'Make You Feel My Love,'" she said, "and I start crying, and then I'll ring them."

When you compare Adele's "Make You Feel My Love" to Jimi Hendrix's "All Along the Watchtower" forty years before, the full spectrum of what can make a great cover song is laid out before you.

Almost everything about the two Dylan covers is different. One is a loud rock anthem, the other a somber piano lullaby. One took months of meticulous perfecting; the other was tossed off in a couple of takes. One saw an artist honoring one of his all-time heroes; the other a singer delivering a song she barely knew by a songwriter she found hard to listen to.

But both covers took a song that few other than big Dylan fans even knew and made it a classic. Both artists heard something in the song and said, "I have something to add to this." In neither case did they end up sounding much like Bob's original recording.

Which, in the end, is why they both work so well. The worst covers aren't the ones that take songs in weird or unexpected directions: they're the ones that take no direction at all. But with "Make You Feel My Love," just like Hendrix and every other artist in this book did, Adele brought something new and personal to someone else's song and gave it a whole new life. ◉

# ACKNOWLEDGMENTS

This book wouldn't exist without many, many people. I'll try to thank as many as I can before the orchestra plays me off.

Thanks to my wonderful wife, Lesley, who was the first person to read every word I wrote, and to my right-hand man at the blog, Patrick Robbins, who was the second. Speaking of which, this book wouldn't exist without the blog, and the blog wouldn't exist without the dozens of great writers, editors, and illustrators who have lent their talents over the past decade.

Thanks to my parents, whose model I've basically been attempting to cover my entire life, and to my little sister, Olivia, who I like to imagine as a far superior cover version of me.

My agent, Helen Zimmermann, expertly helped a first-time author navigate the world of book publishing. My editors at Sterling Publishing, Barbara Berger and Chris Barsanti, primped and polished the text into fighting shape, and Sterling's visual team—Stacey Stambaugh, Christine Heun, Kevin Baier, and David Ter-Avanesyan—made it look as good as it does. I'm eternally grateful also to everyone who gave their time to be interviewed: the musicians, songwriters, producers, engineers, studio players, legal experts, and—in one case—a van owner who was in the right place at the right time.

Oh, and finally thanks to Bob Dylan for playing Billy Stewart's cover of "Summertime" on his radio show back in 2006 and starting this whole thing. ◉

# BIBLIOGRAPHY

## INTRODUCTION

Dylan, Bob. "Episode 10: Summer." *Theme Time Radio Hour*. XM Satellite Radio. July 5, 2006.

Leonard, Will. "Tower Ticker." *Chicago Daily Tribune*. Apr. 16, 1952.

McLean, Don. "'Cover' Versions: On the Incorrect Use of the Term 'Cover'." *Don McLean Online*. Aug. 26, 2004. http://bit.ly/2obZbsE.

Prince. *Lopez Tonight*. By George Lopez. TBS, Apr. 13, 2011.

Rosen, Jody. "Researchers Play Tune Recorded Before Edison." *New York Times*. Mar. 27, 2008. http://nyti.ms/2m4qX4X.

Simon, Bill. "Indies' Surprise Survival: Small Labels' Ingenuity and Skill Pay Off." *Billboard*, Dec. 3, 1949.

"9 Record Labels Vie for Juke Top 10 List." *Billboard*, Nov. 5, 1955.

## ELVIS PRESLEY "HOUND DOG"

Barber, Nicholas. "Hound Dog." In *Lives of the Great Songs*, edited by Tim De Lisle. London: Penguin Books, 1995.

Burke, Ken, and Dan Griffin. *The Blue Moon Boys: The Story of Elvis Presley's Band*. Chicago: Chicago Review Press, 2006.

Collins, Ace. *Untold Gold: The Stories Behind Elvis's #1 Hits*. Chicago: Chicago Review Press, 2005.

Crouse, Richard. *Who Wrote the Book of Love?: The Stories Behind the Hits—From Chuck Berry to Chumbawamba*. Toronto: Doubleday Canada, 1998.

Dickerson, James. *Colonel Tom Parker: The Curious Life of Elvis Presley's Eccentric Manager*. New York: Cooper Square Press, 2001.

Doll, Susan M. *Understanding Elvis: Southern Roots vs. Star Image (Studies in American Popular History and Culture)*. London: Routledge, 1998.

Doss, Erika. *Elvis Culture: Fans, Faith, & Image*. Lawrence, KS: University Press of Kansas, 1999.

Dublin, Sarah. "Turn the Volume Up: The Forgotten Mothers of Rock 'N' Roll." *Medium*, Apr. 14, 2016. http://bit.ly/2nhBLNq.

Dundy, Elaine. *Elvis and Gladys*. New York: Macmillan, 1985.

Fink, Robert. "Elvis Everywhere." *American Music* 16, no. 2 (1998): 135–179.

Greene, Andy. "Songwriter Jerry Leiber Dies at 78." *Rolling Stone*, Aug. 22, 2011. http://rol.st/2nwgbXl.

Guralnick, Peter. *Last Train to Memphis: The Rise of Elvis Presley*. Boston: Little, Brown and Co., 1994.

——— and Ernst Jorgensen. *Elvis Day By Day*. New York: Ballantine Books, 1999.

Hardcastle, Cleothus. "The Backpages Interview: Jerry Leiber and Mike Stoller." *Rock's Backpages*, June 30, 2001.

Hopkins, Jerry. *Elvis: A Biography*. New York: Simon & Schuster, 1971.

"Hound Dog by Elvis Presley." *Songfacts*. Accessed Mar. 28, 2017. http://bit.ly/2nOoPQd.

Humphries, Patrick. *Elvis: The #1 Hits: The Secret History of the Classics*. London: Ebury Press, 2002.

Jeansonne, Glen, and David Luhrssen, Dan Sokolovic. *Elvis Presley, Reluctant Rebel: His Life and Times*. Santa Barbara, CA: Praeger, 2011.

Johnson, Robert. "These Are the Cats Who Make Music For Elvis." *Memphis Press-Scimitar*, Dec. 15, 1956. http://bit.ly/2oMGjxk.

Jorgensen, Ernst. *Elvis Presley: A Life in Music: The Complete Recording Sessions*. New York: St. Martin's Press, 1998.

Leiber, Jerry, and Mike Stoller. *Hound Dog: The Leiber and Stoller Autobiography*. New York: Simon & Schuster, 2009.

Leigh, Spencer. "Freddie Bell: 'Giddy-Up-A Ding Dong' singer." *The Independent*, Feb. 13, 2008. http://ind.pn/2nMELFk.

Lichter, Paul. *Elvis in Vegas*. London: Overlook Press, 2011.

Macfarlane, Malcolm, and Ken Crossland. *Perry Como: A Biography and Complete Career Record*. Jefferson, NC: McFarland & Company, 2009.

Moore, Scotty. *Scotty and Elvis: Aboard the Mystery Train*. Jackson, MS: University Press of Mississippi, 2013.

Olds, Gary. Interview by author. June 11, 2015.

Presley, Elvis. *Milton Berle Show*. By Milton Berle. NBC, June 5, 1956.

———. *Steve Allen Show*. By Steve Allen. NBC, July 1, 1956.

Rohter, Larry, and Tom Zito. "Rock Idol Elvis Presley Dies at 42." *Washington Post*, Aug. 17, 1977. http://wapo.st/2nkgLGy.

Salem, James M. *The Late Great Johnny Ace and the Transition from R&B to Rock 'n' Roll*. Champaigne, IL: University of Illinois Press, 1999.

Silverton, Peter. *Essential Elvis*. London: Chameleon, 1997.

Spörke, Michael. *Big Mama Thornton: The Life and Music*. Jefferson, NC: McFarland & Company, 2014.

Walker, Alice. *You Can't Keep a Good Woman Down*. New York: Harcourt, 1981.

Webb, Robert. *The 100 Greatest Cover Versions: The Ultimate Playlist*. Alnwick, UK: McNidder & Grace, 2012.

Wertheimer, Alfred, and Gregory Martinelli. *Elvis '56: In the Beginning: An Intimate Eyewitness Photo Journal*. New York: Collier Books, 1979.

Zollo, Paul. "Bob Dylan: The Paul Zollo Interview." *American Songwriter*. Jan. 9, 2012. http://bit.ly/2nhBWIA.

## THE BEATLES
## "TWIST AND SHOUT"

Badman, Keith. *The Beatles: Off the Record: Outrageous Opinions & Unrehearsed Interviews*. London: Omnibus, 2002.

Harry, Billy. *The Ultimate Beatles Encyclopedia*. New York: Hyperion, 1993.

Johnson, Phil. "Twist and Shout." In *Lives of the Great Songs*, edited by Tim De Lisle, 62–65. London: Penguin Books, 1995.

Langham, Richard. Interview by author. May 31, 2016.

Lewisohn, Mark. *The Complete Beatles Recording Sessions: The Official Story of the Abbey Road Years 1962–1970*. London: Hamlyn, 1988.

———. *Tune In: The Beatles: All These Years, Vol. 1*. New York: Crown Archetype, 2013.

Margotin, Philippe, and Jean-Michel Guesdon. *All the Songs: The Story Behind Every Beatles Release*. New York: Black Dog & Leventhal Publishers, 2013.

"Please Please Me." *The Beatles Ultimate Experience*. http://bit.ly/2nhGxe1.

Pritchard, David, and Alan Lysaght. *The Beatles: An Oral History*. New York: Hyperion, 1998.

"Recording: Please Please Me Album." *The Beatles Bible*, Sept. 22, 2016. http://bit.ly/2o8JYbr.

Sandercombe, W. Fraser. *The Beatles: The Press Reports, 1961–1970*. Ontario: Collectors Guide Pub, 2007.

Webb, Robert. *The 100 Greatest Cover Versions: The Ultimate Playlist*. Alnwick, UK: McNidder & Grace, 2012.

Winn, John C. *Way Beyond Compare: The Beatles' Recorded Legacy, Volume One, 1957–1965*. New York: Three Rivers Press, 2008.

## THE RIGHTEOUS BROTHERS
## "UNCHAINED MELODY"

"Behind the Song: 'Unchained Melody.'" *MPL Communications, Inc.* http://bit.ly/2nk6tpP.

Crandall, Bill. "Rock and Roll Hall of Fame: The Righteous Brothers." *Rolling Stone*, Feb. 28, 2003. http://rol.st/2nhF2fP.

DeNicola, Linda. "The Sad But True Story of 'Unchained Melody.'" *News Transcript*. http://bit.ly/2oc08B1.

Freeman, Paul. "The Righteous Brothers' Bill Medley: A Voice of Soul and Inspiration." *Pop Culture Classics*, 1990. http://bit.ly/2oc6Jvu.

Garber, Megan. "How 'Unchained Melody' Broke Free." *The Atlantic*, June 13, 2015. http://theatln.tc/2nwsKBM.

Martin, Douglas. "Hy Zaret, 99, Tin Pan Alley Lyricist, Is Dead." *New York Times*, July 3, 2007. http://nyti.ms/2ohWeU1.

Medley, Billy. Interview by author. July 22, 2016.

Munson, Art. Interview by author. July 20, 2016.

Prato, Greg. "Bill Medley of the Righteous Brothers: Songwriter Interviews." *Songfacts*, June 25, 2014. http://bit.ly/1iwYG4c.

Richmond, Peter. "Righteous Brothers/Phil Spector Collectors Items." *Righteous Brothers Discography*, July 2, 2012. http://bit.ly/2oc6T64.

Stitt, Jerry. *Benny to Beyoncé: Finding God's Perfect Pitch for Your Life*. Maitland, FL: Xulon Press, 2012.

"The Interview (September 1996)." *Wayback Machine Internet Archive*, Sept. 1996. http://bit.ly/2nBaKaZ.

"Unchained Melody Publishing LLC." *Unchained Melody Publishing LLC*. Accessed Mar. 29, 2017. http://bit.ly/2nMKH1d.

## ARETHA FRANKLIN "RESPECT"

Bego, Mark. *Aretha Franklin: The Queen of Soul.* New York: Da Capo Press, 1989.

Brackett, David. *The Pop, Rock, and Soul Reader: Histories and Debates.* New York: Oxford University Press, 2013.

Carter, Kelley L. "Sassy Songs Becomes Anthem for an Era." *Detroit Free Press*, June 3, 2007.

Chalmers, Charlie. Interview by author. July 25, 2015.

Dobkin, Matt. *I Never Loved a Man the Way I Love You: Aretha Franklin, Respect, and the Making of a Soul Music Masterpiece.* New York, St. Martin's Press, 2006.

Doyle, Patrick. "Aretha Franklin on Feminism, Beyonce and Who Should Star in Her Biopic." *Rolling Stone.com*, Dec. 11, 2014 http://rol.st/1smCglB.

Franklin, Aretha. *CBS News Sunday Morning.* By Anthony Mason. CBS, Mar. 11, 2012.

────── and David Ritz. *Aretha: From These Roots.* New York: Villard Books, 1999.

Guralnick, Peter. *Sweet Soul Music: Rhythm and Blues and the Southern Dream of Freedom.* New York: HarperCollins, 1986.

Johnson, Jimmy. Interview by author. Aug. 20, 2015.

Jones, Hettie. *Big Star Fallin' Mama; Five Women in Black Music.* New York: Viking Press, 1974.

Llorens, David. "Miracle in Milwaukee." *Ebony Magazine*, Nov. 1967. http://bit.ly/2nMOvzv.

Lordi, Emily J. *Black Resonance: Iconic Women Singers and African American Literature.* New Brunswick, NJ: Rutgers University Press, 2013.

Nathan, David. *The Soulful Divas: Personal Portraits of Over a Dozen Divine Divas, from Nina Simone, Aretha Franklin, & Diana Ross to Patti LaBelle, Whitney Houston & Janet Jackson.* New York: Billboard Books, 1999.

Ritz, David. *Respect: The Life of Aretha Franklin.* New York: Hachette, 2014.

Soeder, John. "R-E-S-P-E-C-T: The Inside Story behind Aretha Franklin's Chart-Topping Anthem." *Cleveland Plain-Dealer*, Oct. 30, 2011. http://bit.ly/2ozxDtf.

"The 500 Greatest Songs of All Time." *Rolling Stone*, Apr. 7, 2011. http://rol.st/2kn9nwK.

Weller, Sheila. "The Untold History of Aretha Franklin's Irrevocable 'Respect'." *Elle*, Apr. 8, 2016. http://bit.ly/1TKqId9.

Werner, Craig Hansen. *Higher Ground: Stevie Wonder, Aretha Franklin, Curtis Mayfield, and the Rise and Fall of American Soul.* New York: Crown Publishers, 2004.

Wexler, Jerry, and David Ritz. *Rhythm and the Blues: A Life in American Music.* New York: Knopf, 1993.

## JIMI HENDRIX "ALL ALONG THE WATCHTOWER"

Buskin, Richard. "Classic Tracks: Jimi Hendrix Experience 'All Along the Watchtower.'" *Sound on Sound*, Nov. 2005. http://bit.ly/2nhJiMd.

*Classic Albums' Jimi Hendrix: Electric Ladyland: Recounting the journey of a legendary music recording.* Directed by Roger Pomphrey. Originally aired July 21, 1997. Burbank, CA: Rhino Entertainment, 1999. DVD.

Cross, Charles R. *Room Full of Mirrors: A Biography of Jimi Hendrix.* New York: Hyperion, 2005.

Dolen, John. "A Midnight Chat with Bob Dylan." *Sun Sentinel*, Sept. 28, 1995 http://bit.ly/2nMTaBq.

Dylan, Bob. *Biograph.* Columbia Records CBS 66509. Nov. 7, 1985. Box set compilation. Liner notes.

Douglas, Alan. Typed 1988 manuscript by Bob Dylan. "The Jimi Hendrix Exhibition." Govinda Gallery. Washington, D.C. July 1993.

Etchingham, Kathy. Interview by author. Feb. 23, 2014.

────── . *Through Gypsy Eyes: My Life, the '60s, and Jimi Hendrix.* London: Gollancz, 1998.

Goldstein, Michael. Interview by author. Feb. 24, 2014.

Hendrix, James A., and Jas Obrecht. *My Son Jimi.* Seattle, WA: AlJas Enterprises, 1999.

────── . *Electric Ladyland.* MCA Records, CAD-10895. Sept. 28, 1993. Compact disc. Liner notes.

McDermott, John, et al. *Jimi Hendrix Sessions: The Complete Studio Recording Sessions, 1963–1970.* Boston: Little, Brown & Company, 1995.

────── and Eddie Kramer. *Hendrix: Setting the Record Straight.* New York: Warner Books, 1992.

Perry, John. *Electric Ladyland.* New York: Continuum, 2004.

Roby, Steven. *Black Gold: The Lost Archives of Jimi Hendrix.* New York: Billboard Books, 2002.

Shapiro, Harry, and Caesar Glebbeek. *Jimi Hendrix: Electric Gypsy.* New York: St. Martin's Press, 1990.

Weller, Sheila. "Jimi Hendrix: 'I Don't Want to Be a Clown Anymore.'" *Rolling Stone*, Nov. 15, 1969. http://rol.st/2nkqGMc.

## JOE COCKER "WITH A LITTLE HELP FROM MY FRIENDS"

BBC Radio 2. "Greatest Cover Versions: Top 50." *BBC Music*, Oct. 13, 2014 http://bbc.in/1w8XKqT.

Bean, J. P. *Joe Cocker: The Authorised Biography*. London: Virgin Books, 2003.

Bell, Max. "Joe Cocker: Friends, Dogs, Drugs, Booze And The Queen." *Team Rock*, Jan. 30, 2013. http://bit.ly/2ozGLxM.

Brandle, Lars. "Paul McCartney Pays Respects to 'Good Mate' Joe Cocker." *Billboard*, Dec. 13, 2014. http://bit.ly/2nklOa3.

Dang, Mike. "How Joe Cocker's Version of 'With a Little Help From My Friends' Ended Up as the Theme Song for 'The Wonder Years.'" *Longreads*, Aug. 7, 2014. http://bit.ly/2nMOITj.

Fornatale, Pete. *Back to the Garden: The Story of Woodstock and How It Changed a Generation*. New York: Touchstone, 2009.

Ebert, Roger. *Awake in the Dark: The Best of Roger Ebert*. Chicago: University of Chicago Press, 2006.

Giles, Jeff. "The History of Joe Cocker and John Belushi's 'Saturday Night Live' Duet." *Ultimate Classic Rock*. Mar. 5, 2015. http://bit.ly/2nkkYtK.

Graff, Gary. "Joe Cocker: Looking Back at 50 Years of Music, In His Own Words." *Billboard*, Dec. 22, 2014. http://bit.ly/2nwusmI.

Hale, Don. *The Joe Cocker Story*. Llandudno, United Kingdom: Coast and Country Productions Ltd., 2010.

Hann, Michael. "Joe Cocker: 'I took black acid once . . . it was a very dark trip'." *Guardian*, Jan. 31, 2013. http://bit.ly/2o9bZQ0.

Knipschild, Harry. "Joe Cocker: van Sheffield naar Woodstock (1968–1970)." *HarryKnipschild.nl*, July 23, 2015. http://bit.ly/2nwTjHe.

Ramirez, Deborah. "A Tribute to Joe Cocker." *Sun Sentinel*, Jan. 15, 2015. http://bit.ly/2nwvmj7.

"Readers' Poll: The Best Vocal Performances in Rock History." *Rolling Stone*, Sept. 5, 2012. http://rol.st/2nwy4oS.

*Saturday Night Live*. "Rob Reiner." Season 1, Episode 3. NBC, Oct. 25, 1975.

Stainton, Chris. Interview by author. Oct. 18, 2016.

"Tony Visconti At GRAMMY Town Hall | New York." Accessed March 30, 2017. *GRAMMYPro.com*. http://bit.ly/2mQFplY.

Visconti, Tony. Interview by author. Oct. 17, 2016.

Webb, Robert. *The 100 Greatest Cover Versions: The Ultimate Playlist*. Alnwick, UK: McNidder & Grace, 2012.

Zimmerman, Lee. "Joe Cocker on John Belushi's Impression of Him: 'I Thought Vocally, He Did Quite a Clever Job.'" *Broward–Palm Beach New Times*, Sept. 28, 2012. http://bit.ly/2nkbcYB.

## THE WHO "SUMMERTIME BLUES"

Barnes, Richard. *The Who: Maximum R & B*. New York: St. Martin's Press, 2000.

Charlesworth, Chris. *Townshend: A Career Biography*. New York: Proteus Books, 1984.

Collis, John. *Gene Vincent and Eddie Cochran: Rock 'n' Roll Revolutionaries*. London: Virgin Publishing, 2004.

Cott, Jonathan. "'Tea with Townshend: A Post-'Tommy' Chat on Rock 'n Roll, Recording." *Rolling Stone*, Mar. 14, 1970. http://rol.st/2omvIJl.

Daltrey, Roger. Interview by author. Oct. 27, 2016

Fletcher, Tony. *Moon: The Life and Death of a Rock Legend*. New York: Spike, 1999.

Hopkins, Jerry. "Keith Moon Bites Back." *Rolling Stone*, Dec. 21, 1972. http://rol.st/1YjAa6q.

Marsh, Dave. *Before I Get Old: The Story of the Who*. New York: St. Martin's Press, 1983.

Marshall, Ben, et al. *The Who: The Official History*. London: Virgin Books, 2015.

Neill, Andrew, and Matthew Kent. *Anyway, Anyhow, Anywhere: The Complete Chronicle of the Who, 1958–1978*. New York: Sterling, 2009.

Pridden, Bob. Interview by author. Nov. 2, 2016.

Segretto, Mike. *The Who FAQ: All That's Left to Know About Fifty Years of Maximum R&B*. Milwaukee, WI: Backbeat Books, 2014.

Smith, Larry David. *Pete Townshend: The Minstrel's Dilemma*. Westport, CT: Praeger, 1999.

Townshend, Pete. *Pete Townshend: Who I Am*. London: HarperCollins, 2012.

Webb, Robert. *The 100 Greatest Cover Versions: The Ultimate Playlist*. Alnwick, UK: McNidder & Grace, 2012.

Wenner, Jann S. "Pete Townshend Talks Mods, Recording, and Smashing Guitars." *Rolling Stone*, Sept. 14, 1968. http://rol.st/2nP3zL7.

## CREEDENCE CLEARWATER REVIVAL "I HEARD IT THROUGH THE GRAPEVINE"

Bordowitz, Hank. *Bad Moon Rising: The Unauthorized History of Creedence Clearwater Revival*. Chicago: Chicago Review Press, 1998.

Bosso, Joe. "John Fogerty Talks about the Creedence Musical Process." *MusicRadar*, July 1, 2013. http://bit.ly/2ozj2xN.

Clifford, Doug. Interview by author. Oct. 18, 2016.

Cook, Stu. Interview by author. Oct. 14, 2016.

Flory, Andrew. "Marvin Gaye as Vocal Composer." *Sounding out Pop: Analytical Essays in Popular Music*, edited by Mark Spicer and John Covach, 63–98. Ann Arbor, MI: University of Michigan Press, 2010. http://bit.ly/2otzGm2.

Fogerty, John. *Fortunate Son: My Life, My Music*. New York: Little, Brown and Company, 2015.

Kirby, Hilary. "The Life of a Song: 'I Heard It Through the Grapevine'." *Financial Times*, Oct. 23, 2015. http://on.ft.com/2oi3Dm6.

Kitts, Thomas M. *John Fogerty: An American Son*. New York: Routledge, 2015.

Masley, Ed. "Interview: Doug Clifford on CCR and John Fogerty." *The Arizona Republic*, July 7, 2015. http://azc.cc/1McgewC.

Moore, Rick. "Marvin Gaye, 'I Heard It Through the Grapevine.'" *American Songwriter*, Nov. 19, 2012. http://bit.ly/2nwyn30.

Murphy, Bill. "John Fogerty: That Old Travelin' Bone." *Premier Guitar*, Nov. 2, 2015. http://bit.ly/2nwruyC.

Webb, Robert. *The 100 Greatest Cover Versions: The Ultimate Playlist*. Carmarthen, Wales: McNidder & Grace, 2012.

Werner, Craig, and Dave Marsh. *Up Around the Bend: The Oral History of Creedence Clearwater Revival*. New York: Spike, 1999.

## GLADYS KNIGHT & THE PIPS "MIDNIGHT TRAIN TO GEORGIA"

Bronson, Fred. The *Billboard Book of Number One Hits: The Inside Story Behing the Top of the Charts*. New York: Billboard Books, 1985.

Cooper, Peter. "Jim Weatherly's 'Train' Never Stops." *Tennessean*, Oct. 27, 2013.

Hall, Michael. "The Secret History of Texas Music." *Texas Monthly*, July 2015. http://bit.ly/2nwInYe.

James, Gary. "Interview With Jim Weatherly." *Classic Bands*, Feb. 21, 2006. http://bit.ly/2nwpIxF.

Johnson, Lindsay. "'I'll Be With Him on the Midnight Train to Georgia': The Traveling Woman in 1920s Blues and 1970s R&B." *American Music Review*, Spring 2014. http://bit.ly/2otOUHT.

Junior, Chris M. "Hop Aboard the Midnight Train to Georgia with Gladys Knight & The Pips." *Goldmine*, Apr. 14, 2010. http://bit.ly/2nkdHdz.

Mironov, Jeffrey. Interview by author. Oct. 2, 2015.

Myers, Marc. "Anatomy of a Song: 'Midnight Train to Georgia.'" *Wall Street Journal*, Aug. 8, 2013. http://on.wsj.com/2otAjwg.

"Sold on Song: Midnight Train to Georgia." *BBC*, Apr. 9, 2004. http://bit.ly/2n4zZ6Y.

Stasium, Ed. Interview by author. Nov. 13, 2015

"Ten Questions with Jim Weatherly." *Nashville Songwriters Hall of Fame*, Sept. 28, 2008. http://bit.ly/2nk1Tbv.

Webb, Robert. *The 100 Greatest Cover Versions: The Ultimate Playlist*. Alnwick, UK: McNidder & Grace, 2012.

## PATTI SMITH "GLORIA"

Amorosi, A. D. "Seventh Heaven." *Philadelphia City Paper*, Nov. 23–Dec. 1, 1995.

Bockris, Victor. *Patti Smith: An Unauthorized Biography*. New York: Simon & Schuster, 1999.

Brazier, Chris. "The Resurrection of Patti Smith." *Melody Maker*, Mar. 18, 1978.

Crowe, Cameron. "Van Morrison Finds Himself on the Road." *Rolling Stone*, May 19, 1977. http://bit.ly/2nAYh4N.

Green, Penny. "Patti Smith." *Interview*, Oct. 1973. http://bit.ly/2nB1wsV.

Gross, Terry. "Patti Smith Recognized as a Rock Legend." *NPR Fresh Air*. Mar. 9, 2007. http://n.pr/2o2u95p.

Hiss, Tony. "'Gonna be so big, Gonna be a star, Watch me now!'" *New York Times,* Dec. 21, 1975. http://nyti.ms/2nwDeiY.

Hoby, Hermione, et al. "Patti Smith: How She Rocks Our World." *The Observer,* May 26, 2012. http://bit.ly/2ozm05E.

Jackson, Blair. "Classic Tracks: Patti Smith's 'Gloria.'" *Mix,* Oct. 1, 2009. http://bit.ly/2nklqrW.

Johnstone, Nick. *Patti Smith: A Biography.* London: Omnibus, 1997.

Kaye, Lenny. Interview by author. Jan. 10, 2017.

Marcus, Greil. "Horses: Patti Smith Exposes Herself." *Village Voice,* Nov. 24, 1975. http://bit.ly/2n4IMWK.

Marsh, Dave. "Patti Smith: Her Horses Got Wings, They Can Fly." *Rolling Stone,* Jan. 1, 1976. http://rol.st/2nSWo6i.

McNeil, Legs, and Gillian McCain. *Please Kill Me: The Uncensored Oral History of Punk.* New York: Grove Press, 1996.

Rockwell, John. "Patti Smith Plans Album with Eyes on Stardom." *New York Times,* Mar. 28, 1975. http://nyti.ms/2nB57Hx.

Shapiro, Susan. "Patti Smith: Somewhere, Over the Rimbaud." *Crawdaddy,* Dec. 1975. http://bit.ly/2nwOzzs.

Sikes, Jason. "The Rock Town Hall Interview: Lenny Kaye's Nuggets of Inspiration." *Rock Town Hall,* Sept. 9, 2011. http://bit.ly/2nwElB4.

Thompson, Dave. *Dancing Barefoot: The Patti Smith Story.* Chicago: Chicago Review Press, 2011.

Patti Smith concert. *WBAI Radio.* May 5, 1975.

Webb, Robert. *The 100 Greatest Cover Versions: The Ultimate Playlist.* Alnwick, UK: McNidder & Grace, 2012.

Wendell, Eric. *Patti Smith: America's Punk Rock Rhapsodist.* Lanham, MD: Rowman & Littlefield, 2014.

## TALKING HEADS
## "TAKE ME TO THE RIVER"

Bowman, David. *This Must Be the Place: the Adventures of Talking Heads in the Twentieth Century.* New York: HarperCollins, 2001.

Byrne, David. *How Music Works.* Edinburgh: Canongate, 2012.

———. Interview by author. Nov. 2, 2016.

Davis, Jerome, and Mark Rowland. *Talking Heads.* New York: Vintage/Musician, 1986.

De Lisle, Tim. "Take Me to the River." In *Lives of the Great Songs,* edited by Tim De Lisle, 29–36. London: Penguin Books, 1995.

Frantz, Chris. Interview by author. Nov. 9, 2016.

Gans, David. *Talking Heads: The Band and Their Music.* New York: Avon Books, 1985.

Gittins, Ian. *Talking Heads: Once in a Lifetime: The Stories Behind Every Song.* London: Carlton, 2004.

Harrison, Jerry. Interview by author. Oct. 7, 2016.

Howell, John. *David Byrne.* New York: Thunder's Mouth Press, 1992.

Sheppard, David. *On Some Faraway Beach: The Life and Times of Brian Eno.* Chicago: Chicago Review Press, 2009.

Webb, Robert. *The 100 Greatest Cover Versions: The Ultimate Playlist.* Alnwick, UK: McNidder & Grace, 2012.

White, Timothy. "Inside Talking Heads: Seventeen years of Popular Favorites and Naked Truths." *Goldmine,* Dec. 25, 1992. http://bit.ly/2nThDEU.

## DEVO "SATISFACTION"

Casale, Gerald. Interview by author. Mar. 10, 2016.

Delliger, Jade, and David Giffels. *Are We Not Men? We Are Devo!* London: SAF Pub, 2003.

*Devo: The Complete Truth About De-Evolution.* Directed by Chuck Statler. Burbank, CA: Rhino Entertainment, 2003. DVD.

Garon, Jon. Interview by author. Nov. 26, 2016

Marshall, Juli Wilson, and Nicholas J. Siciliano. "The Satire/Parody Distinction in Copyright and Trademark Law— Can Satire Ever Be a Fair Use?" *American Bar Association,* May 2006. http://bit.ly/2oBVyc8.

Mothersbaugh, Mark. Interview by author. Apr. 6, 2016.

Rees, Jasper. "Satisfaction." In *Lives of the Great Songs,* edited by Tim De Lisle, 115–121. London: Penguin Books, 1995.

Smith, Kevin C. *Recombo DNA: The Story of Devo, or How the 60s Became the 80s.* London: Jawbone Press, 2013.

Vain, Madison, and Eric Renner Brown. "Mark Mothersbaugh, Brad Paisley, Hilary Duff, and More Honor 'Satisfaction' as It Turns 50." *Entertainment Weekly*, June 5, 2015. http://bit.ly/2obSqa5.

Webb, Robert. *The 100 Greatest Cover Versions: The Ultimate Playlist.* Alnwick, UK: McNidder & Grace, 2012.

## "WEIRD AL" YANKOVIC "POLKAS ON 45"

Levey, Jay. Interview by author. Oct. 21, 2016.

Miranda, Lin-Manuel. *WTF with Marc Maron.* By Marc Maron. Nov. 14, 2016. http://bit.ly/2nwSGM5.

Rabin, Nathan. *Weird Al: The Book.* New York: Abrams Image, 2012.

Schwartz, Jon. Interview by author. Oct. 11, 2016.

"'Weird Al' Yankovic Set Lists." *Wayback Machine Internet Archive*, accessed Apr. 3, 2017. http://bit.ly/2nB9y7C.

Yankovic, "Weird Al." Interview by author. Oct. 21, 2016.

## PET SHOP BOYS "ALWAYS ON MY MIND"

"'Always On My Mind' by Willie Nelson." *Songfacts*. Accessed Aug. 16, 2016. http://bit.ly/2nMUm85.

Brown, Jake. *Nashville Songwriter: The Inside Stories Behind Country Music's Greatest Hits.* Dallas, TX: BenBella Books, 2014.

Edwards, Gavin. "1988 Countdown #92: Pet Shop Boys, 'Always on My Mind.'" *Rule Forty Two*, June 19, 2008. http://bit.ly/2o90qs6.

Heath, Chris. *Pet Shop Boys, Literally.* London: Viking, 1991.

Hilburn, Robert. "The Surprising Saga of 'Always on My Mind'." *Los Angeles Times*, Apr. 24, 1988. http://lat.ms/2oRxHo6.

*Love Me Tender: A Tribute to the Music of Elvis Presley.* Directed by Jon Scoffield. 1987. ITV Central Studios. TV movie.

Lowe, Chris, and Neil Tennant. *Introspective / Further Listening 1988–1989.* Parlophone 7243 5 30507 2 6, 530 5072. June 4, 2001. Compact disc. Liner notes.

Mendelsohn, Julian. Interview by author. Aug. 9, 2016.

Nelson, Willie, and Edwin Shrake. *Willie: An Autobiography.* New York: Simon & Schuster, 1988.

Price, Markie. "Literally Issue 29 Recording." *Absolutely Pet Shop Boys*, July 15, 2005. http://bit.ly/2mQtEfy.

"Splendour: Pet Shop Boys." *Nottingham Post*, July 23, 2010. http://bit.ly/2mQt0yJ.

Studer, Wayne. "Always on My Mind / In My House." *Pet Shop Boys Commentary*, Accessed April 3, 2017. http://bit.ly/2nB7z32.

Thompson, Ben. "Always On My Mind." In *Lives of the Great Songs*, edited by Tim De Lisle, 18–23. London: Penguin Books, 1995.

Webb, Robert. *The 100 Greatest Cover Versions: The Ultimate Playlist.* Alnwick, UK: McNidder & Grace, 2012.

## WHITNEY HOUSTON "I WILL ALWAYS LOVE YOU"

Anderson, Kyle. "An oral history of Whitney's anthem 'I Will Always Love You.'" *Entertainment Weekly*, Dec. 14, 2012. http://bit.ly/2o8LxG0.

"Dolly Parton Reflects on Her Greatest Moments." *CMT News*, July 7, 2006, http://bit.ly/1J1TXP4.

Foster, David. *Hitman: Forty Years Making Music, Topping Charts & Winning GRAMMYs.* New York: Pocket Books, 2008.

Livingston, Ikimulisa. "Whitney's Guardin' Angel." *New York Post*, Feb. 17, 2012. http://nyp.st/2ouzymm.

Parton, Dolly. *Larry King Live.* By Larry King. CNN, July 12, 2003.

Reitzas, Dave. Interview by author. Oct. 4, 2014.

Shelburne, Craig. "Dolly Parton Shares Inspiration of 'I Will Always Love You.'" *CMT News*, Feb. 14, 2011. http://bit.ly/2nwuk6G.

Whalum, Kirk. Interview by author. Oct. 7, 2016.

Yianilos, Peter. Interview by author. Sept. 27, 2016.

## FUGEES "KILLING ME SOFTLY"

Bronson, Fred. *The Billboard Book of Number One Hits: The Inside Story Behing the Top of the Charts.* New York: Billboard Books, 1985.

Chace, Zoe. "The Making Of A Hit Song: Jerry Wonda's Platinum Sound." *NPR All Things Considered*, Dec. 9, 2010. http://n.pr/2nTGkB5.

Flack, Roberta. "Fugee Fever." *Interview*, May 1996.

Fox, Charles. Interview by author. Nov. 22, 2016.

Fox, Killian. "Roberta Flack: soundtrack of my life." *Guardian*, June 29, 2015. http://bit.ly/2nMSUlS.

Harris, Janelle. "The Radical Power of 'Killing Me Softly.'" *The Atlantic*, June 1, 2016. http://theatln.tc/1X18BS4.

Hernandez, Nina. "Thursday Interview: Wyclef Jean." *Austin Chronicle*, Mar. 20, 2015. http://bit.ly/2oi7r6W.

Iandoli, Kathy. "Inside Fugees' The Score, 20 Years Later, With Its Collaborators." *Pitchfork*, Feb. 22, 2016. http://bit.ly/2nkmAUH.

"'Killing Me Softly With His Song' by Roberta Flack." *Songfacts*, Accessed April 3, 2017. http://bit.ly/2ozpk0m.

Lieberman, Lori. Interview by author. July 27, 2016.

Muhammad, Latifah. "A Look At The Fugees' Final Album With The Producers." *Vibe*, Feb. 16, 2016. http://bit.ly/2nB2pEu.

Nickson, Chris. *Lauryn Hill: She's Got That Thing*. New York: St. Martin's Press, 1999.

Pras. Interview by author. July 21, 2016.

Riker, Warren. Interview by author. July 22, 2016.

Shapiro, Marc. *My Rules: The Lauryn Hill Story*. New York: Berkley Boulevard Books, 1999.

Webb, Robert. *The 100 Greatest Cover Versions: The Ultimate Playlist*. Alnwick, UK: McNidder & Grace, 2012.

Wete, Brad. "Fugees Producer Jerry Wonder Talks About the 16th Anniversary of 'The Score.'" *Complex*, Feb. 14,2012. http://bit.ly/2oieMDE.

## THE GOURDS "GIN AND JUICE"

*All the Labor*. Documentary. High Plains Films, 2013.

Bernard, Claude. Interview by author. Nov. 7, 2014.

Berndtson, Chad. "HT Interview: The Gourds." *Glide*, Oct. 13, 2011. http://bit.ly/2ozxkhT.

Haupt, Melanie. "The Gourds: Don't Call It A Breakup." *Austin Chronicle*, Oct. 28, 2013. http://bit.ly/2nwAofy.

Hess, Christopher. "Songs of Innocence and Experience: The Gourds Kiss the Winged Life as It Flies." *Austin Chronicle*, Sept. 22, 2000. http://bit.ly/2n4Gzui.

Langford, Keith. Interview by author. Nov. 5, 2014.

Munoz, Daniel. "Alison Mosshart." *Daily Texan*, Jan. 23, 2012. http://bit.ly/2mQEqlO.

Nardwuar. "Nardwuar vs. Snoop Dogg (2010)." YouTube, Mar. 28, 2010. http://bit.ly/2oieSeu.

Russell, Kevin. Interview by author. Nov. 3, 2014.

———. "Who Listens To The Words That I Speak: One Question with K. Russell." *Gourds News*, Nov. 13, 2009. http://bit.ly/2nhAhCO.

Skolnik, Dan. Interview by author. Nov. 24, 2014.

Smith, Jimmy. Interview by author. Nov. 7, 2014.

"Snoop Dogg Likes Gin and Juice by the Gourds." Video interview. *SPIN.com*, 2008. http://bit.ly/2oi4xzg.

Stewart, Mike. Interview by author. Nov. 14, 2014.

Wildsmith, Steve. "A GOURD NO MORE: Kevin Russell Finds New Musical Life as Shinyribs." *The Daily Times*, Sept. 24, 2014. http://bit.ly/1nKCGpc.

## JOHNNY CASH "HURT"

Associated Press. "MTV awards favorite: Johnny Cash." *Wayback Machine Internet Archive*, Aug. 25, 2003. http://bit.ly/2o1gmKk.

Beard, Steve. "Man in Black." In *Spiritual Journeys: How Faith Has Influenced Twelve Music Icons*. Lake Mary, FL: Relevant Books, 2003.

Brown, Jake. *Rick Rubin: In the Studio*. Toronto: ECW Press, 2009.

Cash, John Carter. Interview by author. Nov. 20, 2014.

Cash, Johnny, and Rick Rubin. *Unearthed*. American Recordings 986 133-5. Nov. 25, 2003. Compact disc. Liner notes.

DeCurtis, Anthony. *In Other Words: Artists Talk About Life and Work*. Milwaukee, WI: Hal Leonard, 2005.

Delaney, Sam. "Final cut is the deepest." *Guardian*, Sept. 23, 2005. http://bit.ly/2oul8TJ.

Evans, Paul. "Johnny Cash: American Recordings." *Rolling Stone*, Feb. 2, 1998. http://rol.st/2nx7V7T.

Ferguson, David. Interview by author. Nov. 11, 2014.

Hilburn, Robert. *Johnny Cash: The Life*. New York: Little, Brown and Company, 2013.

Hormel, Smokey. Interview by author. Nov. 14, 2014.

Kamp, David. "American Communion." *Vanity Fair*, October 2004. http://bit.ly/1UvKzM9.

Kemp, Mark. "Johnny Cash: American IV: The Man Comes Around." Rolling Stone. Accessed via *Wayback Machine Internet Archive*. Nov. 14, 2002. http://bit.ly/2p58S8q.

Anderson, Kurt. "On Johnny Cash's Birthday, a Look Back at His Final Interview." *MTV News*, Feb. 26, 2010. http://on.mtv.com/2nk2UAl.

McKay, Alastair. "Nick Cave On Working With Johnny Cash." *Uncut*, May 12, 2015. http://bit.ly/2oc1Pi3.

"One on One with Johnny Cash: 10 Questions with the Man in Black." *Livewire*, Apr. 1, 2003. http://bit.ly/2o2Nrru.

Orshoski, Wes. "Johnny Cash: An American Original." *Billboard*, Mar. 30, 2002.

Rickly, Geoff. "Idol Worship: New School Meets Old School." *Alternative Press*, Sept. 2004.

Robin, Lou. Interview by author. Dec. 5, 2014.

Silverman, Jonathan. *Nine Choices: Johnny Cash and American Culture*. Amherst & Boston: University of Massachusetts Press, 2010.

Streissguth, Michael. *Johnny Cash: The Biography*. Cambridge, MA: Da Capo Press, 2006.

*The Work of Director Mark Romanek*. Directed by Mark Romanek and Lance Bangs. 2005. New York: Palm Pictures, 2005. DVD.

Thomson, Graeme. *The Resurrection of Johnny Cash: Hurt Redemption, and American Recordings*. London: Outline Press Ltd, 2011.

Turner, Steve. *The Man Called Cash: The Life, Love, and Faith of an American Legend*. Nashville: W Publishing Group, 2004.

Webb, Robert. *The 100 Greatest Cover Versions: The Ultimate Playlist*. Alnwick, UK: McNidder & Grace, 2012.

"6 Music's Cover Lovers." *BBC*, Jan. 27, 2007. http://bbc.in/2obRZwn.

"100 Best Songs of the 2000s." *Rolling Stone*, June 17, 2011. http://rol.st/1tsBuWL.

"100 Greatest Music Videos." *NME*, June 2, 2011. http://bit.ly/2o91Ra2.

## ADELE
## "MAKE YOU FEEL MY LOVE"

Abbiss, Jim. Interview by author. Oct. 28, 2016.

"Adele 'Not Bothered' by Amy Comparison." *Metro News*, Jan. 24, 2008, http://bit.ly/2ozwDp5.

Adkins, Adele. "Adele: My Favourite Musicians." *Observer*, Nov. 15, 2015. http://bit.ly/1MfQC36.

Copsey, Robert. "Adele: 'I aved Bob Dylan'." *Digital Spy*, Jan. 14, 2011. http://bit.ly/2nBapp1.

Cowley, Neil. Interview by author. 3 Nov., 2016.

Dawson, Kim. "Adele: Make Sweet Music to My Songs!" *Daily Star*, Jan. 31, 2011. http://bit.ly/2nBamJR.

Evans, Chris. "Adele: 'My son doesn't like my music, I just sing Twinkle Twinkle.'" *BBC Radio 2*, Oct. 23, 2015. http://bbc.in/2nwwrr6.

James, Sarah-Louise. *Adele: A Celebration of an Icon and Her Music*. London: Carlton, 2012.

Jeffries, Joshua. "Adele 'The Real Deal' Atkins." *Dish Magazine*, May 8, 2009. http://bit.ly/2outqLb.

McCormick, Neil. "Don't Think Twice, Bob Dylan's Still All Right." *Telegraph*, Feb. 2, 2012. http://bit.ly/2o2SFTZ.

Newkey-Burden, Chas. *Adele: The Biography*. New York: Overlook Press, 2015.

Wilkinson, Richard. Interview by author. Nov. 2, 2016.

# INDEX

Note: Page numbers in *italics* indicate/include captions.

## A

Abbiss, Jim, 210–211, 212, 215, 216
Adele, "Make You Feel My Love," 208–217
"All Along the Watchtower," 56–67
"Always on My Mind," 2, *152*, 154–159
*American IV: The Man Comes Around* album, *198*
*American IV: The Man Comes Around* (Cash), 201–202
"American Pie," 4–5, 7, 172

## B

"Bear Cat," 15, 16
The Beatles
    Creedence and, 92–93
    *Sgt. Pepper's Lonely Hearts Club Band* and, *70*, 72, 74, 84
    "Twist and Shout," 26–35
    "With a Little Help From My Friends," 1, 70–71, 74, 77
Bell, Freddie, 15–17, 23
Berle, Milton, 17, 18
Bernard, Claude, 184, 185, *187*, 188, 189, 190, 191
*The Best Little Whorehouse in Texas* (movie), *162*, 164
*Blunted on Reality* (Fugees), 174, *176*
Bob Wills and the Texas Playboys, 18
*The Bodyguard* (movie), *162*, 164, 165–166, 168–*169*
Bowie, David, 22, 121, 134, 135
Branson, Richard, 134
Byrne, David, 118–120, *122*, 123, 126–127

## C

Camillo, Tony, 101–102
Campbell, Mike, 198, 200
Carson, Wayne, 154, 159
Carter, John, 198, 200, 204, 205
Casale, Gerald, Devo/"Satisfaction," 128–137
Cash, Johnny, "Hurt" and, 192–207
    album sales, 194–197
    *American IV: The Man Comes Around* album, *198*, 201–202
    Cash's museum, its contents, 203–205
    exchanging song ideas and, 197
    family responses to video, 205
    good songs quote, 184
    "honesty" in performance, 200
    Mark Romanek and, 202–205, 206
    passing of Johnny, 207
    physical ailments, 200–201

    producer Rick Rubin and, 194, 196–199, 202, 205, 206, 207, 210–211
    recording in L.A., 198–201
    Trent Reznor, Nine Inch Nails and, *194*, 197–198, 199, 203, 207
    video production and success, 202–207
Cash, June Carter, 204
Cash, Rosanne, 196, 201, 204, 205
Chalmers, Charles, 47, 52
Chandler, Chas, 59, 60, 64, 66
Chavis, Ben, 54
Christopher, Johnny, 154, 156
Clifford, Doug "Cosmo," 89–90, 91, 93
Cochran, Eddie, "Summertime Blues," 8, 80–82
Cocker, Joe, "With a Little Help From My Friends," 1, 68–77
Cooke, Sam, 28, 54
Cook, Stu, 90, 92–93, 96
Cordell, Denny, 72–73, 74, 76, 77
Costner, Kevin, 164–165, *166*, 167, 168, *169*
*Cover Me* blog, this book, 9
Cover songs. *See also specific artists; specific songs*
    benefits of, 1–2
    copycat covers, 4–5, 14–15, 24
    cultural shift evolving, 5–7
    defined, 4–5
    history of, 2–7, 35
    performer importance, 5–7
    this book, 5
    today, 7–8
    top bands trajectory of using then writing own songs, 35
Cowley, Neil, 211, 212, 215–216
Creedence Clearwater Revival, "I Heard It Through the Grapevine," 86–95
Curtis, King, 48, 52

## D

Daltrey, Roger, 80, 82, 84, 85
Davis, Clive, 111, 168
Davis, Mark Jonathan "Richard Cheese," 150
*Day of the Dead* (Grateful Dead), 8
Demento, Dr., 143, *144*
Devo, "Satisfaction," 128–137
Dickins, Jonathan, 212–215
Dogg, Snoop Doggy, *182*–183, 185, 188–189
Dowd, Tom, 50, 53, 111

*The Downward Spiral* (Nine Inch Nails), *194*
Duncan, Todd, 38
Dylan, Bob
    Adele, "Make You Feel My Love," 208–217
    Hendrix, "All Along the Watchtower," 2, 56–67
    "Hound Dog" impressing, 22
    photos of, *60, 212*
    *Sgt. Pepper's Lonely Hearts Club Band, 70*
    *Theme Time Radio Hour,* 8
    *Time Out of Mind* album, *212*
    on tour, *212*

**E**

Edison, Thomas, *2*
*Electric Ladyland* (Hendrix), 58–59, 61, 64, 65
"Empty Chairs," 4, *172*
Eno, Brian, 121, *122,* 123–124, 134, 135
Etchingham, Kathy, 58, 61, 64, 67

**F**

Fawcett, Farrah, *98*
Ferguson, David, 198, 199, 200
Flack, Roberta, 2, 173–*176,* 177, 178–179
Fogerty, John, *88,* 90, 91, 93
Fogerty, Tom, 89
Fontana, D.J., 17, 20, 21
Foster, David, 164–165, 166, 167–168, 169
Fox, Charles, *172,* 173, 174, 177
Franklin, Aretha, "Respect," 44–55
Frantz, Chris, 118–119, 120, 122, 126–127
Freddie Bell and the Bellboys, 15–17
*Fried Green Tomatoes* (movie), 164
Fugees, "Killing Me Softly," 2, 170–179

**G**

Gaye, Marvin, "I Heard It Through the Grapevine," 88, 91–92
*Ghost* (movie), "Unchained Melody," 42
Gimbel, Norm, *172,* 174, 177
"Gin and Juice," 180–191
Gladys Knight & the Pips, "I Heard It Through the Grapevine," 92
Gladys Knight & the Pips, "Midnight Train to Georgia," 96–103
"Gloria," 104–115
Gordon, Mike, 188
Gordy, Barry, 88
The Gourds, "Gin and Juice," 180–191
Grateful Dead, 8, 88, 92
Green, Al, 101, 102, 118–121, 123, 126, 127
Gross, Terry, 108, 113, 194

**H**

Haggard, Merle, 156
Hamilton, Roy, 38–39, 40
Hammond, John, 46, 60
Harrison, George, 77. *See also* The Beatles
Harrison, Jerry, 119–121, 122–123, 124, 126, 127
Hatfield, Bobby. *See* Righteous Brothers
Hendrix, Jimi, 2, 56–67, 70, 111, 217
"Hey Joe," 107
Hill, Lauryn, *174,* 176, 177, 178
History of covers, 2–7
*Horses* (Smith), 111–113, 122
"Hound Dog," 10–25
    answer songs, 15
    Big Mama Thornton original, *12*–14, 16, 22–24
    Elvis and, *12, 14,* 15, 16–25
    Freddy Bell and the Belboys, 15–16
    other covers of "Hound Dog," 14–15
    Stoller, Leiber and, *12*–14, 15, 23, 28
Houston, Cissy, *101,* 103
Houston, Whitney, "I Will Always Love You," 160–169
"Hung on You," 39, 40, 41
"Hurt." *See* Cash, Johnny, "Hurt"

**I**

"I Heard It Through the Grapevine," 86–95
Isley Brothers, 28–30, *31,* 33
*I've Never Loved a Man the Way I Love You* (Franklin), 53, 54
"I've Never Loved a Man the Way I Love You," 47–48, 53
"I Will Always Love You," 160–169

**J**

Jagger, Mick, 1, 130, 135, 149
Jean, Wyclef, *172,* 176, 177, 179
Jefferson Airplane, 70, 88–89, 92
Johnston, Max, *187*
Jones, Quincy, 173
Jones, Spike, 143

**K**

Kaye, Lenny, 106, 107, 108–111, 112, 113, 114–115
"Killing Me Softly," 2, 170–179
"Killing the Sound Boy," 177–178
King, Dr. Martin Luther, Jr., 46, 54
Knight, Bubba, 103
Knight, Gladys. *See* Gladys Knight & the Pips
Kramer, Eddie, 64–65, 66

**L**

Langford, Keith, 185, *187*, 188, 190, 191
Lee, Brenda, 154, *156*
Leiber, Jerry, *10*, 12–14, 15, 23, 28
Lennon, John, 30, 31, 32–34, 77. *See also* The Beatles
Lennon Sisters, 38
Lieberman, Lori, 172–174
Lowe, Bernie, 15
Lowe, Chris, 157–159

**M**

Madonna, 5, *7*, 113
Majors, Lee, *98*
"Make You Feel My Love," 208–217
*Mandatory Fun*(Yankovic), 145–147, 149–150, *151*
"Marjorine," 72–74, 76
Martinville, Édouard-Léon Scott de, 2
Mason, Dave, 58, 64, 65
McCartney, Paul, 28, 29, 34, 77. *See also* The Beatles
McCrae, Gwen, 154
McGear, Mike, 59
McLean, Don, 4–5, 172
Medley, Bill. *See* Righteous Brothers
Mendelsohn, Julian, 159
"Midnight Plane to Houston," 98–99
"Midnight Train to Georgia," 96–103
*Milton Berle Show*, 17, 18, 20
Miranda, Yankovic and, 151
Mironov, Jeff, 101–102
Mitchell, Joni, 207
Mitchell, Mitch, 64, 65
Moore, Scotty, 16, 17, 20, 21, 24
Mothersbaugh, Mark, Devo/"Satisfaction," 128–137
Munson, Art, 40, 41
Myers, Alan, 132

**N**

Napster, 182, 185–187, 188, *189*, 191
Nelson, Willie, *1*, 2, *154*–157, *158*
Nine Inch Nails, *194*, 197–198, *199*, 203
North, Alex, 38

**O**

"Oath," 106–107, 110–111, 113
O'Connor, Sinéad, *1*–2
Olds, Gary, 16, 23

**P**

*Pancho and Lefty* (Nelson and Haggard), 156
Parton, Dolly, 162–164, 166, 169
Peñate, Jack, 210, 211
Pet Shop Boys, "Always on My Mind," 152–159
Petty, Tom, 198, *199*
Phillips, Sam, 15
Phish, 182, 185, 187–188, 191
Pickett, Wilson, 46
"Polkas on 45," 145–147, 148
Pras, *172*, 174–179
Presley, Elvis, 2
    "Always on My Mind" and, 154, 156, 157, 158
    "Hound Dog" and. *See* "Hound Dog"
    "I Will Always Love You," 162, 169
    *Love Me Tender* (TV show), 157–159
    Sun Records and, 15
    "Unchained Melody" and, 43
Pridden, Bob, 82, 84–85
Prince, *1*–2, 4, 9
"Purple Rain," *1*, 9
*Purple Rain* (movie), *1*

**R**

"Race Records" chart, 5, *7*, 24
Racism, 5, 9, 23–24
Raney, Wayne, 4, 5
Redding, Noel, 64
Redding, Otis, "Respect," 2, *48*–49, 50, 55
Reitzas, Dave, 167–168, 169
"Respect," 44–55
Reznor, Trent, *194*, 197, 203, 207
Righteous Brothers, "Unchained Melody," 2, 36–43
Riker, Warren, 177, 178
Rivers, Johnny, 132
Robin, Lou, 197, 203, 205
Rolling Stones
    Eddie Kramer and, 64
    live albums, 83
    "Satisfaction" and, 130–131, *132–133*, 137
    trajectory of covering then writing own songs, 35
    translating success to U.S., 61–62
    Yankovic medley of, 147
Romanek, Mark, 202–205, 206
Rotten, Johnny, 134
Rubin, Rick, *194*, 196–199, 202, 205, 206, 207, 210–211
Ruffin, Jimmy, 164
Russell, Kevin, *182–184*, 188–189, 190–191
Russel, Richard, 211

## S

"Satisfaction," 1, 128–137
Schwartz, Jon "Bermuda," 143–144, 147–148, 150
*The Score* (Fugees), *178–179*
"Secret Agent Man," 132
*Sgt. Pepper's Lonely Hearts Club Band* (Beatles), 70, 72, 74, 84
Sholes, Steve, 20, 21, 22
Smith, Jimmy, 184, 185, *187*, 188, 189–190, 191
Smith, Patti, "Gloria," 104–115
Snoop Doggy Dogg, *182–183*, 185, 188–189
Sohl, Richard, 107, 112
Spector, Phil, 39–40, 41
Stainton, Chris, 70, 71–72, 74, 76
Stasium, Ed, 101, 102
Steinem, Gloria, 55
*Steve Allen Show*, 18–20, 23
Stewart, Billy, 8, *9*
Stoker, Gordon, 20, 21
Stoller, "Big Mama" Thornton, *12–14*, 16, 22–24
Stoller, Mike, 12, 15, 23, 28
Stuart, Marty, *199*
Sullivan, Ed, 17, 18–20, 24, 34
"Summertime," 8, *9*
"Summertime Blues," 78–85
Swayze, Patrick, 42

## T

"Take Me to the River," 116–127
Talking Heads, "Take Me to the River," 116–127
Tench, Benmont, 198, 200
Tennant, Neil, *154*, 157–159
"The Man Comes Around," 201, 203. *See also American IV: The Man Comes Around* (Cash)
Thomas, Rufus, 15
Thompson, Wayne Carson. *See* Carson, Wayne
Thornton, "Big Mama," *12–14*, 16, 22–24
*Time Out of Mind* (Dylan), *212*
Townshend, Pet, 80, *83*, 84, 85
Turner, Ike and Tina, *93–95*
"Tutti Frutti," 24, 184
"Twist and Shout," 26–35

## U

"Unchained Melody," 2, 36–43

## V

Visconti, Tony, 72–76

## W

Wagoner, Porter, 163–164
Watchtower ("All Along the Watchtower"), 56–67
Watts, Charlie, 21, 149
Weatherly, Jim, 98–99, 101
Wexler, Jerry, 46–47, 48, 50, 52, 53, 55
Weymouth, Tina, 118, 119, 124
Whalum, Kirk "Bishop," 166, 167, 168
"What Becomes of the Brokenhearted," 164
White, Ted, *47*, 50
The Who, "Summertime Blues" and, 78–85
"Why Don't You Haul Off and Love Me?," 4, *5*
Wilkinson, Richard, 211, 212
Wills, Bob, 18
"With a Little Help From My Friends," 1, 68–77

## Y

Yankovic, "Weird Al," 140–151
    accordion lessons and background, 142
    artists' responses to parodies of, 149
    cover royalties for parodies, 148–149
    debut album, 144
    Dr. Demento, 143, *144*
    early polka-fied medleys of, 142–144
    inspiring imitators/followers, 150–151
    legal issues for parodies, 148, 149
    *Mandatory fun #1* album, 145–147, 149–150, *151*
    Miranda on, 151
    parody success of, 142
    perfectionist attitude toward parodies, 147–148
    "Polkas on 45," 145–147, 148
    Spike Jones comparison, 143
Young, Neil, 92, 197
Young, Paul, 164

## Z

Zaret, Hy, 38

# PHOTO CREDITS